Dave Schell
July 7, 1969

BEHAVIORAL THERAPY

HALMUTH H. SCHAEFER, Ph.D.

Chief of Research
Patton State Hospital, California
Professor of Clinical Psychiatry
Loma Linda University
Loma Linda, California

and

PATRICK L. MARTIN, Ph.D.

Staff Psychologist
Patton State Hospital, California

The Blakiston Division
McGRAW-HILL BOOK COMPANY, INC.
New York Toronto Sydney London

Over the years, psychiatric nurses, technicians, and attendants have become increasingly involved in the treatment of the mentally ill. There is no longer room for passive helpers, blind executors of orders—mere bystanders while treatment goals and treatment plans are being formulated. Behavioral therapy challenges these professionals to broaden their knowledge and increase their responsibilities. It is to those who will fulfill this new professional involvement that we dedicate this book.

Preface

This text is a handbook to aid in the education of psychiatric personnel. It is for the men and women who are or will be applying behavioral techniques in the treatment of mental patients in our society.

Although based on rigorous scientific research, it deliberately shuns either scholarly or technical presentation. Rather, in everyday language and with numerous examples and exercises, it seeks to provide practical help for psychiatric nurses and technicians and for all others whose work brings them into contact with mental patients. As is necessary when describing a new area of human knowledge, new terms will be used, and some familiar terms will be used in novel ways. One such term is the word *behavior*. In English usage *behavior* is commonly considered non-countable. In normal speech one rarely says, "His behaviors need to be studied." In behavioral science, however, it is useful to treat *behavior* as a countable word. That is to say, we might speak of "one behavior" or of a patient who "emits six behaviors which upset his family." Also, the behavioral scientist regards many human acts as behaviors which are not usually so considered. Reading these lines, for example, is one behavior which in turn elicits many other behaviors: eye movements, the firing of cells in the optic nerve and others in the cortex, thinking, recognizing, feeling in various ways, discriminating between stimuli—all these are behaviors of interest to the behavioral scientist. All can be affected by the environment, all can be shaped, modified, and controlled.

In this context it is perhaps in order to dwell on one particular term which we have come to use and which we use throughout this book: *odd behavior*. To the behavioral scientist a mental patient is treated differently because he behaves in ways that are unacceptable to society, or because he shows otherwise common behaviors in highly inappropriate situations. In short, he is behaving oddly. It is true that the word *odd* is not commonly used in this connection, but then, the behavioral view of mental illness is also not common. Provoked by friendly critics and by our own initial discomfort with this word (although it is amazing how swiftly one can become used to a useful term) we have searched hard for a better word. We found none that is at once so brief and so descriptive and, in one way of looking at it, so shocking and thought-provoking. We considered *abnormal, anomalous, bizarre, comical, droll, eccentric, extraordinary, fantastic, grotesque, peculiar, quaint, queer, rare, strange, unacceptable, uncommon, undesirable, unique, unmatched, unusual,* and *whimsical,* to mention a few. Odd behavior is some of these but not all of them. To speak of psychotic behavior, as some behaviorists have, is to ask for the problem of having to explain the difference between neurotic and psychotic behavior and thus to fall into a trap from which others are vainly trying to escape.

We attach no value judgment to *odd.* We know that there are some odd (in the sense of unique) behaviors that are highly desirable and others that are not. But we think that all of the possible words one can use in describing the behavior of the mentally ill, *odd* is the one that has least surplus meaning and carries the least amount of implied value judgment. The word has also been useful in helping us guard against insensitivity to changes in mores and cultural habits. What was odd years ago may not be so any more. A woman who wore knee length skirts in 1910 might have required psychiatric help. Today she would not. In short, *odd* as a word always forces us to consider the circumstances. And that really is what behavioral science is all about.

Behavioral techniques are only now beginning to find acceptance in the treatment of mental illness and mental deficiency, although a substantial body of laboratory evidence provides the basis of these techniques. By their very nature, behavioral techniques rule out the notion that there is a single right procedure for each contingency, a single correct way to help patients. This poses problems, since effective behavioral therapy depends on personnel who are not only familiar with the fundamentals of both operant and classical conditioning, but also self-reliant and imaginative in using what they know. The success of this new technique depends more than any previous one on the skill and knowledge of the nursing personnel of our health services.

On the basis of our own practical experience we know that those who already work with the mentally ill will experience a profound change in their function as they become accustomed to the use of behavioral techniques. Those who are students without experience will discover in themselves fundamental attitudinal changes toward cultural beliefs about mental illness and life in general. Those working with behavioral therapies come to understand that their contact with patients affects their behavior, even as by living, by our very existence, we affect the behavior of those around us. Behavioral technology, essentially the theme of this book, permits prediction and suitable use of the influence we all have on others. Good therapy requires such prediction.

Because we believe that nothing teaches, or nothing changes behavior, as well as practical experience, we have provided exercises and examples in this handbook which should provide the student with insight and understanding of what is expected of him in his new role. In using these examples the student will learn to rely on his own judgment and experience. He will learn that he must be able to determine what his—and his patient's—needs are at a given time. He will come to realize that it is up to him to help set up and enforce schedules of reinforcement which eventually lead to a patient's acceptance as a human being in a human society. The student will find that as a behavioral technician he is directly concerned with treatment that conditions the behavior of human beings, that it is because of what *he* does or does not do that *his* patients will assume responsibility for themselves and thus once again take their places in society as free and responsible individuals.

If good therapy is the modification of behavior toward desired ends, a goal on which both traditional and behavioral therapists agree, the hoped-for influence of this book is that it will modify the behavior of its readers sufficiently so that they in turn can be efficient modifiers of the behaviors of persons who are mentally ill.

HALMUTH H. SCHAEFER

PATRICK L. MARTIN

Acknowledgment

We are deeply indebted to O. L. Gericke, Superintendent and Medical Director of Patton State Hospital, for the initiative, guidance, practical help, and moral support he has given.

The empirical evidence which forms the basis for the methods we advocate and the advice we give in the following pages would not have been available to us without the perseverance, the eagerness to learn, the willingness to work harder and longer, the professional integrity, and the loyalty of the nursing personnel—both technicians and nurses—in the Behavioral Therapy Project at Patton State Hospital. To name them all for acknowledgment is an impossible task. But, to thank here all of those who have helped in the writing of this book as well as in the project through which it grew is our humble and most pleasurable duty.

Contents

Part I

Introduction to Behavioral Therapy

.

1

Behavioral Attitude toward Mental Illness

Your study of this chapter should help you answer the following questions:

1. What is the aim of behavioral therapy?
2. What objections are there to a behavioral approach to mental illness?
3. What is the role of a behaviorist in the control of human behavior?

The terms listed below are introduced and defined in this chapter:

behavior
therapy
contingency
control

THE AIM OF BEHAVIORAL THERAPY

The word *behavior* has become such common coin that like all common coins it is shiny but faceless. Over the last forty years its use has increased twenty-fold in titles of scientific articles alone, but the number of behavioral scientists has not. And all that is called behavior today is not necessarily behavior in the sense in which a behavioral scientist uses the term.

Behavior is what an organism does including actions that take place inside the organism's body and therefore cannot be seen. But this definition is valid only if it is taken literally and not used to describe what an organism *is*. For example, the statement that a person is "depressed" says nothing about what the depressed person does, although one gets the idea that it is behavior which is being labeled. When it is said that somebody is "lazy," no description of behavior has been given. True, terms such as "lazy" and "depressed" can be, and are, used to summarize detailed descriptions of behavior under carefully enumerated circumstances. But without such descriptions and enumerations, the labels mean nothing to the behaviorist as a scientist.

Many so-called descriptions of behavior are really value judgments. They do not fall under the definition of behavior used in this text. Behavior cannot be good or bad. Behavior invariably has consequences labeled desirable (good) or undesirable (bad). But here the difficulty starts: Desirable or undesirable for whom? For what? The organism emitting the behavior? His health? His standing in the community? His friends, parents, wife, or children? The law of the land? The common good? It is well to remember that behavior in itself is neither good nor bad; the circumstances and conditions under which it occurs give it its value.

It is a giant step from acceptance of the behaviorist's definition of behavior to pursuit of the study of behavior. If behavior is merely what an organism does, then it might be said that behavioral science cannot do more than catalog what organisms have done. But this is not true. Behavioral science can also record the prevailing conditions and circumstances under which a certain behavior occurred. This is not done to arrive at ready value judgments, but rather for the purpose of being able to predict under what conditions that same behavior may be expected to recur. Therein lies the basis for a science of behavior. If a study is scientific, it must provide for the prediction of future events. The reliability with which predictions can be made is one of the factors determining the value of a science.

Once a description has been made in behavioral terms, many questions which seemed to lie beyond the scope of behavioral science become meaningful. For example, what of intentions? The behaviorist answers that intentions can be regarded as environmental factors which make the appearance of a given behavior highly probable. The factors may, but need not, include verbal statements; in any event they include the internal environment of the behaving organism.

Wishes, wants, needs, drives, hopes, choices, decisions, dreams, visions—all these and many more can, like intentions, be couched in behavioristic terms and then studied with the same techniques and methods which have proven fruitful in other areas of science. The extent to which behavioral science has addressed itself to these traditional questions has made possible behavioral therapy.

Therapy is any set of procedures which produce a beneficial change in a patient. Ideally, therapy results in permanent change. A surgeon seeks to permanently alter a malfunctioning heart; a behaviorist seeks to alter overt behavior. If the patient uses speech which society finds completely unacceptable, the aim of behavioral therapy is to modify the patient's words and sentences. If the patient exhibits extremely poor grooming habits, the aim of behavioral therapy is to bring about acceptable grooming habits. Behavioral therapy concentrates on developing or reinstating behaviors which are necessary for effective functioning in a social context.

The student familiar with other kinds of therapy may be prompted to ask, "Why isn't the alteration of ego structure, the enhancement of self-esteem, or self-realization the aim of behavioral therapy?" A change in ego structure cannot be seen, even as the ego itself is invisible. The ego, as well as any change in it, is an inference based on visible behavior. An alteration of self-esteem or an approach to self-realization are similar inferences. If there is a way to change ego, self-esteem, etc., the behavioral therapist would begrudge no one to go that way. But he doubts the usefulness and the reality of these concepts and hence makes no use of them in his approach to therapy.

Behavioral therapy takes as its basic problem human action, whether the action is an obnoxious way of eating, a habit of talking to voices no one else hears, or the practice of lying under a chair all day. Behavioral therapy can be distinguished from other therapies primarily in terms of its reliance upon principles of learning theory. Its basic method of procedure is to arrange *contingencies* between the patient's behavior and the consequences of that behavior. Consequences are events which closely follow an instance of behavior. They are often arranged in contingencies—in other words, a certain behavior must occur for a specific consequence to take place. If you watch behavior, it becomes quite clear that what an organism does always brings about change in some way. Verbalizations bring others to act, to answer, or simply to acquiesce in what is being said. Turning and pulling a doorknob usually permits access to whatever is on the other side of the door. Working a certain number of hours each week results in payment of a wage. All these examples point to something fundamental regarding behavior—that behavior operates upon the environment.

Behavior also has consequences, and these frequently become the contingencies of life with which everyone is familiar. Whether a person does something, answers, or simply listens to what is being said depends upon whether he has heard a command, a question, or a statement. Whether or not a closed door opens often depends on someone turning a knob and pushing or pulling the door. Whether or not money is found in a pay envelope depends upon the performance of certain tasks. Behavioral therapy capitalizes on this fact of life by arranging contingencies between behavior and its consequences.

For therapy, however, the arrangement of contingencies is not enough unless the kind of consequence is considered. In greatly simplified form, there are two kinds of consequences—"good" and "bad." A good consequence is typically referred to as a reward (positive reinforcer), while a bad consequence is viewed as something that is undesirable (negative reinforcer). The behavioral therapist is always on the lookout for these two kinds of consequences relative to a particular patient and purposely structures an environment so that behavior becomes the vehicle by which rewards are acquired or undesirable events terminated.

Nurses who have worked in a hospital know, of course, that such contingencies are traditionally used (for example, when ground privileges are made contingent upon acceptable ward behavior). The behavioral therapist, however, insists that complete consistency be maintained in manipulating such an arrangement. He also insists upon many more immediate consequences for the patient. Behavioral therapy involves the complete structuring of a patient's environment and is made as all-encompassing as possible. Not only ground privileges but almost all necessities as well as luxuries of daily life are made contingent upon some behavior.

For the conventional therapist, odd behaviors are symptoms. For the behavioral therapist, they are not. They are behaviors which can and should be changed. The mentalistic and the behavioral therapist agree, however, on the final goal of what is to be accomplished: They both want to change the patient's behavior, or more exactly, the patient's probable behavior under given circumstances. The disagreement lies in the techniques and the general approach that is to be used. The mentalist believes that by curing the mind, the behavior will automatically change. The behaviorist would change the behavior itself.

It is often thought that what makes working in a mental hospital, or more generally, working in the field of mental health, most difficult is the large number of different mental conditions and diseases that must be recognized. As long as mental illness in various forms is accepted as reality, this is certainly true. But today in psychiatry, as well as in the social sciences, the concept of mental illness is increasingly regarded as a hindrance to progress rather than a help. Thomas S. Szasz, a leading American psychiatrist, has gone so far as to call mental illness a myth.

> I submit that mental illness is a myth. Bodies are physical objects; minds, whatever they may be, are not physical objects. Accordingly, mental diseases (such as depression or schizophrenia) cannot exist in the sense in which bodily diseases (such as broken bones or ulcerated skins) exist [1].*

Thus, while a nurse or psychiatric technician should be familiar with the usage of psychiatric diagnostic labels, he should regard them more as legal classifications rather than as guides for behavioral therapy.

OBJECTIONS TO A BEHAVIORAL APPROACH

Today it is no secret that behavioral techniques and their therapeutic applications were developed in animal laboratories through experiments with such organisms as rats and pigeons. Therapeutic drugs were also

---

* Numbers in brackets refer to "References and Notes," pp. 219–220.

developed and tested in animal laboratories. There is a striking contradiction in the readiness with which many men expect, nay demand, that drugs be tested on animals before they are used on man, and their unwillingness to believe that behavioral laws derived from animal experimentation are also valid for human beings.

Historically there exists a well-rooted tradition that human beings are separated by a wide and sacred gulf from all other living creatures. The behaviorist, of course, concedes that man is different from other organisms, but at the same time he points to the difficulties that arise when an attempt is made to define particular differences. It has been commonly held, for example, that man alone uses tools. Field studies and research show that this is simply not true: Apes, ants, and other animals use tools as well.

It has long been believed that man is the only animal who utilizes symbols and rituals as, for example, in religious services. Investigation has shown that the use of symbols and rituals does not provide a criterion for difference between man and other animals: Bees use symbols to communicate, and animals do have rituals.

But man does indeed differ from other animals. He differs in ways such as speech habits, record keeping, care of the young, and kinds of disease. And even as man differs from other animals, so too, do they differ from one another. A cockroach breathes differently from a dog, and so does a fish. The locomotion of a camel is different from that of a woolly monkey or a pelican. The means of defense used by a porcupine are quite different from those used by a cobra or an octopus. Seeking to bring order to the seeming confusion of the world, man sorts and classifies. This he does without any compulsion to make value judgments, but merely for the sake of convenience. He simply observes that some organisms have backbones and some do not. It turns out that when man himself is classified this way, he falls into the same category as dogs, fish, birds, and the long extinct dinosaur. But this does not make man a dog or a dinosaur, any more than it makes a fish a bird or a man.

Anatomical variation is not, of course, the only basis for classifying organisms. Some kinds of behavior are clearly common to man and other animals. Both men and dogs follow patterns of sleeping and waking and apparently even dreaming. Similarly, human beings and other animals eat and both procreate their own kind.

If the scientist is to study such functions experimentally, he must in some measure control the environment. But in the study of human behavior, ethical and aesthetic considerations have so far limited the possibility for control. It comes, then, as no surprise that in psychological, as well as in medical research, much effort has been made to find lower animals in which some human function is adequately represented for study. Some tissue in dogs, for instance, is so much like human tissue that a surgeon can reasonably practice on dogs before plying his skill on a man. It is true, such problems as blood sugar levels and metabolism of proteins can be studied directly in human beings but not under conditions as conveniently controlled as in lower organisms. As long as the findings in lower animals can be demonstrated to hold true for man (and the evidence is increasingly certain that they can), such practice will continue, with due humanitarian concern for the comfort of the animals as is now shown in all modern research laboratories. Because of this valuable experimentation with animals, study of the same processes in human beings means less risk and fewer variables to control, either because these variables have been found irrelevant or because they are understood through other methods.

Someone may object: "Yes, it's true that such mechanical processes as digestion, circulation, and tissue growth are common to man and beast. But you say, also, that a dog sleeps, eats, and procreates like a man. That is where I part company with you. I don't know about sleeping, but when I eat, I don't eat like a dog. And sex, well, you ask me to consider the mechanical similarities. As I do, I cannot help but agree that mechanically and superficially the dog and I do the same thing. But there is a world of difference between the dog and me. I don't sleep just anywhere, but in an appointed room especially designed for me; I don't eat just because I am hungry, but for various social reasons and to cater to my refined appetite. I don't simply mate as a dog does, but I court and adore the woman I love; I marry and plan a future: I am in ecstasy when the dog is merely in heat."

But there is no need to part company over such matters. Surely from these differences it is not to be assumed that there can be no universal laws of behavior. The laws sought by a behaviorist, however, will not be derived from experiments on ecstasy.

Even though it is agreed that men and animals share some aspects of behavior, many men contend that unlike animals, human beings do more than "just behave." Traditionally, man has seen himself as more than animal. He has placed himself at the center of a world which revolves around him. Yet, with time, man's position in the universe has steadily shifted from the center of first one sphere and then another, as he learned that the sun does not revolve about his planet. Biologically speaking, man is not a special case but one in a long evolutionary chain; man is not the only animal that uses tools, not the only creature that forms societies, not the only one who communicates through symbols, and so on. Yet each time a daring thinker advanced one of these notions—so commonplace today—he risked not only his professional respectability but his very life. And now comes the behavioral view which seems to demote man further from his one-time central position. Even tentatively accepting man as different from other animals—in that animals are guided by their immediate environment, by instincts, and by physiological processes, while man in his humanity is guided by forces like spirit and intellect—even this seems an assertion that man is special and surely "higher" than other organisms. But man is not at the center of the universe, and a condescending smile is all that is offered those who only recently, as history goes, still believe that he is.

Besides the objection that what is known about behavior rests on experiments with lesser animals and does not consider man's "humanness," there are philosophical objections likely to be raised to a behavioral approach for the treatment of mental illness. Generally these objections address themselves to the question of whether or not a science of behavior (on which behavioral therapy is based) is possible at all. An argument frequently heard is that human behavior is not amenable to causal description and treatment (that is, to scientific study) since each human being is unique and therefore necessarily eludes description by scientific method. But even the most rigid scientist readily concedes that everything in the world is unique in some way or other. No ball bearing manufactured by machine is exactly like any other. Yet, in many aspects, they are alike. The kind and degree of difference are well known to both manufacturer and buyer; certainly the differences do not interfere with a scientific study of ball bearings.

It is conceivable that the following psychological law is valid: If an organism has been rewarded every time for a given response, that response will, upon absence of the reward, cease swiftly. If this law holds, then it should be true that a given response under such conditions as the law describes will cease swiftly *regardless of the differences that prevail in human beings.* A case in point is the continuous reinforcement the operator of a gum-ball machine receives. For every penny he puts into the machine he receives a gum-ball. No other variables, no individual differences, are relevant here. It does not matter whether a child, a man, or a woman; a Negro, an Oriental, or a Caucasian; a Jew, a Gentile, or a Moslem puts the penny in, if the machine breaks down, he will use at most one more penny before ceasing to respond in this fashion. Here individual differences, which quite assuredly are observable, play no role at all; nor do they restrict in any way the validity of the general law illustrated.

A second argument against the sheer possibility of a behavioral science is that even if there were a causal order in the phenomena of human behavior, such an order would of necessity be so complex as to escape understanding *prior* to the formulation of laws about them. The "blooming buzzing confusion" of life as William James saw it is no more than the apparent absence of order which human ingenuity has been steadily supplying. He who despairs of discovering order in the confusion might have sought to discourage Mendeleev who couched the stuff of nature in his periodic table of elements.

A third objection to behavioral study being scientific is that science, by definition, attempts to explain a present fact by reference to a past fact. Since human behavior is held to be always directed toward a goal—that is, a fact that lies in the future—the study of behavior cannot be a science in the sense that physics or chemistry is so regarded. This argument seems plausible until it is understood that a future goal, as such, never guides behavior, but rather it is past experience which determines the course of action (i.e., directs behavior) although there is an illusion that it is a future goal.

A fourth objection takes this course: Granted, for argument's sake, that behavior is determined by material, cultural, and social environment; then no one could be held accountable for what he is doing. Under such circumstances one would deserve no praise for his good deeds nor blame for his bad. This argument rests on the curious supposition that man cannot foresee the outcome of his deeds. But he can, and this is where so much confusion enters. In short, to base behavior on scientific causality denies the known fact that people respond to moral imperatives. Surely, in postulating a science of behavior, what is known to be real about human behavior does not need to be disregarded. The thief may well be impelled by manifold environmental factors. Included among those, however, is one by which he can quite justly be held responsible; he knows that by stealing he wrongs society. This knowledge is very much a part of the environment which influences him, and to excuse him—that is to say, not to hold him responsible for his act—would require proof that such knowledge was not part of his environment at the time he committed the act. And, indeed, this is sometimes the basis for legal defense of the thief.

There are other challenges to the usefulness of a science of behavior, some of which are so subtle as to amount to hairsplitting. But the present task is not to answer all possible arguments, nor to attempt to defend systematically all arguments for a science of behavior on which behavioral therapy might be based. Mainly the intent is to establish common ground on which living examples can be understood rationally and in reasonable agreement. No general panacea for mental illness is offered. There is much in behavioral science still to be achieved, yet the time seems to have arrived for assessing and sharing that which is known.

THE CONTROL OF HUMAN BEHAVIOR

There is an unsavory flavor about the word *control* and when the word is used in the sense of "controlling other human beings," reactions are downright negative. The fact is, however, men constantly control the behavior of other men whether they wish to do so or not. The worker on a sit-down strike controls the behavior of his employer even as a dictator orders a whole people around, although each uses different means. The sergeant who orders his squad to march right, left, or straight ahead controls behavior, but so does the beggar girl who cries, "Buy my matches," on an icy winter night. The father who never once looks at his children, let alone at their homework, controls their behavior just as much as the father who tightly supervises his children's homework and is frequently at their side. All other conditions being equal, we know that the children of the attentive father will do well in school and those of the father who does not care will do less well and that both results are directly attributable to the actions of the respective fathers.

Control most commonly implies taking action to make others perform in a certain way, but this implication is one-sided. *Not* doing anything just as surely has its effects and thus controls the behavior of others. It is upon the recognition of this fact that behavioral science is founded. If it is true that control of some kind takes place all the time—and it clearly is—then it cannot but benefit mankind to learn about the laws according to which control takes place. The behaviorist insists that even though knowledge stemming from the pursuit of science may be put to evil use as well as to good, the body of knowledge itself cannot be good or evil. It simply is. In behavioral science, control is the core of knowledge. It follows, therefore, that control as such, and an understanding of control, is neither good nor evil of itself.

Control of behavior then is not something to be feared, nor should its exercise be regarded as either weakness or strength of character. That men control one another's behavior is a fact of life as real as any other aspect of human living.

To many these are novel thoughts, thoughts not yet widely reflected in our literature or textbooks. Even books which ostensibly deal with the control of behavior rarely admit this purpose in these terms. Textbooks on education, for example, should seek to train teachers who will by their control of students, make useful citizens of them. This implies the shaping of the behavior of these students in many different ways. And even though that is generally what happens, the almost hysterical fear of even mentioning anything that smacks of behavioral control of human beings leads to circumlocutions in these textbooks. Mystical forces are invoked, forces which lie latent within each child but which can be brought out by a good teacher provided he or she skillfully nourishes, unfolds, develops, bends, and encourages.

In clinical psychotherapy it is no different. Here, too, the objective most clearly is to change unacceptable behaviors to acceptable behaviors. But many traditional therapists go to great lengths to make sure it is understood that they are in no way controlling either their patient's outlook on life or his behavior. They say they are freeing the patient to decide for himself. They set the stage, they claim, for the patient to find himself. They most emphatically deny that in many ways they function even as a mechanical controller, conditioned by a culture which makes it difficult, if not impossible, to act otherwise.

The behavioral therapist, on the other hand, is not beset by such fears. He recognizes that he controls the behavior of those who come to him for help, regardless of whether he wants to or not and, indeed, irrespective of whether or not he believes that he does. Every time he agrees with the patient he reinforces what the patient at that moment has done (not necessarily what the patient has said), because social agreement is a strong reinforcer. If the patient is telling the truth, the therapist has strengthened truth telling; if the patient is not telling the truth, then by agreeing, the therapist has strengthened lying. The behavioral therapist recognizes the unavoidability of control and has accepted its moral and ethical implications. He realizes that he is responsible for what his patients do while they are in his care and that he cannot hide behind the pretense that it is up to the patients to make their own decisions to do what is "right."

The control of behavior takes place all the time. Certainly, therefore, studying the laws of control is bound to make for better mental health if for no other reason than avoiding any knowledge about control must inevitably lead to some misapplications. The study of behavioral control, surprisingly enough, reveals that all the punitive sort of control which dictators, benevolent or otherwise, have used is not at all that which is most powerful. Rather, the gentle though lawful granting of the wishes and needs of the controlled exercises the greatest amount of control. For example, on the basis of behavioral laws, there are ways to teach animals to do nearly unbelievable acts—guiding missiles, inspecting drugs, or reading simple numbers—all without ever punishing the animal or even touching him. All that is necessary is to arrange the animal's environment in such a way as to elicit the desired response. A basic exercise in undergraduate classes in behavioral science requires students to teach a laboratory animal to press a lever to obtain food, something the animal has never before done. Without knowledge of behavioral laws, students could not hope to accomplish this in the lifetime of the animal. Armed with an understanding of behavioral control, however, most students succeed in less than thirty minutes.

There is no way to describe the profound emotional experience of the experimenter as he successfully completes this exercise. And neither is there a substitute for the actual procedure as a means of demonstrating the underlying principles of behavioral control. Probably the most valuable insight the experimenter gains is that the behavior of the organism he is shaping controls his own behavior.

On the surface it may sometimes seem as if through skillful control anyone can willfully influence what somebody else is doing. This, of course, smacks of brainwashing and a kind of manipulation which is highly objectionable to civilized man. But scientific experiments, such as teaching an animal to press a lever, point out that the "controller" is not really independent of the "controlled." If the experimenter does not take into account the idiosyncrasies, wishes, intentions, and aversions of the animal or person whose behavior he hopes to influence, he simply will not succeed. Thus, the sooner a behaviorist learns that his techniques do not place him above those whom he controls, the more successful he will be. All modes of psychiatric therapy, for example, require that the patient be understood and respected. Behavioral therapy, by its very nature, makes it necessary to understand the patient; it requires that the therapist subjugate his own inclinations to the behavioral makeup of the patient. Most important, the behavioral therapist is continually aware that his actions are controlled by the patient as much as he controls those of the patient.

EXERCISES, CHAPTER 1

1. What is behavior? Explain why the following are not adequate descriptions of behavior: lethargic, happy, sad, withdrawn, agitated, and mad. Pick two of these terms and write an adequate behavioral description for each. Ask yourself, "What overt behaviors correlate with each of these terms?"
2. Therapy is any set of procedures which produce a beneficial change in a patient. Write a definition of behavioral therapy.
3. Which argument against using a behavioral approach seems most salient to you? Why?
4. The classroom presents numerous instances of attempts at behavioral control. List several, couching them in terms of the behavior involved and its possible consequences.
5. Briefly explain why the controller is not independent of the controlled. Why is this especially true in a behavioral therapy?

Part II

Fundamentals of Behavioral Techniques

2

Two Models of Conditioning

Your study of this chapter should help you answer the following questions:

1. What are the basic units of measurement in behavioral science?
2. What are the main characteristics of Pavlov's classical conditioning?
3. What is operant conditioning?

The terms listed below are introduced and defined in this chapter:

response
stimulus
S-R psychology
classical conditioning
respondent conditioning
second-order conditioning
first-order conditioning
operant conditioning
schedule of reinforcement
continuous reinforcement
extinction
strength of response
reinforcer
reinforcement
variable ratio schedule

BASIC UNITS FOR MEASUREMENT

Every science uses some kind of basic unit for measurement and description. Chemistry and physics have the atom; biology, the cell; and astronomy, the light-year. In behavioral science the basic unit is the response. A response may consist of the firing of a single neuron within the body—an electrical change measurable but not visible to the naked eye—or it may be the complex response of clenching a fist or writing a novel. This shifting scale may at first seem confusing. Some early behaviorists defined the response as the "smallest conceivable unit of behavior," but this proved to be inadequate. At best they allowed that a response, if not "atomic" (i.e., like atoms in physics), should be considered at least "molecular," (i.e., like the molecules in physics, which always contain several atoms).

Much in the way that chemistry developed rapidly with the concept of atoms and molecules, behavioral science sought to make strides by proceeding analogously with the response. This analogy is indeed satisfactory because even as every atom and every molecule is not a unit of standard simplicity or complexity, neither is the response. To most laymen *atomic* implies uniformity, simplicity, and minute parts, an implication which does not necessarily help in understanding the function of the larger entity which consists of atoms. Thus, by inference, a definition of response was introduced which rested essentially on the difficulty of appreciating that a response, even though atomic, might just as likely be highly complex.

The word *response* has its root in the Latin *respondere* meaning "to answer." Hence, the response is an answer to something, which in turn is generally called a *stimulus* from the Latin word *stimulare*, "to goad." There is sound justification for allowing basic units in behavioral science to be defined relatively. No science can claim to have established an ultimate and indivisible unit for describing and measuring. Chemists, for example, once believed that the atom was a uniform and final unit, but now it is known that atoms can be split and that atomic particles can be studied in great detail. A response, like any molecule, atom, or particle, amounts to whatever a scientist happens to find most useful for the purposes of his particular study. One behaviorist might wish to examine the effect of different intensities of light on the human retina. For him, the firing of a single cell, or the firing of the whole optic nerve, could be taken as a response. Similarly, when the eye blink is studied, the closure of the eyelid, involving the firing of many cells, constitutes the single response. For children learning to write, the making of a single straight line may at first be called a response. Later, it becomes more meaningful to regard the formation of a whole letter as a response. Still further along in the learning continuum, the writing of a word, a sentence, a paragraph, an essay, or even a book might be considered an individual response. Clearly, the term *response* needs to be defined and redefined in the particular context of each study to which it applies.

What is true for the response applies equally to the stimulus, which may be an object, like a street sign, a rock, some food, or a picture or may be an event, like an eye blink, a musical tone, or the movement of a hand. An event, such as the change in a person's blood sugar level, which is a response to certain physiological conditions, may also be regarded as a stimulus for this change gives rise to yet further consequences. All responses are potentially stimuli; but, of course, not all stimuli are responses. Responses are always emitted by an organism; that is to say, they are actions of one kind or another. Stimuli, on the other hand, may exist outside and independent of the organism. A fallen tree across a pathway is a stimulus for one's turning around to take another direction, but the log is not necessarily a response. In a recitation of the Gettysburg Address the first word "fourscore" is a response, but it also acts as a goad, or a stimulus, for the next word "and" which, in this context, in turn becomes a response. Thus, "fourscore" is both a response and a stimulus. Reciting the whole address may be a response to the stimulus of the teacher's saying, "Please recite the Gettysburg Address." The recitation, in turn, may be the stimulus for applause by the audience. Plainly, whether something is called a stimulus or a response is determined by whatever aspect happens to be of interest at the time. A stimulus, together with its response, forms the next larger unit that is of interest to the behavioral scientist.

The concern with stimuli and responses in behaviorism has given rise to the term *S-R psychology* which in turn is the matrix of behavioral science. To base the entire science of human behavior on such arbitrary units as the stimulus and the response may at first seem austere and limited, especially if one assumes that stimuli and responses are invariably trivial events in the vast environment of living beings. But, on the contrary, the widely ramified effects of stimulus and response, no matter what the definition, bear on every concern in daily living, on abnormal and industrial psychology, and on any other conceivable area of interest to persons concerned with human behaviors.

Sometimes behavior is observed which could be regarded as a response, but for which there does not seem to be a stimulus. In such a situation, if it seems important enough, experiments are undertaken which can eventually show what the stimulus is. It may well be, however, that whatever the stimulus, the response in question can also be brought about in answer to other stimuli which may easily be introduced in the laboratory and used to serve the purposes of the study. It is therefore unnecessary to worry about the original unknown stimulus. For example, a glass of milk may be the stimulus for someone to say, "Ah! There is milk!" If a linguist now wishes to study a person's pronunciation of "milk," he need not, in his lab, always provide glasses of milk for his subjects. He need only elicit the response "milk" regardless of the original stimulus. In other words, an understanding of behavior based on experimentation with responses need not falter through the uniqueness of particular stimulus-response combinations.

Classical Conditioning

There is rarely a one-to-one relationship between a given stimulus and a given response. The same stimulus may well elicit different responses in different people, or it may elicit different responses in the same person under different conditions and at different times. Thus, a soldier in battle hearing the word "duck" will fall flat on his face;

a hunter in the Wisconsin woods upon hearing the same word will sight over his shotgun.

There are some stimuli that always do elicit the same responses. A drop of vinegar on the tongue of a living animal will always elicit some salivation. It is this regular occurrence of a given response to a given stimulus which first attracted the attention of the Russian physiologist, Ivan Pavlov. He found that if two stimuli were presented simultaneously, only one response would be elicited. Assume that the aroma of food and the sound of a bell are presented at the same moment and followed by salivation. That stimulus which could by itself elicit the response, in this case the aroma of food, was recognized as the stronger of the pair of stimuli. But to Pavlov's surprise, he found that if the pair of stimuli are presented together often enough, then the weaker stimulus by itself eventually elicits the same response which previously only the stronger stimulus could elicit without the other. That is, the bell alone could stimulate the salivary glands. Pavlov called this pairing of stimuli *conditioning*, in recognition of the manipulation of conditions to bring about predictable consequences. Figure 2-1 shows a schematic presentation of Pavlov's discovery.

The arrow between the top boxes indicates that the stimulus "vinegar on tongue" always causes salivation. If the presentation of the vinegar

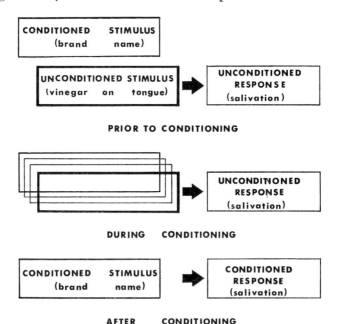

Fig. 2-1. Schematic diagram for Pavlovian conditioning (also called respondent or classical conditioning).

is always paired with the brand name of the bottle containing the vinegar the brand name alone will later elicit salivation. This pattern of behavior is called *classical,* or *Pavlovian, conditioning.* Other terms used to designate this same pattern of behavior are *respondent conditioning* and *Type-S conditioning.* Both of these were coined to illuminate the fact that it is manipulation of the stimuli which plays the important role here, and without any doubt the stimulus which plays the role in eliciting the response is identified by these alternate terms. Since Pavlov's work, much research has been done on classical conditioning, which has led to a rather thorough understanding of both the power and the limitations of this concept. A simultaneity of presentation, for example, of the unconditioned and the conditioned stimulus is important: If the conditioned stimulus follows the unconditioned one by even a fraction of a second, it is next to impossible to achieve conditioning. It is, however, possible to gradually let the conditioned stimulus *precede* the presentation of the unconditioned stimulus. Under such circumstances, passage of time itself seems to become a conditioned stimulus. The number and variety of *unconditioned* stimuli are not great. Most typically, if not always, unconditioned stimuli are tied to responses involving involuntary (smooth) musculature such as the salivary gland, the digestive glands, and similar organs.

There have been impressive attempts to account for all behavior of organisms through classical conditioning on the basis that once a certain stimulus has been paired with an unconditioned stimulus, the resultant stimulus-response unit may serve as a basis for the introduction of a new stimulus to be conditioned. Thus, a *second-order conditioning* is possible in which a stimulus is paired with one that had been conditioned previously to an unconditioned stimulus during *primary,* or *first-order, conditioning.* For example, a baby given food is at the same time exposed to the presence of a human being, typically his mother. The food, of course, is the unconditioned stimulus and the mother's smell, her hair, her features are the conditioned stimuli. Later, these conditioned stimuli by themselves may serve to condition yet other stimuli in the childs environment. But what is being conditioned here? The salivation which occurred originally in response to milk? Does mother's voice elicit salivation? Is the reason one's sweetheart often has the same hair color as one's mother reducible to the fact that salivation occurred at one time? It could be postulated that in addition to salivation there were other responses, perhaps sexual ones, which played an important role during the original conditioning, and that through subsequent second-order, third-order, and, in short, higher-order conditioning, stimulus-response bonds were established which account for behaviors seemingly far removed from the original presentation of baby food followed by salivation. A first- and second-order conditioning sequence is presented in Figure 2-2.

Originally the unconditioned stimulus "presenting baby with baby food" brought on the unconditioned response "salivation" (with perhaps evidence of happiness and contentment). The unconditioned stimulus "seeing mother's features" brought the unconditioned response "firing of visual nerve cells" (Fig. 2-2A). Always pairing "mother's features" with "presenting baby food" meant that eventually the baby salivated whenever he saw his mother's features (Fig. 2-2B). Thus, through first-order conditioning, a new stimulus-response unit became available. Always pairing the stimulus of the now conditioned stimulus-response unit with a picture of the flag (Fig. 2-2C) meant that eventually the baby would salivate (and also be happy etc.) whenever he saw a picture of the flag (Fig. 2-2D). This response would be elicited as a result of second-order conditioning.

Extensive laboratory work has shown, however, that higher-order conditioning is not as strong as it would have to be to account for man's habits, nor can it be carried beyond third-order conditioning with any degree of reliability.

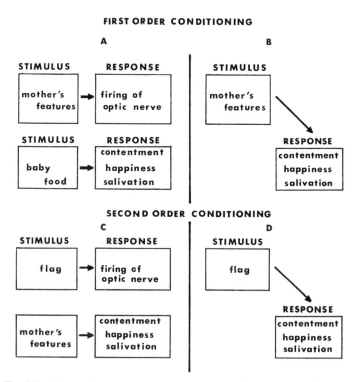

Fig. 2-2. Schematic diagram for second order Pavlovian conditioning.

Thus, it is not surprising that there have been no recent serious attempts to explain all behavior on the basis of classical conditioning. On the other hand, stimuli conditioned through classical conditioning—that is, by being paired with unconditioned stimuli—are extremely powerful in eliciting predictable responses. Much as a person might tell himself intellectually not to, he will salivate at the sight of a lemon or a vinegar bottle. The observation that somebody who has never seen a lemon does not salivate merely proves it is conditioning and not something else which plays a role here.

A striking aspect of classical conditioning is that the response in no essential way operates on the environment such as, perhaps, to influence the stimuli which elicited it. Say, a man is feeling the sting of a mosquito. His response to that stimulus is to slap where he feels the sting, and in doing so he sometimes effectively eliminates the source of stimulation, the mosquito. Within the framework of classical conditioning it would be difficult to deal with this situation: The response (slapping) is complex when compared with the glandular responses which are studied in classical conditioning; also, there were no frequent pairings of stimuli. A more elegant and doubtless broader frame of reference is needed to account for responses which cannot be analyzed according to the classical conditioning model.

OPERANT CONDITIONING

Through the genius of B. F. Skinner, an American psychologist, another kind of conditioning was formulated, called *operant conditioning*. In the 1930s Skinner noted that every response emitted by an organism has some consequence. In making this statement he observed that it is of less interest to know what elicited the response—that is to say, it is less important to inquire about the stimulus—than it is to inquire about the effect of the consequences on the response. Now, once the simple fact that responses necessarily have consequences is understood, it is difficult to see why it had not been spelled out and studied before. But all great discoveries are invariably statements about conditions and facts so self-evident as to be easily overlooked. Galileo, for instance, noted that things always fall downward. To be sure, people had observed the same thing for thousands of years, but only after Galileo stated this formally and began to conduct measurements, was significant progress made in the study of gravity. Einstein, too, noticed something that everybody had known for a long time: Measurement of space invariably involves measurement of time. On the same order of significance was Pavlov's discovery that some stimuli always elicit the same response. Once a common observation has been formally stated as a principle, it is usually not difficult to explore its relevance to heretofore puzzling questions. It is often said that the achievement of a discovery lies in giving a common observation new meaning.

What did Skinner mean when he said that every response has some consequence? He was stating that it is impossible to emit even the smallest response without in some way changing the world as it existed before that response was emitted. Even if the response is merely the firing of a nerve cell, one consequence, at least, could be the firing of another cell. But even if that does not happen, a certain consequence is the change of electric potential in that cell for some time after the firing. That condition, of course, is a consequence in the cell of having fired. If a further consequence is, say, the movement of an arm, then the surrounding air gets moved about, muscles tire, skin is stretched and restretched, a vase might be knocked off the table, a cheek might turn red—a chain reaction of consequences. It is impossible to think of a single response that does not involve necessary consequences, some of them doubtless trivial, but some also of literally vital importance.

Skinner decided to experiment by manipulating some of the consequences which he could observe. At first he worked with a hungry rat for whom he built a device which delivered a small food pellet every time the rat pressed a lever. It soon became evident that the rat pressed the lever whenever that action was followed by a release of a food pellet. It also became evident that the high frequency of lever pressing ceased quickly when the food pellet no longer followed.

This brief example contains the elements which started basic behavioral experimentation beginning in the 1940s and continuing today at an accelerating rate. The rat could first have operated the lever by accidentally leaning on or bumping it. What stimulus or stimuli elicited this original response is not clear and is of little or no concern. Measuring the rate of the response, however, should show that the rat responds perhaps once every hour (on the average) or perhaps only once a day. Whatever the frequency, it is very low. Why? Because operating the lever has as yet no important consequences for the organism. But quite a change occurs when the environment is manipulated so that every time the lever is depressed a pellet of food falls into the cage. Soon the rate of response sharply increases. The animal now is on a *schedule of reinforcement,* one called *continuous reinforcement,* since for every response the same positive consequence occurs. In this case for every lever pressing a food pellet is delivered. Now, instead of pressing the lever once per hour or per day or some such low rate, the animal might press the lever as often as ten times per minute, or six hundred times per hour.

To continue the experiment the consequence is again manipulated. Now not a *single* response is followed by a food pellet. This new schedule is called *extinction.* The effect of an extinction schedule is to lower the rate of response so that in a very short time it is back to its original level. Manipulating the consequences of a response makes it possible to change the rate of its occurrence, that is, the *strength of response.* Again, this situation can be presented schematically, as in Figure 2-3.

The question mark after the word *stimulus* means that the cause of the first lever press made by the animal is unknown. The broken arrow indicates, however, that some stimulus, whatever it may have been, led to the first response. The solid arrow then shows that this response led to what is called a *reinforcer,* in this case, food. The reinforcer, in turn, increased the rate at which the response was emitted, hence the recircling arrow. The process diagramed here is called *reinforcement.*

Skinner saw that the response had operated on the animal's environment in a very important way: After the response had been emitted there was a pellet near the animal where none had been before. He therefore called the response an *operant.* He also observed that he could control the strength of a response, just as Pavlov had many years earlier controlled the strength of stimuli. Consequently, he called his total procedure *operant conditioning.* Since the response is instrumental in obtaining the reinforcer, *instrumental conditioning* is sometimes used as synonymous with *operant conditioning.*

This example of operant conditioning demonstrates a very important law of behavior: *Extinction is swift after a schedule of continuous reinforcement.* In other words, the animal did not maintain the high rate of response which took place with a schedule of continuous reinforcement when the environment was manipulated to introduce a schedule of extinction. In the law the term *extinction* describes a fact about an organism's behavioral pattern. Previously the word *extinction* described a procedure. The animal could, of course, have ceased to respond for any number of reasons: He might have been distracted by the introduction of other stimuli, he might have been chased out of the chamber, or he might have suddenly died. Each of these instances would have resulted in a change of rate. (When no response is emitted the rate is, of course, as low as it can be.) But only under the conditions described does the technical term *extinction* refer to a changed rate. If it is known that an animal does not emit a certain response but the conditions which preceded the low rate of responding are unknown, there is no justification for speaking of extinction. Extinction involves a return to an original state; therefore, the original state must be known before extinction can be said to take place.

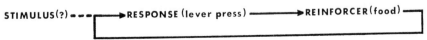

Fig. 2-3. Schematic diagram for operant conditioning (also called instrumental or Skinnerian conditioning).

As the story goes, Skinner one day had difficulty with his apparatus and, when the lever was pressed, the food magazine delivered pellets only occasionally. In effect, the rat was now working on a schedule of occasional reinforcement or, since the ratio of lever presses to reinforcements varied, a *variable ratio schedule*. After some time, Skinner arranged for an extinction schedule again, exactly as he had done before. But now he found that the effect of extinction was quite different from what it had been following continuous reinforcement: The animal kept responding for a very long time before the rate at which the responses were emitted gradually diminished. Here a second law of behavior had been established: *Extinction is slow after variable ratio schedules.*

Rather than speculate as to the reasons for this difference, Skinner began to experiment with other rats and other animals as well. He felt that if the laws just stated were of any importance they should have generality. Experimentation showed that both these laws did, indeed, have generality. They hold for all living organisms and, thus, are to be regarded simply as a fact of nature.

To what human behavior do these laws apply? Whenever someone operates a cigarette vending machine or a postal meter, he is, like the rat, on a schedule of continuous reinforcement. When the machine breaks down he will emit a response once more (will drop in another coin), but then extinguish (stop responding), at least with this machine and under these conditions.

Likewise, the man in Las Vegas operating a "one-arm bandit" is very much like the rat on a variable ratio schedule: Occasionally his response is reinforced, and much of the time it is not. What will happen if this machine breaks down? Of course, the man will go on throwing in coins; he will be slow to extinguish.

These examples serve well to illustrate an important merit of behavioral analysis: Explanations for a given behavior are provided by direct reference to the environment of the behaving organism and the conditions under which his behavior in this environment occurred. Behavioral explanations differ quite sharply from traditional ones. It is customary to explain the gambler's behavior by saying that he gambles because he has a compulsion—in effect a little demon that dwells inside him and prods him into doing what he does. That he has such a compulsion is inferred from the fact that he is seen doing something which, lacking knowledge of behavioral laws, is difficult to explain. And so, exactly as primitive man has done for many millennia, a little devil is invented that makes men do things. Efforts to change the behavior within the nonbehavioral frame of reference naturally are directed at changing the inner force. But how does one chase the devil away? How can one stop the compulsion from exerting its evil influence? Where is the compulsion located? What feeds it? Can it be measured directly? Does it ever die? How did it get there in the first place? Men are still trying seriously to answer these questions.

True, the behavioral scientist has not yet answered the question of why extinction after variable ratio schedules is slower than extinction after continuous reinforcement. He accepts these laws as facts about nature much as magnetism or the existence of life itself are accepted as facts about nature. But he certainly has found a useful, practical explanation for the high rate of responses that the gambler emits even in the face of seemingly insufficient reinforcement for his behavior.

Most human behavior is on a variable ratio schedule and, consequently, very difficult to extinguish. In bringing up children the parents cannot be there every time the children speak the truth. Consequently, they cannot continuously reinforce the children for veracity. This is desirable in a culture which values truthfulness, because there will be a time when the parents are no longer around to reinforce their offspring for telling the truth. In an adult world in which reinforcement for honesty is not abundant, this behavior would extinguish quickly had it not been on a schedule of variable ratio reinforcement during childhood training. But this holds true for undesirable behaviors as well. Suppose Johnny throws a temper tantrum every time he does not want to eat his cereal in the morning, and suppose further that his mother occasionally gives in and allows him not to eat his cereal. Johnny's temper tantrums then are on a schedule of variable ratio reinforcement. It is safe to predict that Johnny will have difficulties in the adult world. He will continue to throw temper tantrums for a much longer time than will Tom, Dick, and Harry whose mother, let us say, gave in to every temper tantrum of her boys and who, in effect, placed the boys' temper tantrums on a schedule of continuous reinforcement. These examples are oversimplifications because it is difficult to conceive that any child would be consistently reinforced under any conditions for throwing temper tantrums. Their purpose here is merely to show how the analysis of behavior forces a new look at the mechanisms of behavior in general, a new look which in many respects differs from traditional approaches.

Some human behaviors *are* on schedules of continuous reinforcement: Gravity is with us at all times and reinforces muscle movements continually in the same manner. From this, one could have predicted that man would adapt easily to movement in outer space, since his earthbound habits of movement would be extinguished quickly once the reinforcer (gravity) was no longer present.

It is interesting to think in behavioral terms of human habits and especially of the tenacious way they seem to cling. Once the schedule under which a particular habit functions is known, many of the puzzling aspects of habits—as for example, why some cling tenaciously and others do not—become quite understandable.

The fact that a stimulus through pairing with another can come to elicit a response it normally would not have elicited and the fact that responses have consequences which influence the probability with which these responses are emitted are the roots from which behavioral science and subsequently behavioral therapy have grown. Facts can, of course, be trivial or fundamental. If they are fundamental, they lead to implications which are likely to influence our lives.

EXERCISES, CHAPTER 2

1. In any science, why is it necessary to have basic units of measurements?
2. To which kind of conditioning is the term *response* more appropriate: classical or operant?
3. A stimulus may be a response and some responses may be stimuli. Why then make a distinction between the two? (Give examples.)
4. Reconstruct the basic model of classical conditioning with an example different from that given in the chapter.
5. Discuss the importance of higher-order conditioning.
6. Explain why classical conditioning is not as widely used as operant conditioning in explaining and understanding human behavior.
7. What did Skinner mean when he pointed out that every response has some consequence?
8. How does the speed with which extinction occurs relate to the schedule under which the behavior to be extinguished was acquired?
9. Give examples of continuous reinforcement schedules with human beings.
10. Comment on the reasons for the greater number of variable ratio schedules one may find with humans compared to the number of continuous reinforcement schedules.

3

Basic Schedules

Your study of this chapter should help you answer the following questions:

1. How does deprivation affect behavior?
2. How may aversive stimulation affect behavior? How does punishment?
3. What can be done when a behavior that is not normally emitted is to be reinforced?

The terms listed below are introduced and defined in this chapter:

differential reinforcement for low rates
fixed interval schedule
fixed ratio schedule
aversive stimulus
negative reinforcer
conditioning through reinforcement
reward
punishment
successive approximation
handshaping
magazine training

DEPRIVATION AND BEHAVIOR

Anyone investigating behavior soon realizes that no attempts at behavioral modification would be successful without reinforcers. Food evidently can function as a reinforcer, so can water or money, so can a friendly smile or a kind word. In fact, it may well be that anything at all—any subject, any material, any event, any situation—can function as a reinforcer in some environment and under some conditions. But it is, of course, also true that nothing functions as a reinforcer all the time. A man who has starved for three days is likely to do anything for a morsel of bread. On the other hand, someone who has just finished a rich meal would hardly consider a morsel of bread a reinforcer. Thus bread can be a powerful reinforcer in one instance, capable of eliciting a variety of behaviors of great strength, or it may also be quite useless as a reinforcer. The difference clearly lies in what deprivation precedes the use of a reinforcer. A rat who is not hungry is unlikely to perceive a food pellet as a vital consequence of pressing a lever. A man who is not thirsty is unlikely to do anything just to get a drink.

The reflection that deprivation is always necessary for a reinforcer to be effective easily leads one to conclude that the relationship between deprivation and reinforcer, quite independent of the schedule of reinforcement, determines the rate at which a certain behavior is emitted. In other words, it is commonly thought that the primary factor which causes the rat to press a lever is the hunger which resulted when food was withheld. The relationship between deprivation and the subsequent need or drives which such deprivation may establish in an organism has, in fact, been the basis of various psychological systems which see in the reduction of these drives the origin of all behavior. To show the fallacy on which such attempts at analyzing behavior rest, it is necessary to consider an additional schedule of reinforcement.

Of the many schedules which Skinner and his coworkers investigated, the following have thus far been presented in this text.

1. *Continuous reinforcement*—every response is followed by the same consequence or reinforcer
2. *Extinction*—no consequence that earlier functioned as a reinforcer follows the response
3. *Variable ratio reinforcement*—according to a specified average, only some responses are followed by given consequences

In order to fully appreciate the relationship between deprivation and behavior, it is important to understand the schedule called *differential reinforcement for low rates* (drl for short). This schedule works as follows.

Suppose that as an animal emits a given response; he starts a clock which has been regulated to run out within a second. If the animal responds again within that second, he resets the clock but receives no reinforcement. However, if he postpones his next response until the clock has "timed-out" (i.e., if he does not respond again until after the second is up), he is reinforced and the clock starts timing once more. Now suppose that gradually the clock is set to run longer and longer before reinforcement occurs. The animal learns this, of course, and soon responds at the highest rate the clock allows, which actually may be quite low, depending on how the clock has been set. In effect, no reinforcement is given for responses that are emitted at a rate higher than has been arranged. Differentiation is simply made between whatever higher rates the animal might respond on and the low rates which are possible under a particular arrangement.

Now, suppose there were two animals side by side, one of whom had been on a high variable ratio schedule and another who had been on a schedule of differential reinforcement for a very low rate. Suppose also that the animal on the variable ratio schedule is not particularly hungry and that the animal on the differential low rate schedule has not eaten for a whole day. What the naïve observer sees is one animal who furiously operates a lever and another who presses a lever only once, then dawdles in his cage, cleaning his paws, licking his tail, and after what seems like hours, presses the lever again and receives a pellet. The observer would be prone to conclude, quite wrongly, that the rat on the variable ratio schedule is hungry and that the other is not hungry at all.

Even had the animals been equally hungry, the results would still be the same: The one on the variable ratio schedule would respond at a high rate; the one on the schedule that reinforced low rates would respond at whatever rate his schedule had been arranged. If neither of the animals were hungry, neither of them would respond. Thus, deprivation is a necessary prerequisite but not the only or most important determiner of the *rate* at which a response is emitted.

To investigate the role which deprivation plays in influencing the occurrence of responses, it would be necessary to place similar organisms on the same schedule and vary their respective deprivation times. Under such conditions it would be likely that an animal that has just been fed would not operate the lever because, for that animal, food at that time is not an effective or functional reinforcer.

Merely observing two rats, one pressing a lever at a high rate while the other dawdles in a corner, is not enough to draw valid conclusions concerning the reasons for their difference in performance. As soon as the schedules these animals are on are known, the suspicion that one animal (the one who is not responding) is either sick or has just been fed is valid. But this suspicion should be voiced after knowing what schedules these animals had been subjected to. Hence, an analysis of behavior becomes valuable only when it takes into account the schedules of reinforcement which precede the observation. Most significantly, investigators no longer look for inner states and jump to unwarranted conclusions.

Use of this particular schedule (drl) demonstrates the relative importance of environmental manipulation involving schedules of reinforcement on the one hand and deprivation on the other. The importance of knowing both the deprivation and the schedule of reinforcement in order to make accurate judgments about behavior applies to schedules other than drl. One of these is the *fixed interval schedule*. As the name implies, a fixed interval of time must elapse before the same response will be reinforced again. On a fixed interval schedule an organism most typically learns not to emit relevant responses immediately following the delivery of a reinforcement, but to respond at an ever-increasing rate as the time for delivery of the next reinforcement approaches. One is tempted to think, not altogether incorrectly, that employees who are paid by the week or by the month are on a fixed interval schedule. But even though a rest period follows the delivery of the reinforcer, it is quite evident that many other schedules, all of which counteract the usual effect of a fixed interval schedule, are concurrently in force for humans. That is to say, in the example given, there is no question that people would fail to come to work if no contingencies were imposed on them other than showing up on payday.

Another schedule that must be considered when establishing the relationship between deprivation and behavior is the *fixed ratio schedule*. Its application is seen with employees in a paper bag factory who are on piecework. They must fold a certain number of paper bags (emit a fixed number of responses) before they are paid (reinforced). The rate of responding is steady and typically high between reinforcements under a fixed ratio schedule.

With both the fixed interval and the fixed ratio schedules, it is, of course, necessary for the reinforcer, whatever it is, to be something that is needed or desired by the organism. Whatever is used becomes effective only when it is preceded by deprivation. Deprivation, however, assures only that there is likely to be activity. The rate at which this activity occurs, or is likely to change, depends on what schedule of reinforcement has been arranged.

AVERSIVE STIMULATION AND PUNISHMENT

Under the schedules of reinforcement discussed so far the response was invariably an agent leading to a consequence. In all these instances the response, as it were, brought about something that did not exist immediately prior to its occurrence. But a response may, of course, also terminate a prevailing state, that is to say, remove something from the environment. Someone who is itching and responds by scratching alleviates (at least most of the time) the itch and thus terminates an unpleasant event. Technically, an unpleasant event such as being bitten by a mosquito is called an *aversive stimulus*. This term permits generality in referring to any event or action which goads an organism into doing away with it. Hence, the situation is much as before: A given response is strengthened because of its consequences. When a man scratches in response to an itch, however, the reinforcement consists in terminating an aversive state of affairs. Schematically this condition can be presented as in Figure 3-1.

This method of notation, first proposed by F. Mechner, a behavioral psychologist, is borrowed from electronic circuit diagraming. Horizontal arrows mean that a condition to the left of an arrow continues in time

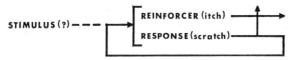

Fig. 3-1. Schematic diagram for reinforcement through the termination of an aversive stimulus.

either for an unknown period (if nothing is written beyond the tip of the arrow) or until the event toward which the arrow points occurs. Upward arrows mean the cutoff of events whose arrows they cross. In the example above, the upward pointing arrow's response presumably terminates the itch. (It is irrelevant that there are certainly conditions where scratching not only does not terminate itching but actually makes it worse. In such instances other schedules hold.) In this representation the arrow originating at the right of the word *response* branches into two: One turns upward and terminates the itch; the other continues on, then circles back to the bracket. This means that the response in question (in this case scratching), having once been successful in alleviating an itch, will be emitted again whenever a similar pairing of reinforcer and response occurs. (In the schematic, the bracketing of *reinforcer* and *response* signifies that they always exist together.) Again, as in the previous schematic (p. 25), one may presume that originally there was some other stimulus which led to the first scratch, although for an understanding of the process described this is not important.

But surely there must be some difference between the reinforcer represented here and that diagramed on page 25. There is. The reinforcer in the present example is a *negative reinforcer;* that is, it strengthens all those responses which terminate it. In all the previous examples, *positive reinforcers* such as food pellets strengthened the responses which brought them about. This difference can be understood by comparing the two diagrams in Figure 3-2.

In either case the response is strengthened; that is to say, it is likely to occur with greater frequency in the future due to the function of

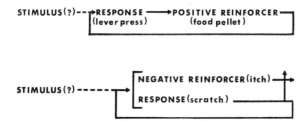

Fig. 3-2. Two schematic diagrams of reinforcement, showing processes by which a response can be strengthened either through termination of a negative reinforcer or granting of a positive reinforcer.

either the negative or the positive reinforcer. The entire procedure is called *conditioning through reinforcement*. Incidentally, it is quite true that negative reinforcers could function as stimuli which actually elicit the response that removes them from the environment of the organism. But it is not definite that they do function this way. It may well be that some other stimulus actually elicits the response. This may or may not be of importance in a given situation, but it does not affect the basic principle involved. In other words, the itch in the example may well have been the stimulus itself. But it need not have been, and in this context, it would not matter whether it was or not.

Designating a reinforcer "positive" or "negative" depends on the effect the reinforcer has on the rate of response. If a reinforcer *precedes* the response and subsequently strengthens it, then it is by definition a negative reinforcer. If it *follows* a response and that response is strengthened, then by definition it is a positive reinforcer. Such definitions are not uncommon in science. In physics, for example, that pole of a magnet which points toward north is by definition different from that which does not. The definitions do not say anything about why things happen as they do. But they do allow reference to replicable procedures and thus allow for communication among people interested in the same field. Through the application of either a positive or a negative reinforcer, the future occurrence of a response, under the conditions described, can be increased. In both situations one might say that the organism was "rewarded."

Using the term *reward* in this context requires considerable curtailing of its common meaning. It is not commonly thought that rewarding someone means giving him what he regards as a normal condition or as his just due in the first place. Also, there are some events, such as mild electric shock, which are certainly not thought of as rewards at all but which can function as effective reinforcers. Consequently, while it is not wrong to use the term *reward* in its restricted sense, *reinforcer*, the technical term, is much to be preferred.

An even more important reason for avoiding the term *reward* is that it has as its most common antonym the term *punishment*. Thus, by analogy, one might infer that the opposite of reinforcement is punishment, an inference which is quite wrong. Here is one instance where behavioral research quite unequivocally contradicts popular belief. Reinforcement is useful to strengthen a behavior, but to weaken a behavior requires the procedure of extinction, not punishment.

Figure 3-3 shows what punishment looks like in schematic form. This time no arrow circles back to *response*, and therefore no indication

STIMULUS (?) ---→RESPONSE——→NEGATIVE REINFORCER

Fig. 3-3. Schematic diagram for punishment.

is given that the occurrence of the response will be increased. The effect of a punishment schedule is not analogous to the effect of a reinforcement schedule. The strength of the response is, indeed, not in the least affected by punishment. True, all responding, including the response which brought it about, ceases for a time after punishment. But when the punishing conditions no longer prevail, the response not only returns to its former rate but increases temporarily, as if to make up for time lost under the punishment schedule. Thus punishment can be used to suppress a behavior, but it cannot be used to change it. To change behavior requires schedules of reinforcement. Table 3-1 shows what

Table 3-1

Comparison of the Effects of Reinforcement, Punishment, and Extinction on Behavior

Conditioning Using Positive Reinforcer	Conditioning Using Negative Reinforcer	Punishment	Extinction
Original eliciting stimulus is unknown	Original eliciting stimulus is unknown	Original eliciting stimulus is unknown	Original eliciting stimulus is unknown
Response produces the positive reinforcer	Response removes the negative reinforcer	Response produces negative reinforcer or removes positive reinforcer	Response does not result in the usual consequence
Response is strengthened	Response is strengthened	All responding is temporarily suppressed	Response is weakened

is involved when aspects of reinforcement and punishment are compared. The conditioning schedule designed to weaken a response or, indeed, to remove it entirely from the behavioral repertoire is, of course, extinction. With the procedure of extinction, an organism emits a response but receives no positive reinforcer or removes no negative reinforcer. This gradually weakens the response to the level of frequency which existed prior to the deliberate use of any reinforcement procedure. If the response was not originally in the organism's behavioral repertoire, it disappears altogether after extinction.

Under a procedure of punishment, a response is neither weakened nor removed. Instead it emerges in unchanged form under different conditions or under the same conditions if the punishing event no longer follows.

However, when some behavior prevails which cannot be reinforced and which prevents behavior that can be reinforced from occurring, punishment is appropriate. In such a situation the user of punishment must be skillful in ascertaining that during the brief period following punishment some response can be elicited and reinforced which precludes the reappearance of the punished response. A good example is the completely rowdy classroom. The skilled teacher in such a situation may well use punishment to establish momentary quiet. But during that quiet he needs to quickly catch the children's interest in the subject matter and thus elicit responses, especially from the ringleaders, which can be reinforced. If he fails in this, he will either have to continue to punish or else resign himself to an unruly group of students. Punishment does not and can not teach anything. Punishment suppresses responding.

One might well wonder why the notion that punishment has the opposite effect from reward is so prevalent and also why the process of extinction is so little understood and used. Behavioral science can readily answer this question: Punishment is widely used for the simple reason that it is instantly reinforcing to its user. The person who uses punishment typically wants to stop some ongoing behavior. He wants a quick change in behavior—and, of course, he gets it. At that time—that is, at the time when he gets the change he wanted, when he stops whatever behavior he wanted to stop—it is not evident that the change he produced is merely temporary. And of course, sometimes that is not important either. But the point is that punishment, its prevalence in law enforcement, teaching, and the rearing of children notwithstanding, does not change behavior and thus is used only in circumscribed ways in mental hospitals.

SUCCESSIVE APPROXIMATION OR HANDSHAPING

What if there is a kind of behavior that should be reinforced but which never occurs? How can a behavior be strengthened that is not there to begin with? Fortunately, this seeming dilemma can be handled with ease through operant conditioning. A behaviorist begins by thinking of a continuum of behaviors. At one end of that continuum is what the organism is expected to do; at the other end is what the organism does now.

Suppose a behaviorist is asked to train a retarded child to button his own shirt. The child does not do this. The behavior that is wanted constitutes one end of the behavioral continuum. At the other end are things the child does now: He holds buttons in his fingers; he can show them to the therapist.

As he begins the child's training, the behaviorist reinforces for the already existent behavior. This does no more than permit the therapist to identify with certainty effective reinforcers which control this original behavior. Suppose that small candies function as reinforcers for the retarded child. Gradually, and in small, successive steps, the therapist reinforces what he wants to achieve by handing the child a candy. First he might reinforce the child for merely showing a button, but only for showing buttons that are sewn on the shirt. Once this is under control the next step might be—but need not be—to reinforce only when one hand shows the button while the other holds that part of the shirt containing the buttonhole.

For some children this might be too large a step, for others it may be too small. In behavioral shaping, failure is most often due to steps that are too large. Too small a step cannot cause problems because there is always a response that can be reinforced. But suppose that the child performs satisfactorily. The next step might be to reinforce only when the buttonhole is brought ever closer to the button. Then reinforcement might be granted only after the button has been thrust into the buttonhole. For the final step, candy is given only after the button has been shoved through the buttonhole. Each step, in effect, contains elements of the one previously reinforced. In the process the therapist extinguished parts of the behavior over which he had just achieved control and simultaneously began to reinforce a behavior which was a short step away from the old behavior and a short step closer to the one he sought to establish.

This behavioral technique is called *successive approximation,* or *handshaping.* The term *handshaping* is widely used, perhaps because it suggests the emergence of sculpture from a blob of clay under the hands of a skilled artist. Actually, it comes from the laboratory where this technique was initially developed. There the experimenter holds an electric pushbutton switch in his hand by means of which he can deliver reinforcement to an animal. Use of the term *handshaping* stresses the important quality of reinforcing by hand and not through automatic means.

To understand this process, it would be well to handshape a pigeon or rodent either alone or with help from a behavioral laboratory. A good experiment to begin with is the following which can easily be performed as a classroom demonstration.

Assume that the response to be shaped is a clockwise full-circle turn by a pigeon in his cage. The animal must first be *magazine trained.* This means that the click of a food magazine must have come to function as a stimulus which causes the pigeon to go to the feeding trough when he hears it.

For the experiment the pigeon stands in his cage and the experimenter watches it. In his hand he holds the pushbutton switch which will be used to trigger the food magazine whenever appropriate. In this case, since the experimenter wants the pigeon to turn a full circle in a clockwise direction, merely a slight tilting of the animal's head to the right or a tiny step with the right foot would be the appropriate time to activate the food magazine. Just as soon as the animal makes such a movement the experimenter immediately presses the button in his hand, thus closing an electrical circuit and bringing food within reach of the pigeon.

Since turning the head or moving a foot occurs frequently in a pigeon's behavioral repertoire, an experimenter rarely has to wait long for this response or an approximation of it. What happens next? According to behavioral law, a response that brings a positive reinforcer is likely to occur in the future with high frequency. In this experiment, any clockwise turn of the animal's head is the response, and grain in the food magazine is a positive reinforcer. If the law holds, the pigeon will very soon turn his head clockwise again and instantly his behavior is reinforced by access to food.

Before reinforcing the next response, the experimenter waits ever so little longer, that is, until the animal has turned his head in the desired direction a little more than he did at first. This procedure continues until the turning head pulls, as it were, the body after it.

A critical step is reached when the animal makes a half-turn prior to reinforcement. Sometimes the skilled experimenter can press the switch at just that moment when the bird's body is just slightly beyond the half-turn. If he does, the bird will then and there complete the full turn as he goes to peck at the food. This establishes the full response. But the half-turn is somewhat tricky. It must be remembered that up until then the bird was really being reinforced for turning and then for re-turning as he went to get food. At the half-turn point, the bird must continue to turn or the desired terminal behavior will not have been reached. Thus, at the halfway point of the turn a large behavioral step must be taken. Yet with a well-magazine-trained pigeon the whole procedure should not take more than ten to twenty minutes, and sometimes as little as two minutes.

The salient points about handshaping are as follows:

1. *Both the initial behavior and the terminal behavior must be clearly defined.*

Obviously, if the experimenter does not know or knows only vaguely what it is he wants to accomplish, he cannot expect to be successful with techniques which are highly specific.

2. *There must be a chain of behavioral links between the initial and the terminal behaviors.*

Now, this chain cannot be thought of as rigid. It usually is not the only way to get from the initial to the terminal behavior. Suppose that by chance the pigeon in the previous example had completely turned around the first time the experimenter was ready to reinforce. Clearly it would not make sense here not to reinforce simply because the experimenter had guessed quite soundly that the first response to be reinforced would be far short of the complete response.

3. *The experimenter must be willing to quickly change his strategy if at one point he designed too large a step and the organism does not emit the desired behavior.*
4. *The reinforcer to be used must be available in small quantities, so that at a critical time the organism does not satiate.*

With rats and pigeons this is easily arranged through small food pellets. Many of the widely used reinforcers for human beings permit the same arrangement. Small candies for children, puffs on a cigarette for adults, glimpses of pictures, sips of a favorite beverage, all have been used successfully.

5. *There must be assurance that the response to be shaped can physically be emitted by the organism.*

For human beings this most typically is a medical judgment. It is clearly not determined by what people might commonly think an organism is capable or incapable of. On the other hand, it is equally clear that rats cannot be shaped to fly like birds or that a child without arms can be trained to button his shirt. These examples may seem quite trivial, but they are given to make an important point: If, due to some brain damage or some other physical deficiency which may not be visible to the layman, there is no possibility that a given response can be emitted, then any attempt at handshaping is a waste of time.

Both from a general scientific as well as a therapeutic point of view, deprivation and handshaping are powerful techniques which demand responsibility on the part of their user. They are tools like others which technology has provided over the years. And like all tools they can be put to good or to evil use. Fortunately, there is little if any chance in a modern hospital that these techniques can be abused, because inherent in their application is the close observation of the persons on whom they are applied. If the results are detrimental—and this will show within days if not within hours—the technique can and must be changed. Then, too, the techniques are quite public in the sense that the user can exactly describe what he is about to do, and in modern hospitals, he is required to give such descriptions. Finally, there is ample assurance through competent professionals that the personal welfare and safety of patients is safeguarded. If, for example, a physician has diagnosed that there is no organic reason for a patient's nonspeaking and if he requests a handshaping regimen which entails deprivation of one sort or another, he also ascertains with the help of dieticians that a balanced diet is maintained for such a patient. Thus, no patient is "starved" into submission in any sense of the word. Behavioral techniques are new though, and as such they perhaps frighten and cause criticism. To be sure, a critical attitude is desirable and can only result in a more thoughtful and thus more effective application of these techniques. How desirable it would be if everyone had similarly critical attitudes toward widely used techniques, such as punishment, which can be shown to be not only ineffective but even detrimental!

EXERCISES, CHAPTER 3

1. Give examples of schedules of reinforcement (and their results) which are in effect for greatly divergent living organisms.
2. Give an example of differential reinforcement for high rates with human beings and another for low rates with human beings.
3. Speculate why two children who were equally loved or unloved (or, to put it behaviorally, whose state of deprivation of parental love is equal) may behave differently under similar situations.
4. Speculate why aversive control is so common in American culture.
5. Reinforcement can occur either by the appearance of a positive reinforcer or the avoidance of a negative reinforcer. In either case the response in question is strengthened. Give examples for this.
6. The term *reward* is used as equivalent to *reinforcement* or *reinforcer*. Why should the technical terms be preferred to the popular one?
7. Wise parents use successive approximations of given behaviors with their children. How might this possibly affect the mental health of the children?
8. Discuss the extent to which handshaping requires flexibility.
9. Think of an unusual behavior in an animal (such as a rat taking a shower) and design schedules which would establish this behavior. List reinforcers you would use and the chain of behaviors which you successively would reinforce.
10. Express schematically the case where a nurse scolds a patient for lying on his bed; then draw a diagram for the case where the nurse rewards the patient for not lying in bed. Predict the consequences of the two techniques on the basis of what you know so far.

4

Stimulus Discrimination

Your study of this chapter should help you answer the following questions:

1. What is the importance of stimulus control?
2. What is a suitable environment for the treatment of mental illness and how is it achieved?
3. How is rate of response used in behavioral therapy?

The terms listed below are introduced and defined in this chapter:

stimulus discrimination
control stimulus
conditioned reinforcer
superstitious behavior
suitable environment
total environment

CONTROL STIMULI

There is a procedure so basic to behavioral science that without it severe limitations would be placed on the use of behavioral techniques. This procedure is used to teach different responses in the presence of different stimuli. It most commonly is referred to as *stimulus discrimination,* or simply *discrimination.* Its basis is another of those facts so obvious as to escape attention—i.e., that every behavior is emitted in a real environment which contains many stimuli. Most typically, any given behavior is acquired in a fairly limited environment which contains the same stimuli throughout the period of acquisition. These stimuli, therefore, eventually function as *control stimuli* for this behavior. They set the stage, as it were, for the emission of the behavior.

To see how this works, think of any schedule of reinforcement discussed so far. The schedule you select is operating naturally in an environment containing numerous stimuli other than those the experimenter may consider relevant. These might be the reinforcers, the levers or manipulanda the organism uses in his response, and so forth. Possibly some of these stimuli are perceived by the responding organism, although they are not necessarily of any relevance to the particular schedule being used. Yet, willy-nilly, these stimuli are being paired with the reinforcer much in the way in which Pavlov deliberately paired food and the sound of a bell.

Suppose that every time an organism is subjected to a schedule of continuous reinforcement a certain stimulus complex A (for example, a green illumination of the experimental chamber) is also introduced. Suppose further that every time this schedule alternates with extinction, stimulus complex B (for example, a red illumination of the chamber) is introduced and complex A is removed. It should not be long before the organism perceives this and promptly ceases to respond as soon as B appears, yet responds again upon the reappearance of A. When this happens, the organism is said to have learned to *discriminate* between A and B.

To the casual observer, A and B appear to control the behavior in question. That is, as long as it is understood that the control exerted by A and B was made possible only through the control over behavior by the original reinforcer, there is no reason why A or B cannot be called *control stimuli*. And indeed they are. Investigations of this principle lead to another general law of behavior: *Control stimuli may function for organisms generally, no matter to what biological classification the organism belongs.*

Some control stimuli play a strong role in the life of rats. Others are important in the life of human beings. Some affect both men and rats. One of the most obvious control stimuli to which all organisms are more or less subjected is daylight. Its counterpart is the absence of daylight. Many stimulus-response sequences are reinforced in the presence of daylight and are not reinforced in the absence of daylight; e.g., for being active, daylight is a control stimulus for most people, though not for all.

In classical conditioning the range of unconditioned stimuli is more limited than the range of neutral stimuli which can be conditioned. Likewise in operant conditioning, probably few stimuli may serve as unconditioned reinforcers, but practically anything can—and does—function as a control stimulus.

A clear understanding of control stimuli is an essential part of the analysis of behavior. Certainly one cannot practice behavioral therapy without it. Suppose, for example, that a psychiatric nurse in a mental hospital reinforces a patient for engaging in a variety of activities on the ward instead of for sitting in a corner all day long. Suppose also that the ward is one in which a "token economy" has been established; that is, patients receive brass tokens as reinforcers for doing work or behaving in appropriate ways. The patients use these tokens to obtain both luxuries and necessities. Accordingly, the patient who is supposed to engage in a variety of activities is given a token whenever the nurse sees him talking with other patients, looking at TV, having his hair cut—in brief, when he is *not* sitting in a corner by himself.

Practically, the nurse cannot closely observe the patient's behavior all day long; consequently, he is on a schedule of variable ratio reinforcement. This is good, for once the desired behavior has been established in this way, it will not easily extinguish. As time goes by the patient responds beautifully to the treatment, and the nurse is delighted. Confidently she goes on a three-week vacation, but, lo, what happens to the patient? Within a few days the new behavior has completely extinguished, and the patient is back where he was before the nurse worked with him. In this case, the nurse was that stimulus A in the presence of which reinforcement was given. If the other nurses on this ward are considered stimulus complex B, then an ideal situation exists for stimulus discrimination. Every time stimulus complex A (the psychiatric nurse) was present, a variable ratio schedule with tokens for reinforcers was in force. Every time only stimulus complex B (everyone else on the ward excluding the psychiatric nurse) was present, an extinction schedule was in force during which no reinforcements were forthcoming for engaging in a variety of activities. That the psychiatric nurse actually functioned as a control stimulus can be tested when she returns from her vacation. If she really functioned as a control stimulus, the behavior which she had established would *at once and in full force be emitted by the patient.*

Consider another example. Suppose that a group of summer tourists is visiting a picturesque small town. Its members gaily chatter and joke as they walk through the streets and visit curio shops. Their tourist guide banters with them as he relates local anecdotes and points out sights. Now they are entering the local ancient cathedral. Instantly their voices become subdued, and the guide reverently explains the history of the cathedral, pointing out famous murals and other art works. Once outdoors again, the group is as gay and as noisy as it had been before. A behaviorist would say that the entire cathedral constituted a control stimulus in the presence of which silence and decorous behavior have been traditionally reinforced.

It is worth noting that nothing about a control stimulus is intrinsically reinforcing. Nor is it necessary that the behavior controlled by the stimulus be continuously reinforced, once it has been established.

Control stimuli can be almost unbelievably powerful. The skilled behavioral scientist always worries about control stimuli as much as he does about the schedules with which he is working. Overlooking the presence of a control stimulus, which by hindsight becomes an obvious one, can only lead to failure to accomplish the desired behavioral goal. The psychiatric nurse, for example, might have thought she had established new behavior in her patient. She had indeed done so, but the desired behavior was also tied to a control stimulus, in this case, her own person. Therefore, she did not accomplish the behavioral goal she had set.

Employment of useful control stimuli can be as beneficial as unplanned control stimuli can be detrimental. If it is known, for example, into what environment a mental patient is to be discharged, the skilled behavioral therapist will search this environment for stimuli which can be introduced into the therapeutic situation. Their introduction assures that the behavior, once established and under the control of these stimuli, will be maintained after the patient's discharge.

The room in which therapy sessions are held can become a control stimulus. In his lectures J. Greenspoon, a psychologist who has applied behavioral therapy principles in clinical counseling, reports the case of a man with a Napoleon delusion. With this man, Greenspoon used social approval as a reinforcer. In the course of a clinical session in his office, Greenspoon would listen attentively and reply cheerfully as long as the patient talked about reasonable things. As soon as the talk shifted to the patient's delusions, Greenspoon would look bored, begin to leaf through magazines, and look out the window. The instant that the patient said something that made sense to Greenspoon, he again gave his full attention. Within a very short time this patient ceased to refer to his delusions during therapy sessions. But nurses on the ward reported that the patient was as delusional as ever as soon as he left the therapist's office.

A little reflection on this state of affairs suggests that if therapy is to be successful, it should be practiced in as varied an environment and by as varied a number of therapists as possible. It is for this reason that the best success is obtained where not just one person or a small group of interested professional personnel is engaged in this form of therapy, but where the entire hospital staff from superintendent to janitor understands the principles of behavioral therapy and is in some way or another involved.

It is impossible to overestimate the importance of control stimuli. Much has been made, for example, of fetishism in mental illness. Yet, even though no thorough study in this area has been made from a behavioral point of view, it is safe to guess that most fetishes are no more than control stimuli powerfully attached to some behavioral pattern, such as sexual orgasm, that carries its own natural reinforcers.

To prove the importance of control stimuli one has only to analyze those that affect his own behavior. For many of us, talking on the telephone is a strong control stimulus for smoking. For all of us, food colors are control stimuli: If food is not of the right color we can hardly bring ourselves to eat it. Violet potatoes or green meat need but be imagined to make clear what is meant. The most disconcerting aspect of control stimuli is that they show no established generality; one man's crow is another man's nightingale. Cultural conditioning sometimes makes it appear that this or that control stimulus is universal, or as people often say, "human nature." But that is not true. Anything at all can function as a control stimulus for practically any behavior. All that is needed is a consistent pairing of the reinforced behavior with the stimulus in question.

An understanding of control stimuli is also helpful in appreciating the fact that there are some stimuli which can universally be used as reinforcers—sex, food, and water are examples—and others which must be conditioned before they can become effective—for example, money in all its forms. *Conditioned reinforcers* often allow parceling into small bits a major reinforcing event which itself cannot be broken up. A trip abroad, a visit, a dive into a cool pool on a hot day, a car, a dress—all these can be reinforcers, but they cannot be chopped up to sustain long periods of responding as they are needed, for example in shaping a behavior. But the money necessary to buy these things can be divided into units small enough to serve this purpose. In a culture with relatively stable currency, it is sometimes hard to grasp the fact that the little pieces of green paper or silver used for money have, in and of themselves, no value whatsoever. The experience of legendary King Midas is relevant here. Completely unaware that gold is a conditioned reinforcer, Midas wished that everything he touched would turn to gold. When his wish was granted, he soon felt hungry enough to pray to have his wish undone.

To be effective, conditioned reinforcers must make obtainable an effective reinforcer, i.e., something an organism needs or wants. In many behavioral therapy programs tokens and other nonofficial money are used as a conditioned reinforcer. Both daily necessities and privileges should, of course, be available in such programs only by means of these conditioned reinforcers. In effect, the reinforcers that are effective for individual patients, such as sweets for one, cigarettes for another, should be available to them also only through the tokens or whatever the conditioned reinforcers are.

Unfortunately, the experimenter cannot always easily undo the control some stimuli may exercise over a given behavior. Consider the following situation which could occur when a pigeon is being magazine trained. The animal might be standing on one foot the first time the food magazine is activated. Since a reinforced response is strengthened, the bird will more often than not stand on one foot during the next few minutes. If, again by chance, the reinforcer is given when the animal happens to be standing on one foot, this response will be further strengthened. There is, of course, no causal relationship between lifting one foot and receiving food. But no such relationship is required for reinforcement to be effective. The pigeon in this case has acquired what one might call a "superstition." What is more, exactly because there is no planned relationship between the presentation of the reinforcer (which is regulated by a clock) and the *superstitious behavior,* in effect the animal is being reinforced on a variable ratio schedule for this behavior. Extinction after variable ratio reinforcement is slow, and thus, predictably, superstitions are quite resistant to extinction.

Skinner, who first noticed superstition of this type in pigeons, remarks how such behavior often develops in the physical vicinity of control stimuli. Hence, the environment, or at least those parts of it which functioned as control stimuli, will often elicit superstitious behavior even in the absence of the original reinforcer responsible for the acquisition of such behavior. For the pigeon, superstitious behaviors themselves are, of course, control stimuli simply because they are events, i.e., stimuli, which were present when reinforcement was given during a learning process.

All that has been said here about pigeons applies to human superstitions as well. Magic "wishing for something" or "not walking under ladders" is quite probably reinforced by chance some of the time (a variable ratio schedule) and hence is resistant to extinction.

Control stimuli can be a powerful tool for shaping behavior. Their identification leads to understanding of behavior, and their use provides a means of helping mental patients acquire those behaviors expected of them for life in a community outside the hospital.

The old expression, "There's a time and place for everything," contains a great deal of truth. Observation of behavior verifies that the surroundings influence what is done and said. Behavioral scientists are describing the processes by which this happens and call it discrimination learning. The behavior of the mentally ill is not controlled by the same stimuli that function for normal individuals. To a large extent, then, behavioral therapy aims at bringing the patient's behavior under the control of stimuli appropriate to a given situation.

THE SUITABLE ENVIRONMENT

One often hears that schools should be architecturally designed to provide an environment suitable for learning; churches, for worship; and offices, for work. Such statements imply that somehow there is a kind of material environment which will be most conducive to the goals of any given endeavor. By analogy, mental hospitals are to provide an environment suitable for patients to recover from mental illness.

Behavioral studies concerning control stimuli do indeed show that building design is important but quickly make it apparent that people are an all-important part of an environment. If the environment in a mental hospital is to be suitable for recovery from mental illness, then the nurses, doctors, other patients, visitors, and, in fact, anyone with whom a patient comes in contact must also be suitable since they are part of the environment. Yet meeting this requirement is not as easily accomplished as furnishing a ward, using a certain color wall paint, or providing soothing music—elements more commonly thought of as part of the environment.

The fact that some patients may require stimulation while others need none at all points out that even if it were possible to establish an environment suitable for one purpose, this very achievement would make that same environment quite unsuitable for another.

What then is the answer? It lies in the fact that behaviors (responses) can be stimuli. A patient's environment includes the actions of those in the environment as well as the physical features. In fact, since actions in some way or another reflect on the physical aspects of an environment, they are perhaps the most important aspect of environment. Intuitively this has always been recognized. The young lover who assures his sweetheart that "the humblest abode is heaven with you . . ." merely expresses in poetic form the meaning, "being with you makes drab surroundings unimportant . . . ." A behavioral approach makes these statements understandable since every response is considered part of the total environment and as such affects not only one person, but all who exist in that environment. Now, responses (stimuli as parts of an environment) can be friendly or unfriendly in a cultural context. That is to say, they become control stimuli for other behaviors which typically occur along with them. A smile, for example, is a control stimulus which, most commonly, elicits a smile from others. Nodding signifies agreement.

But, again, there is still individuality even to control stimuli as culturally conditioned as a nod or a smile. Whether a smile or a frown is involved or whether tender loving care (mostly shown through many small responses) or firmness are being used, it is the therapeutic goal which determines their employment. In other words, tender loving care, as such, is neither good nor bad for therapy. It is the use which is made of it which can be beneficial or, as the following example shows, disastrous.

In a certain Eastern hospital for the mentally retarded there was an unusually large number of so-called "headbangers." The superintendent, alarmed at this state of affairs, observed conditions on the wards and found something which anybody unfamiliar with behavioral analysis could not help but approve: The nurses were most loving and kind with their patients. As soon as a patient began to hit his head against a wall, the nurse would rush to him and comfort him. In addition, to calm him down or to show her acceptance of him, she would give him a bit of chocolate or other candy. But this superintendent saw that the nurses were using the most powerful behavioral techniques toward a horrible purpose: They were giving tender loving care to patients smashing themselves bloody against a wall. Not only that, the reinforcers they used had become control stimuli, so that any time a nurse would appear with chocolate or other candy, patients instantly began their headbanging.

It is at once an obvious and at the same time a difficult goal to achieve that every smile or frown, every friendly approach or firm one, detailed attention or complete disregard be suited to the therapeutic goals of the individual patient. What is suitable for one may be exactly wrong for another.

The same goes for other aspects of the environment. Should nursing personnel, for example, wear uniforms or civilian clothes? It is difficult to research this question because of the emotional overtones which the pros and cons are likely to take. For the patient who sees the mental hospital as a refuge from a hostile world, the nurses who wear uniforms are most reassuring. They personify the authority and orderliness which strengthen his delusions. Nurses who wear uniforms around him help him stay in the hospital. On the other hand, for the patient who is withdrawn and for whom civilian clothing is a control stimulus for remaining silent the nurse who wears a uniform may be beneficial. Toward her he will open up, and it is she who can most easily make a list of reinforcers effective for him.

At the moment no hard data exist which categorically support the wearing of uniforms or the wearing of civilian clothing. In our own behavioral hospital program, however, we explored the question of whether uniforms should or should not be worn by having nurses wear civilian clothes on duty. The first day this was tried, the experience shocked the nurses and started them thinking: When they walked down the corridors of the administration building, people whom they had known for years apparently did not see them; did not respond to their nods; looked, as it were, right through them. Again, the power of a control stimulus had been demonstrated. Administrative personnel rarely interact with patients; for the most part, patients might as well be furniture. To the nurses this was a sobering insight. As it developed, the data which were obtained in this project did prove that in general it would be more beneficial to wear civilian clothes rather than uniforms, but these findings certainly cannot be generalized to all mental hospitals nor to all other conditions involving nursing personnel and patients.

In deciding what is suitable and what is not, the issue of illness crops up. As long as mental patients are regarded as sick in some way, personal comfort for that patient is an important consideration. But in the behavioral view the patient is not sick in any physical sense. He is in the hospital to find himself again, to find modes of behaving which are acceptable in the outside world. Yet, in the outside world, no one normally makes your bed, ties your shoes, helps you with your bath, or performs services traditionally accepted as part of nursing. Thus, if hospital treatment is directed toward getting patients out in society again, its environment should not be made too comfortable for the patient. The patient should never be able to regard the hospital as a haven, for then, of course, no more therapy would be possible. (It may be quite true that places are needed where a person can withdraw even to the extent of spending the rest of his days apart from general society, as perhaps elderly senile people might want to do. But a hospital which has as its aim the recovery of patients should not be abused for this purpose.)

As a final consideration regarding a suitable environment, the physical building within which therapy is conducted should be used therapeutically. Since buildings usually already exist when a behavioral program is begun, the question typically is not how to design such buildings, but rather how best to use those that are available. Who is to decide this? Logically, the daily psychiatric staff meeting attended by the psychiatrist, behavioral therapist, nurses, social workers, and whoever else is concerned with the patients' recovery program, provides the platform for such decisions. Here is decided which rooms are to have curtains, which ones not; which patients are to have nightstands, which ones not; who is to eat at single tables, and who at a community table. Clearly, therapeutic needs should dictate what is to be done and how a building is to be utilized to serve as a control stimulus.

Older, less "antiseptic" looking buildings probably are more suited for behavioral therapy programs than many modern structures. In the older building it is often easier to arrange for a variety of settings from the coldest and most sterile to the warmest and most homelike. In the modern buildings, beds are too often in a row in a single, large room that can easily be supervised from an observation post (the nursing station) not unlike the way a jail yard is controlled from a guard tower. A modern building doesn't necessarily defeat a behavioral program. Its use simply calls for greater ingenuity on the part of the staff so as to create a control environment suited to the purposes of a behavioral program.

EXERCISES, CHAPTER 4

1. Explain why a behavior observed in one environment cannot be predicted for another without reference to prevailing control stimuli.
2. List control stimuli that are present when you eat dinner.
3. How many of the stimuli listed under (2) are present when you eat popcorn while watching TV? While you eat a hot dog at a ball game?

4. How does clever advertising make use of control stimuli when you shop for groceries?
5. Discuss sexual fetishism in terms of control stimuli.
6. Why are modes of behaving to be considered in discussions of an environment?
7. People sometimes say that they "have always used operant conditioning." This is, of course, true. Discuss the terrifying results to which such applications without understanding of the principles involved may lead.

5

Desensitization

Your study of this chapter should help you answer the following questions:

1. What is desensitization?
2. What is the theoretical background of desensitization?
3. How is desensitization used in behavioral therapy?

The terms listed below are introduced and defined in this chapter:

anxiety
desensitization
antagonistic behaviors

DESENSITIZATION DEFINED

Most human beings are familiar with the intense fear that accompanies an accident, many have experienced stage fright, and still others report they feel uncomfortable when meeting people for the first time. In clinical psychiatry and psychology such responses are called *anxiety*. J. Wolpe defines anxiety as the "autonomic response pattern or patterns that are characteristically part of the organism's response to noxious stimulation" [2]. Responses to anxiety include raised blood pressure, higher pulse rate, sweating, muscle tension, verbal reports of intense fear, and in extreme cases, defecation, micturition, and avoidance behavior. *Desensitization* is a behavioral method of reducing or eliminating anxiety.

Almost fifty years ago Watson and Rayner [3] demonstrated that fears could be developed using the classical conditioning presented in Chapter 2 of this text. In an experiment with a young child they systematically paired a noxious stimulus with the close physical proximity of a white rat. After a few pairings the child showed signs of fear of the rat. This fear had not been present prior to conditioning. Tests of generalization indicated that the fear spread to other furry objects.

M. C. Jones [4] demonstrated methods of overcoming these fears by pairing eating with graded presentation of the feared object. At first the conditioned stimulus was displayed at a distance, but over successive exposures it was moved ever closer to the subject. Gradually fear disappeared.

This evidence supports the belief that these potent stimulus-response connections can be dealt with behaviorally. The various therapies providing additional support are presented under the following names:

Conditioned reflex therapy [5]
Reciprocal inhibition therapy [6]
Systematic desensitization [7]

They all adopt the classical or respondent paradigm as shown on page 20 as a theoretical basis for their work.

The technique known as *desensitization* has been selected for discussion in this chapter because it is widely used and is currently receiving experimental investigation. Of the eighty-eight cases summarized by Wolpe in 1958, fifty-seven were treated with desensitization techniques either alone or in conjunction with another method. Experimentation conducted by Lang has placed this approach under the scrutiny of systematic investigation.

THEORETICAL BASIS FOR DESENSITIZATION TECHNIQUE

The desensitization procedure developed by J. Wolpe is attracting wide attention to its quick and lasting results. The procedure is based on but one of the many behavioral laws which have come from the laboratory: *A stimulus cannot be conditioned to two stimuli which require different responses.* A completely neutral stimulus, such as a few squiggles on paper, can come to elicit a response which is normally elicited by an altogether different stimulus. The example (in classical conditioning) was salivation. Salivation is naturally elicited by acid (vinegar) on the tongue but can also be elicited by a manufacturer's trademark. Pairing of the unconditioned and the conditioned stimulus makes it possible to give the conditioned stimulus power which it did not have before.

The same process is seen in the internal stimulus of *fear* which always results in the response of tensing the muscles. This stimulus is frequently bonded to neutral stimuli, thereby becoming biologically useful for the survival of the species. For example, if man had not learned to fear poisonous snakes, he would soon have become extinct. Sometimes, however, fear is evoked by neutral stimuli which have little or no survival value. Some people are afraid of being high above ground level. Their muscles tense, they are unable to move, and they may even scream in panic. This can occur even in safely enclosed rooms if they are on the upper floors of a tall building. In such a case the conditioned stimulus *height* is bonded to the unconditioned stimulus *fear*. Thus, in due course, height alone comes to elicit all the responses that normally only fear elicits.

By itself height is a neutral stimulus in some people. It could be, and often is, bonded to extreme relaxation. Some airplane pilots say that they are not really relaxed until they are high in the air.

Both tensing and relaxing are human responses which can be verbally induced. Suppose that fear is an unconditioned stimulus which also can be used to elicit the response of muscle tightening, and that soothing sounds constitute another unconditioned response that elicits relaxation. From a scientific point of view, both muscle tensing and relaxing are behaviors incompatible with one another, that is, they are *antagonistic*. Once one of these behaviors comes under the control of a stimulus (this might be spider, snake, height, or whatever), the other cannot be emitted at the same time.

This rationale differs from that given by Wolpe in that it stresses relevant aspects of the operant conditioning model which might underlie a phobia. Wolpe reasons in accord with the classical conditioning model. He states that any formerly neutral stimulus which is now conditioned to an unconditioned stimulus (such as fearwhich by itself elicits tensing of muscles) cannot also be conditioned to another unconditioned stimulus (soothing sounds) which elicits relaxation. This demonstrates the basic behavioral law cited above: *A stimulus cannot be conditioned to two stimuli which require antagonistic responses.*

It was on this premise that Wolpe performed experiments with cats in which a strong neurosis had been deliberately established. He summarized this work as follows:

> . . . neurotic cats were treated by getting then to eat in the presence of small and then gradually increasing "doses" of anxiety-evoking stimuli. The treatment was uniformly successful and I gave reasons for concluding that this was so because the anxiety responses were inhibited by the eating, which resulted on each occasion in setting up a measure of conditioned (learned) inhibition of the anxiety responses to whatever stimuli had evoked them. With repetition more and more conditioned inhibition was built up, so that the anxiety-evoking potential of the stimuli progressively diminished—eventually to zero.
>
> The observations led to the framing of the following general principle:
>
> *If a response antagonistic to anxiety can be made to occur in the presence of anxiety-evoking stimuli so that it is accompanied by a complete or partial suppression of the anxiety responses, the bond between these stimuli and the anxiety responses will be weakened.*
>
> This hypothesis does not deny the possibility that these bonds may be weakened by other means, too . . . [8].

The basic procedure for desensitization technique is to pick some bodily condition which is present whenever the neurotic stimulus is present and then to try to find some diametrically opposed bodily condition with which to pair the neurotic stimulus. Good examples are phobias of the type mentioned earlier, such as *acrophobia* (fear of heights) and *claustrophobia* (fear of closed spaces). Others are possible.

Wolpe reported, for example, sexual responses where stimuli via the *nervus erigens* cause erection in the human male and swelling of the labia in the human female. Suppose that a particular stimulus, perhaps the sight of shoes, causes erection in a man. He becomes worried and seeks clinical aid. The traditional therapist would seek to establish under what conditions the shoes acquired their strange power. The behavioral therapist, on the other hand, recognizes that for this man, shoes are stimuli conditioned to a response which is not normal. Explaining to the patient what is already evident, even if it were possible to be sure about the original conditioning, would in no way weaken the bond between the existing stimulus and response. But let the sight of shoes of every kind become conditioned to nervous processes which do not permit erection (specifically of the *nervus erigens*), and the difficulty is eliminated.

The question arises as to why extinction schedules are ineffective in such situations. The answer lies in the fact that extinction can occur only when a response is emitted *without reinforcement.* As long as the experimenter controls reinforcement, he can extinguish a response. If he does not control reinforcement, by definition, he cannot practice extinction. The man who experiences an erection upon seeing shoes, frequently, but not always, also experiences sexual gratification; thus he is on a variable ratio schedule of reinforcement. Even if it were possible to control his reinforcement, it would be difficult to extinguish shoes as a control stimulus. Since the reinforcement cannot be controlled, the control stimulus needs to be paired with some other behavior, specifically, with behavior incompatible with erection. How this can best be done clinically is left to the ingenuity of the therapist.

For those stimuli which elicit tensing of the muscles, increased heart beat, increased pulse rate, sweating, and so on, there are known diametrically opposed responses which can be induced. Any means to induce them suffices. For example, relaxation can be brought about by soothing sounds, hypnosis, drugs, alcohol, or conditioned stimuli such as poetry, music, height, noise, and closed spaces. But suppose one of these stimuli, perhaps closed spaces, *does not* elicit relaxation but instead causes tensing of the muscles and the verbal report, "I'm afraid." What is called for is induction of relaxation by any suitable means at a time when the person is not afraid. This might even be sitting with the therapist in an open meadow. As soon as the patient is relaxed, the stimulus which has become conditioned in this patient to tensing of muscles should be gradually introduced.

A "closed space" can be gradually introduced by describing situations which involve closed spaces. Then, if relaxation continues, the therapist becomes more specific in his talk about closed spaces. Finally he may show pictures of closed rooms, then pictures showing the patient in a closed room. Obviously, this may take much time. Still later the patient is asked to imagine himself in a closed room, and finally he is asked to go alone, or with the therapist, near and then into a closed room. At every step care must be taken so that verbal statements and all graded experiences with closed rooms are unfailingly accompanied by relaxation in the patient. With the patient's cooperation, the treatment desensitization is successful when the stimulus "closed space" has become conditioned to a relaxed state.

USING DESENSITIZATION IN BEHAVIORAL THERAPY

During the first few therapy sessions the patient and therapist identify the stimuli which elicit anxiety. To do this the therapist asks the patient to imagine various scenes and situations. In addition to helping provide identification, this takes advantage of the fact that often the thought is not as anxiety provoking as the actuality of what the patient fears. The therapist may administer a psychological test which is designed to identify anxiety provoking stimuli. The patient is asked to list stimuli which he knows make him afraid.

When potential stimuli have been identified, the therapist and patient arrange them on a continuum which ranges from the least provoking stimuli to the one most likely to elicit anxiety. A simplified hierarchy of this kind is given in Table 5-1 for a person who might express an abnormal fear of horses. The hierarchy includes the attributes of size (dogs and young horse), similarity (dogs, young horse, stuffed horse), and intensity (in terms of distance).

Desensitization sessions formally begin when the therapist presents stimuli to the patient. The patient is asked to imagine a neutral stimulus whereupon the patient is expected to report whether he experienced any fear or discomfort. Even if the reply is negative, the therapist may present the stimulus again to ensure the absence of anxiety. He then moves one step up the hierarchy and repeats the procedure.

Consider the protocol presented in Table 5-2, which gives the course of therapy for a patient who had an intense fear of horses. The words in the body of the table indicate the patient's estimate of the intensity of his anxiety. In actual therapy, the patient might simply be asked to state the rating or to hold up fingers corresponding to the degree of anxiety.

Table 5-1

Stimulus Hierarchy for Treating Fear of Horses

Imagine: Dog
                  Chihuahua
                  Fox terrier
                  Labrador retriever
                  Saint Bernard
            Foal
                  Newly born
                  One month old
                  Five months old
                  Six months old
            Horse
                  At 100 feet distance
                  At 75 feet distance
                  At 50 feet distance
                  At 25 feet distance
                  At 10 feet distance
                  At   8 feet distance
                  At   6 feet distance
                  At   4 feet distance
                  At   2 feet distance
Presented: A stuffed horse
                  Touching its back
                  Touching its neck
                  Touching its nose

The patient moved through the first two levels rapidly. Once he repeatedly responded negatively to the stimulus of the Labrador retriever the session was terminated. However, this same stimulus was used again to begin the second session. Since anxiety was seemingly not present, the therapist soon moved up the hierarchy. The patient reported greater anxiety present with the newborn horse than at any time previously. At this point the therapist might better have adopted a new tactic. He and the patient could have analyzed the stimulus more closely and perhaps introduced additional steps in the hierarchy—the newborn horse viewed from a distance or even just part of the horse. In the fourth session this method was adopted.

Behavior disorders related to anxiety have been widely treated with systematic desensitization. An excellent example is provided by Kraft and Al-Issa [9]. The patient was a twenty-five-year-old female whose frigidity was referable to "social" anxiety evoked in the presence of men. At the time of treatment she stated that she hated all sex, never thought of men as potential sex partners, could not bear to have her husband's arm around her, and refused sexual relations. She was admitted for hospital care after an attempted suicide and an extensive psychiatric history. Her husband divorced her. Previous treatment

Table 5-2

Possible Course of Therapy for Patient under Treatment for Fear of Horses

Imagined stimulus	Anxiety engendered by repetitions of the imagined stimulus*								
	1st	2nd	3rd	4th	5th	6th	7th	8th	9th
Session One									
Small dog	None	None	None						
Fox terrier	None	None	None						
Labrador retriever	Some	Some	Some	None	None	None	None	None	None
Session Two									
Labrador retriever	None	None	None	None					
Saint Bernard	Some	Some	None	None	None	None			
Newly born foal	Mod.	Mod.	Some	Some	None	None	None		
Foal—1 month old	Mod.	Mod.	Mod.	Some	Some	Some	Some	None	None
Session Three									
Foal—2 months old	None	None	None	None	None				
Foal—3 months old	None	None	None	None	None	None			
Foal—4 months old	None	None	None	None	None				
Session Four									
Full-grown horse at 200 feet	None	None	None	None	None	None	None		
Full-grown horse at 150 feet	None	None	None	None	None	None	None		
Full-grown horse at 100 feet	None	None	None	None	None	None	None		
Full-grown horse at 50 feet	Great	Great	Mod.	Mod.	Some	Some	Some	Some	None

* Degrees of anxiety: none, some, moderate, great.

modes had been abreaction, electroshock, and various combinations of drugs.

Behavioral treatment commenced following three interview sessions devoted to identifying anxiety provoking situations. A hierarchy of twenty-six items was formulated starting with "talking to a man in a crowd," and ending with "sexual intercourse." Intermittent items included "men smiling at her," "dancing with men," and "kissing men."

In addition to desensitization, the patient was thoroughly relaxed by means of hypnosis. The total course of treatment consisted of eighty-four sessions in which the therapist asked her to imagine various scenes on the hierarchy. Table 5-3 summarizes the result of treatment. After nine months, a follow-up indicated complete recovery. Psychometric indices showed marked reduction in neuroticism and anxiety.

Table 5-3

Summary of Treatment of Fear-induced Frigidity through Desensitization*

After 9 sessions	Patient became more sociable with men and women.
After 22 sessions	Patient reported she could move around and not experience anxiety.
After 33 sessions	Took on a part-time job. Could read "sex books." Could watch a television show with kissing scenes. Went to hospital dances. Went on a dinner date with a man and reported that she thoroughly enjoyed it.
After 64 sessions	Patient took on a part-time job and terminated therapy. (Returned to therapy after four and a half months—return of an ex-boyfriend prompted this plan.)
After 84 sessions	Married a man in her office. She reported that she could completely cope with intercourse without difficulty. Became pregnant and looked forward to forthcoming child.

* After Kraft and Al-Issa.

The patient achieved recovery in spite of opinions that she might have "aversions" which support a rejection of the feminine role. Traditional therapeutic theory would predict a relapse since no attempt was made to alter the presumed basic problem. The patient was not asked to achieve insight into her problem nor was she asked to make other adjustments of her personality. Perhaps it can be assumed that an individual does not have to probe the inner depths of his soul or modify other psychic entities in order to change his behavior if throughout treatment he gradually experiences the consequences of his newfound abilities. After treatment, he easily perceives the most important result of therapy. He has changed.

Wolpe [10] believes that desensitization is not an appropriate treatment mode for psychotic patients. He reserves its use for neurotic behaviors which are associated with intense anxiety or neurotics misdiagnosed psychotic. Yet, psychotic patients often display the characteristic indicators of anxiety. One of our patients engaged in avoidance behavior and showed signs of panic whenever discharge from the hospital was pending. She paced back and forth and stated that she was extremely frightened.

The difficulties of applying desensitization to psychotic behavior have been outlined by Cowden and Ford [11]. They point out that psychotic patients may not be able to participate as thoroughly as neurotic patients during therapy. They attribute this to inability to discriminate between anxiety provoking and non-anxiety provoking stimuli. They also found that psychotic patients are less cooperative during sessions, are inattentive, and have difficulty concentrating. Despite these conditions, Cowden and Ford met with some success using desensitization when they depended more on physical signs of anxiety and placed less reliance on the patients' verbal reports.

One patient was unable to talk with other people. When confronted with the prospect of conversation, he would tremble, smoke numerous cigarettes, and become tearful. After volunteering for the experiment, the patient and therapist worked out a hierarchy directed toward dealing with anxiety provoked by social conversations. At first the patient imagined himself talking freely about a film he had seen, then progressed to talking about future plans with close relatives. He was also trained to relax. Throughout the therapy, both the patient and ward personnel stated that he became more friendly and relaxed. He was more talkative and reported a reduction in unusual thoughts and vivid dreams. After desensitization, he communicated in regular therapy sessions and brought in material which he had not talked about in years. Cowden and Ford consider this a successful demonstration of the usefulness of densensitization with psychotic patients.

Our own experience indicates that desensitization can be useful in ward situations. Customarily a daily pay call is held on the female ward. This involves not only the distribution of tokens for performance of various work tasks, but also an opportunity for patients to make deposits and withdrawals from their bank accounts.

A young female patient reported to the pay window and indicated the number of tokens she was to be paid for her work that day. It occurred to us that her performance warranted extra consideration. Therefore, when delivering the tokens several complimentary statements were made to her. She looked surprised, then backed away. About five minutes later she reappeared at the pay window in an agitated state shouting, "You had better stop that! I don't like it one bit!" and then fled from the ward.

Fifteen minutes later a telephone call informed us that the patient was running up and down the halls of the administration building screaming, "He's trying to hit me with a hammer! He's trying to do all kinds of bad things to me!"

Apparently, for this patient, complimentary statements functioned as stimuli which elicited undesirable behavior. The notion was tested. At the next pay call no compliments were made. The patient was merely asked how much she had earned, and payment was made to her. The next day, however, compliments were reintroduced. When she was given her tokens we said, "You've not only worked well today, but you also look very nice." Our comments triggered reenactment of the agitation occurring previously.

We decided to introduce treatment based on desensitization. For this patient the hierarchy presented is shown in Table 5-4. Care was taken not to move from one level of the hierarchy to the next until the patient had apparently adapted to the current level. In the treatment outlined, when the patient showed no signs of apprehension she was given extra reinforcement in the form of additional tokens. Within one month (approximately thirty interactions) the patient had been guided through the entire hierarchy. Initially she showed signs of apprehension and made negative commentary, but flight from the ward did not recur.

Table 5-4

Elements of Interaction at Pay Call

1. Place tokens on pay window shelf and say "Hello" in a matter-of-fact manner.
2. Place tokens on the pay window shelf and say "Hello" more pleasantly.
3. Place tokens on the pay window shelf and say "Hello" together with the patient's name.
4. Place tokens on the pay window shelf and say "Hello, you've had a good day."
5. Place hand close to tokens on pay window shelf so patient has to come into physical proximity. Use pleasant greeting.
6. Hold tokens in hand so patient removes them. Use pleasant conversation about how well she is working in the program.
7. Hold tokens in hand so patient removes them. Make statement concerning how nice the patient looks.
8. Hold tokens in hand so patient removes them. Increase emphasis on patient's attractive appearance.
9. Gently grasp patient's hand and place tokens in it.

Another example of successful desensitization came shortly after the hierarchy had been completed. A male nurse assigned to the ward complimented the patient and his remarks induced agitated screaming and running away. When the patient was returned to the ward she asked the therapist who had worked with her on the hierarchy what she should do about the new nurse and his remarks. She was told to calm down and everything would be all right.

In turn, the nurse was instructed to desensitize the patient gradually by regulating his behavior in terms of a hierarchy. This was successful, and the patient learned to appreciate compliments from male staff members.

Our experience verifies that desensitization procedures can be applied to the treatment of psychotic as well as neurotic patients in a ward situation.

Doubtless there are instances where behavioral patterns look like a phobia but are really reinforced by social reactions. For example, a young girl may find that it is considered unladylike to handle worms and then behave as if she had a phobia of worms. Or a patient may profess a phobia of dark rooms with the result that he is not asked to do cleaning chores which require getting a mop from a dark closet. In such cases there will probably be none of the cooperation required to make desensitization techniques successful. Even if the procedure is applied as skillfully as possible, the patient will simply insist that whatever was feared in the first place is still being feared.

If such a functional relationship is suspected, a simple technique can be used to verify the existence of a real phobia. The availability of the patient's most effective reinforcer is made contingent on some behavior which involves exposure to the phobic stimulus. The patient for whom cigarettes are reinforcers and who allegedly fears dark rooms would, if a real phobia were involved, not get cigarettes from the dark room. If he does get the cigarettes, he has no serious phobia of dark rooms. If he does not get them, he does have a phobia. In the latter case he is likely to cooperate with desensitization procedures. In that case, too, no other behavioral measures should be taken to attempt changing the behavioral pattern as if it were not a genuine phobia. As usual, not opinion but behavioral data provide the basis for this decision.

EXERCISES, CHAPTER 5

1. Construct a hierarchy of scenes for use in therapy for someone who has an extreme fear of enclosed places, taking the following information into account:

   a. He only is severely disturbed when alone in an enclosed location.

   b. The mere thought of an enclosed space causes him to perspire.

   c. He can with effort just barely tolerate an enclosed space if it is not also dark.

2. Describe the theoretical basis for desensitization presented in the chapter using the example above as illustrative material.

3. John is a psychotic patient who reports that he has an irrational fear of insects. An attempt to help him using desensitization procedures has failed. He always says he is extremely afraid at even the lowest levels of any hierarchy. What is John's problem?

4. What role, if any, does hypnosis play in desensitization therapy?

5. Frequently, individuals with phobias faint when confronted with a fear provoking stimulus. How does this relate to the belief that extinction schedules are ineffective in treating phobias?

6. Why is desensitization termed a behavioral therapy?

7. Under what condition is systematic desensitization successful in treating homosexuality?

8. How can stage fright be remedied with a desensitization procedure?

Part III

Data Collection

6

Record Keeping and Quantification

Your study of this chapter should help you answer the following questions:

1. Why are records important and what must be considered when preparing to record behavior?
2. What sources of information are available for baseline data?
3. How are data obtained using time sampling? Rating scales?

The terms listed below are introduced and defined in this chapter:

baselines
data, datum
time sampling
mutually exclusive behaviors
concomitant behaviors
apathy score
rating scale
validity
reliability
coefficient of correlation
response rate
cumulative record

MAKING RECORDS

Behavioral therapy developed from scientific consideration of relationships between organisms and their environment. One's own considerations can, of course, be conducted without reference to notes or records of any kind. Yet man's memory, however keen, is inevitably influenced by shifting frames of reference or personal bias and feeling. Carefully kept records are far more dependable than human recollection for they do not change with time or circumstances. Then too, in any scientific pursuit, different men often work on the same problems at different times and places. If each man keeps records, his findings are available to the others for study and comparison.

Records are also valuable in that they promote consistency by making it possible to base decisions upon an exact and unchanging representation of past events. In behavioral therapy this is crucial since nursing personnel are frequently required to implement given procedures relative to changes in behavior. A patient's program may require that reinforcement occur every fifth occasion of a particular response. However, the responses may be spaced over a period of several hours and be interspersed with many interesting but irrelevant events. One way to make sure reinforcement occurs when it is called for is to refer to a record of frequency rather than simply to rely on memory.

Records provide the only precise method of looking back over a course of therapy. Behavioral therapy is a new discipline, one that is in a state of rapid development and constant change. A behavioral therapist needs some objective method for evaluating the success or failure of the techniques he has been using. By keeping and referring to records, he has readily available the details which may be crucial to the further development of the techniques he seeks to perfect.

Because behaviors (or their consequences) can be seen, they are quantifiable. Behaviors can be counted, and numbers can be assigned to represent their various dimensions. Quantification thus can eliminate a great deal of ambiguity and provide standards useful as a basis for judgment. For example, consider the subjective measurement, "The patient often becomes angry." Does the quantity "often" refer to the same circumstances which might prompt the same measurement by someone else? Surely a record showing that the patient in question becomes angry six times per week communicates a more precise meaning for "often." In this instance, "often" simply means "six times a week."

One of the characteristics which make data useful is conciseness. To compile data which meet this criterion, it is wise to do as follows.

1. Decide exactly what behavior is to be observed.
2. Define the terms that will be used to represent an observation.
3. Determine precisely how often an observation is to be made.
4. Determine where observations are to occur.

For example, suppose that patient A is considered a "pacer" and it is desirable to know how much pacing she actually does. Prior to starting actual observations and making a record, the observer must know exactly what behavior should prompt him to record an instance of pacing. If he has a specific description against which he can compare his observation, he will be able to record the behavior concisely.

One description might be as follows: Pacing—walking with no particular goal. This definition is weak, however, because of its highly subjective character. How can the observer know whether or not the patient has a goal or, for that matter, intentions of going anywhere? What is the goal of any pacing? A better description is: Pacing—a number of ambulatory circuits between points in the patient's environment. But this, although more precise, is still inadequate. The observer needs to know the meaning of "a number of" and how many points are involved. A good definition meeting the requirements for concise record keeping is: Pacing—making five or more complete ambulatory circuits between any two points in the patient's environment.

Once having defined the observations that are to be recorded, the observer must also decide when each observation shall be made and from what location. Does he have to keep track of a patient all day long or may he make regularly spaced observations throughout the day? Might it be better to make recordings on a random time basis? Should the observer be required to approach within a specified distance (perhaps five feet) of a patient before making an observation, or should his record be made from any location where the patient can be seen? Answers to such questions form guidelines for concise record keeping.

The importance of records cannot be overestimated in a behavioral program. They are far more reliable than most people's memory; they make possible a review of what has been accomplished and at the same time provide a base for considering what should be done next. They can be used for purposes of comparison and evaluation both by people in the program and outside the program. But a record is of little value unless its information is both accurate and concise. These qualities are achieved in part, at least, through careful preparation and definition before actual observation is begun.

SOURCES OF INFORMATION FOR BASELINE DATA

In any behavioral treatment program the patient's current behavior should be the basis upon which his treatment plan rests. Which behaviors need to be developed or reinstated? Which need strengthening and which need to be extinguished? Information containing answers to such questions is called a *baseline* and comes primarily from the following sources:

1. Patient's psychiatric and medical records
2. Interviews with patient
3. Interviews with persons who have at any time created or helped with the treatment of the patient
4. Direct observation of the patient's behavior

The patient's *psychiatric record* sometimes may contain records of direct patient observation; it usually gives information in the form of impressionistic comments which may provide tentative focal points for treatment planning. The psychiatric record might indicate that the patient is frequently depressed, but systematic observation should be undertaken to verify or refute this impression.

The patient's *medical record* should also play a role in treatment planning. Behavioral therapy should never be attempted if there is anything in the patient's medical history that is clearly the cause of an odd behavior. Attention should also be given to the patient's drug history. Many tranquilizers cause side effects which are similar to behavior associated with institutionalization. A program to combat pacing should not be entered into without making sure that this is in no way associated with the kind of drug the patient is on. If it is, merely changing to a new drug may be all that is needed to extinguish the undesirable behavior.

Interviews with the patient are a valuable part of baseline information because the patient's behavior during an interview often alerts personnel to particular oddities which are considered prima facie evidence of a psychotic state. Interviews can also provide information about possible reinforcers. For example, the patient's attitude toward visits from his family and friends may not appear on his record but can be brought out in an interview; his smoking habits, desire for sweets, and interest in food can often be ascertained. The general direction of treatment may be suggested from what is learned in an interview with a patient. Upon coming into our own behavioral therapy program one man stated, "I'm no good. I can't do anything right. You can't expect me to do anything, because I'm a loser. I got this way because I masturbated and that made me retarded." Such comments, combined with other baseline information, were instrumental in our treatment decision. He was placed on a program which required work tasks of increasing responsibility.

Interviews with psychiatrists, psychologists, social workers, nurses— anyone who has previously been in contact with the care or treatment of the patient for mental illness can help provide answers to questions such as the following and thereby direct the course of treatment.

1. Does the patient work? Too much? Too little?
2. Does he like to eat? What kind of table manners has he?
3. Does he like to stay in bed all day? To sit? To pace?
4. Is he willing to follow instructions?
5. How does he get along with other patients?

Again, information regarding the patient's behavior must be verified through direct observation, but the opinions of those who have worked with the patient can be helpful in suggesting what may be needed in a treatment plan and should not be overlooked. We have sometimes persuaded personnel on the wards from which patients are transferred to the behavioral program to conduct systematic observations prior to transfer. In this way objective data are acquired which provide a comparison with the observations made following a patient's arrival in the behavioral program.

Data from direct observation of a patient's behavior should without question be the primary source for baseline information. Properly carried out, observation of a patient provides objective data and most clearly shows a patient's behavioral strengths and weaknesses. Some patients who have a prior history of hospitalization may also have previous records based on direct observation of their behavior. If so, comparing this information with baselines taken at the time of readmission can prove helpful when making up a treatment plan.

A single entry in a graph, record, or observational account is called a *datum*. Two or more entries are *data*. The term *baselines* most often refers to connected points on a graph (hence "line") or, in other words, consists of several observations. The term *baseline information*, therefore, while strictly a generalization, is not altogether inappropriately used when actually *baseline data* are referred to.

OBTAINING BASELINE DATA

The value of any record lies, of course, in the data it presents. One of the best known methods for obtaining reliable data in a behavioral program is *time sampling*. This procedure is carried out by making observations at stated intervals over a given period of time.

In our own program, once the criteria have been established of exactly what is to be observed under what conditions, some member of the nursing staff makes an observation each half hour between 0630h and 2130h. By the end of each day of the study, thirty notations have been entered on a standard form which nursing personnel use.

Many notation systems are possible, but we use the symbols on the card presented in Figure 6-1. The symbols, as well as instructions on their use, are always given at the top of the card. Suppose that a patient is being observed for the behavior "lying on bed" and that this behavior has been defined as "patient is on his own bed in a prone position—one which would normally be used for sleeping." Utilizing the time sampling method, the nurse looks at the patient's bed each half hour. If the patient is indeed lying there, the observer enters this information on the observation form, marking a plus sign after the appropriate time. If the patient is not lying on bed a minus mark is entered.

Quite obviously the symbol + has a highly specific meaning, and a person examining the record could be sure that at the time shown, the patient was certainly "lying on bed." On the other hand, the symbol − does not carry this degree of specificity since it represents all behaviors except the one called for in the observation. The patient might be sitting on his bed, working in the kitchen, or even be AWOL. The record shows only whether or not the patient was "lying on bed." Each

Instructions: Patient's name _George P._

    Plus (+) = Patient in <u>prone</u> position on own bed
    Minus (−) = All other events

Observer: _P. M._   Time Sampling Interval: _½ hr._

Date: June 1, 1967				Date: June 2, 1967	
0630	+	1400	+	0630	1400
0700	+	1430	+	0700	1430
0730	+	1500	+	0730	1500
0800	−	1530	+	0800	1530
0830	+	1600	+	0830	1600
0900	+	1630	+	0900	1630
0930	+	1700	+	0930	1700
1000	+	1730	+	1000	1730
1030	+	1800	−	1030	1800
1100	+	1830	−	1100	1830
1130	+	1900	−	1130	1900
1200	−	1930	−	1200	1930
1230	−	2000	−	1230	2000
1300	−	2030	−	1300	2030
1330	+	2100	+	1330	2100

    Total +'s = **20**   Total +'s =

    Total −'s = **10**   Total −'s =

Fig. 6-1. Format of a typical observation card used in a behavioral therapy program.

day's data are easily summarized simply by counting the number of pluses and the number of minuses and entering the totals in the appropriate blanks at the bottom of the sheet.

For George P., the patient whose record is shown in Figure 6-1, there were twenty pluses and ten minuses. When the performance and needs of this patient are subsequently considered, these figures provide an accurate, quantitative basis for decision making.

Time sampling can be used for recording more than a simple observation such as "lying on bed." For a record of a patient's general ward behavior, new instructions are prepared defining the behaviors under observation, and a time interval is set. For observation of complex behavior, the nurse is occasionally required to write a brief description of what the patient is doing as well as use a number and letter code when entering frequent behaviors. A sample of this more elaborate record form is shown in Figure 6-2.

In this system the observer's notations must include the number symbol of one of the following *mutually exclusive behaviors.*

1 Walking   2 Running   3 Standing   4 Sitting   5 Lying Down

All behaviors on a ward can be classified under one or another of these categories, and being engaged in one mutually excludes the others. It is true, however, that a patient can emit certain responses *concomitantly*. For example, he can be both sitting and smoking, or he may be standing and eating, or lying down and talking, or running and screaming. In our system of collecting data by time sampling, the observer is instructed to watch the patient for one second and then enter a coded notation on the record sheet in the appropriate hour blank. If the patient is simply standing, just this fact and the location where the behavior occurred is recorded. For example, see 1830h, on the sample sheet in Figure 6-2. The entry for the observation "standing while working on assigned task in the dining room" is shown at 0900h. The notation "unavailable" signifies that the patient could not be found. If an observation

Watch Especially for:
19- head in hands HH
18- Working-assigned
16- Talking to others

GENERAL CODE

Mutually Exclusive Behaviors

1 Walking	4 Sitting
2 Running	5 Lying down
3 Standing	

Concomitant Behaviors

6 Drinking
7 Eating – meals
7a Eating – other than meals
8 Grooming (describe)
9 Group meeting
10 Medication
11 Reading
12 Receiving pay
13 Rocking
14 Pacing
15 Smoking
16 Talking to others
17 T V
18 Working – assigned
19 Other

Location

A Dining room
B Hall of lounge
C Sleeping quarters
D Lavatory
E Outside

Patient____*Susan R.*____
Admission____
Followup:
① 2 3 4 5 6 7 8 9
Date:____*August 24, 1967*____

0630	*3-8*	D
0700	*3-6*	B
0730	*4-15*	B
0800	*3-10*	A
0830	*4-18*	A
0900	*3-18*	A
0930		
1000	*4-19 HH*	B
1030	*4-19 HH*	B
1100	*3-19 Buying item*	B
1130	*3-18*	A
1200	*4-7*	A
1230	*3-16 (Employee)*	B
1300	*4-11*	A
1330	*4-9*	A
1400	*4-9*	A
1430	*4-9*	A
1500	*Unavailable*	
1530	*1*	E
1600	*3-11*	A
1630	*3-18*	A
1700	*3-18*	A
1730	*4*	D
1800	*4-16*	E
1830	*3*	C
1900	*3-16*	C
1930	*4-17*	B
2000	*3-11*	A
2030	*2-19 (screaming)*	B
2100	*5*	C

Fig. 6-2. Sample of record used in a special study within a behavioral therapy program.

is missed, no entry is made. With every use of the symbol 19, the nurse is expected to add a brief word description.

Close examination of the Behavioral Study Form gives further details of a day's observations that were made and recorded to show the behavior of a patient for whom we particularly wanted the information. These are listed in the upper left-hand corner.

If this is the first study of a patient's general behavior (i.e., is a baseline study), the nurse making the observations (or the person in charge of records) enters a check mark after the item "admission." If it is a follow-up study, the appropriate symbol is circled. The number of follow-ups made will depend on two factors: (1) the needs of the patient and (2) the ratio of personnel to patients.

Follow-up observations are made in order to determine a patient's progress under treatment. They provide feedback and also give a quantitative basis for making changes once treatment has begun. Figure 6-3 gives data gathered during observations made for the first eight days of a patient's stay on the ward, and for one month after the start of treatment. The numbers scaled on the vertical axis refer to the percentage of the total observations made each day. The horizontal axis represents the times of observation.

Inspection of Figure 6-3 reveals that during the patient's initial eight days on the ward, undesirable categories comprised a higher percentage of the observations than desirable ones. After treatment, this situation

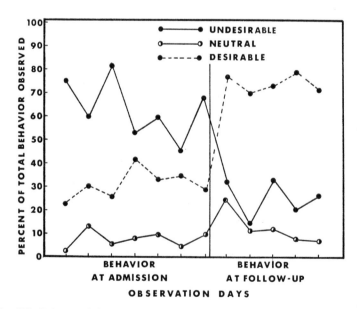

Fig. 6-3. Behavioral data in graphic form showing progress of treatment.

was altered. The bulk of observations were then desirable behaviors with a sharp reduction in the emission of undesirable behavior. This information strongly suggests that the treatment program formulated for this patient was effective. An examination of the patient's behavioral records would clearly indicate exactly which behaviors had been changed.

Summarization of concomitant behavior data is somewhat more complex than of single behavior observations but is based on the same procedure.

1. Count the occurrences of each of the mutually exclusive behaviors and enter the figures as subtotals. This count should include instances with an accompanying concomitant behavior.
2. Make a similar count for just the concomitant behaviors and enter these items as subtotals.
3. Count and record each instance of mutually exclusive behavior *without* concomitant behavior, and also record any "missed observation" or "unavailable."
4. Total each of these divisions and check the totals against the thirty possible observations per day.

The sample form represented in Figure 6-4 summarizes in this way the data of the Behavioral Study Form of Figure 6-2.

Behavior forms and summary sheets such as those shown yield an enormous amount of data. To transpose this plethora of information into effective treatment programs, we take the following steps.

1. Determine a patient's apathy score from mutually exclusive behaviors.
2. Work out values for concomitant behaviors.
3. Set treatment plans.

By definition, an *apathy score* is simply the total number of occurrences of mutually exclusive behaviors observed *without* concomitant behavior. Susan R., some of whose data are shown on the sample Behavioral Study Form (Fig. 6-2) and the summary sheet (Fig. 6-4), had an apathy score of 3 for one day of the first follow-up. Her low score means that whenever under observation she was almost always involved in a concomitant behavior. Had her apathy score been high, her therapist would have known that she rarely interacts with her environment. He would then have planned treatment designed to change her behavior to ways that would prepare her for life outside the hospital, where a high degree of social interaction is required. (Of course, no judgment would be made or treatment set on the basis of a single day's

STUDY FORM SUMMARY

Date: _26 Aug. 1967_

Admission:_____

Patient:

Susan R.

Followup:
① 2 3 4 5 6 7 8 9

Mutually Exclusive Categories + Concomitant Categories		Concomitant Categories	
Activity	Frequency	Activity	Frequency
1 Walking	0	6 Drinking	1
2 Running	1	7 Eating – meals	1
3 Standing	12	7a Eating – other than meals	0
4 Sitting	11	8 Grooming	1
5 Lying down	1	9 Group meeting	3
	24	10 Medication	1
Mutually Exclusive Categories		11 Reading	3
Activity	Frequency	12 Receiving pay	0
1 Walking	1	13 Rocking	0
2 Running	0	14 Pacing –	0
3 Standing	1	15 Smoking	1
4 Sitting	1	16 Talking to others	3
5 Lying down	1	17 TV	1
	4	18 Working – assigned	5
Location		19 Other	4
A Dining room	13		24
B Hall or lounge	5		
C Sleeping quarters	3	Missed Observation	1
D Lavatory	1	Unavailable	1
E Outside	1		
	28		

Fig. 6-4. Summary sheet for behavioral study form shown in Fig. 6-2.

observation.) The authors found this index very sensitive to the application of techniques used to combat apathy in a whole-ward behavioral program.

To establish *values,* we gave one of the following ratings to each concomitant behavior.

Desirable	Behavior desirable for *this* patient and to be maintained or reinstated
Neutral	Behaviors about which nothing will be done
Undesirable	Behavior undesirable for *this* patient and to be extinguished or replaced

Admittedly, these are subjective choices based on the opinions of nurses, psychiatrist, psychologist, and social worker, but they are made with the patient's needs in mind. What was considered desirable for patient A might not have been for patient B. For example, if a patient comes from an environment where table manners are considered highly important and his behavior in this regard was a significant factor in his commitment, table manners would probably fall in the desirable-undesirable ratings. For another patient, the same behaviors might be classified neutral.

Values can and do shift. Upon admission, a patient might eat three meals a day with no disturbance and without snacking unduly between times. His eating behaviors would probably be rated neutral. In a follow-up study made three months after the start of treatment for other behaviors, the patient might be eating too much or throwing his food. In such a case, his eating behaviors would be assigned new values and take an entirely different role in his treatment program.

Some kind of *rating scale* is always used in recording observations. A rating scale allows an observer to compare his perception of events within the preestablished categories of the scale. For example, a rating scale might use the twofold classification severe—not severe. As soon as an entry reflects this choice, a rating scale has been utilized.

In time sampling, an event is perceived, a choice made according to a rating scale, and the information immediately recorded. But with the use of many rating scales, there is a time lag between perception and notation. One scale which has proven useful in many research situations is the NOSIE-30. This scale is for nurses observation for inpatient evaluation. It presents thirty behaviors which have been statistically classified into three positive categories and three negative categories. Nurses are directed to rate the patient's behavior as they "observed it *during the last three days only.*" The scale has been validated on a sample of 1,100 psychiatric patients and has an acceptable level of reliability. The Ellsworth MACC Behavioral Adjustment Scale, which is widely used for the selection of patients for open-ward programs, has no period of observation specified.

When selecting a rating scale its validity and its reliability are of paramount importance. *Validity* refers to the ability of the scale to measure what it is supposed to measure. For example, most rulers are valid tools for measuring length because the manufacturer takes precautions to ensure that the units of measure are exactly those specified by the National Bureau of Standards. A ruler is used with the knowledge that an inch will be an inch as long as the instrument is used correctly.

Reliability refers to the ability of the scale to perform its function consistently on each occasion of measurement. A voltmeter is a device for measuring electrical voltage levels. Prior to its use a good electrician always checks the meter's accuracy by measuring the voltage output of new batteries. Suppose that three measurements were taken on a new 2.5 volt battery, with readings of 1.5, 2.3, and 2.5. This discrepancy suggests that the meter is not reliable—it is not consistently performing its function.

The results of tests for validity and reliability accompany established rating scales. Both statistics are reported in terms of a *coefficient of correlation* which is a statistical index ranging from -1.00 through 0.00 to $+1.00$. Behavioral rating scales show good reliability and validity if their coefficients are in the $+.70$ to $+1.00$ range.

RESPONSE RATES

It is now time to examine the importance of a basic datum in behavioral science—the *response rate*. The physical sciences progressed as rapidly as they did mainly by formulating reliable techniques of measurement. In medicine, for example, a basic datum is the body temperature. If it is high, it tells us something about the person. It allows us to measure the effect of a drug, usually long before the patient himself is able to report that he feels better.

Measurement and quantification make it possible to describe a given state in terms of what is "normal." To stay with the medical example, at 40°C a patient's temperature is clearly higher than at 37°C (his temperature before he became sick). Since this patient's temperature usually stays at the lower figure, 37°C is considered his normal temperature. Measuring and finding that the temperatures of many other people center about 37°C means that this value can be set as the basis for "normalcy." Regardless of the procedure, whether the patient's own standard is used or reference is made to a statistical average, the ability to measure and compare makes possible a statement about "normal" or "abnormal" temperature.

In behavioral science the rate of response has, similarly, long proven to be the single most useful datum. A rate always combines two measures. Miles per hour, for example, is a rate which measures distance (as expressed in miles) and time (as expressed in hours). Commonly, overall or average rates are used, as when we say that this car can go 40 miles per hour while that one can do 60 miles per hour; this chess player finishes his game in 22 moves per game (on the average) while that one takes 68 moves; this person's pulse rate is 100 beats per minute while that one's is 110 beats per minute. In other words, we usually encounter rates as a single figure which expresses a relationship between two measurements.

Rates are easily expressed graphically. In Figure 6-5, the time (in hours) is entered along the horizontal axis and the distance (in miles) along the vertical axis. If a car covers a distance of 40 miles in one hour a single dot (at A) can give this information. The slope of a line drawn between A and the point at which the horizontal and vertical axis meet (the zero point) shows in graphic form the *rate* at which

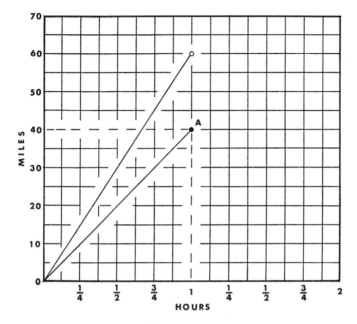

Fig. 6-5. Rates of movement (speeds) of a slow moving (40 mph) and a faster moving (60 mph) car shown as sloped lines.

the car travels. Another line drawn for a car that can go 60 miles per hour makes instantly possible many comparisons about the performance of these two cars. At a glance, one can see that in half an hour the slower car would cover 20 miles; during the same time the faster car would cover 30 miles. A great advantage of expressing speeds and similar rates in graphic form is the ease of representing changes. When changes are shown the line is no longer straight but curves. Also, the steeper the slope the greater the speed. A horizontal line along the hours axis would indicate that absolutely no distance has been covered. A straight up-and-down line along the miles axis would indicate an impossible case in which an infinite distance is covered in no time at all!

One way of imagining a graphic presentation of rates is to watch a pen moving across a paper from left to right as time goes by. Now, as the pen moves in this horizontal direction, imagine also that some event (such as a patients' heartbeat) moves the pen simultaneously upward on the paper. If the heart beat is even, its representation should look like the line in Figure 6-6. If in the middle of the observation the patient's heart should for some reason slow down to exactly one-half the rate at which it had been beating, a graph representing this change should contain a noticeable difference in the slope of the steplike line, as shown in Figure 6-7. Graphs of this kind are called *cumulative records*

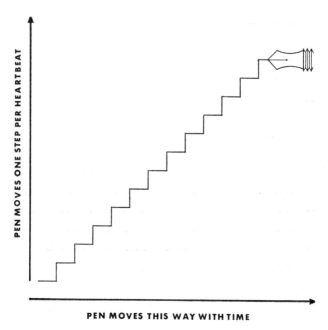

Fig. 6-6. Presentation of a rate as a succession of events (heartbeats) over time.

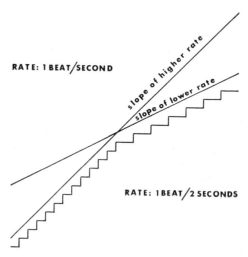

Fig. 6-7. The effect of a change in rate on the slope of lines representing these rates.

because responses are cumulatively added vertically one on top of the other while the pen moves horizontally along the paper. Obviously, the steeper the slope of the cumulative record, the more frequent has been the response, i.e., the greater the rate.

Graphs need not be feared. Many can be and are quite simple. They are so important in behavioral analysis that they soon become an indispensable tool. In a behavioral program, graphs can help a nurse measure the success of her techniques. Graphs make it possible to readily compare one performance with another. Graphs are an effective way to show that a certain behavior occurs at a high rate during one time and at a low rate during another. For instance, it might be said that two patients smoke "all day long." Very well, this knowledge is of importance whether they are to be cured of their chain-smoking habit or whether their smoking is to be used as a reinforcer for other behavior which is to be changed. Before setting up a schedule of reinforcement for these patients, a somewhat cautious (and skeptical) behaviorist would want to see a *baseline* on the smoking behavior of the patients in question. In this case the baseline is a cumulative record of firsthand observations of what an organism does.

In the case of the two smokers, a baseline was made to establish whether or not they were actually smoking at the time of each observation. Thirty observations, one every half hour starting at 0630h and ending at 2100h were made. Figure 6-8 shows the way the findings appeared on a graph. The graph shows that one patient (Mr. B) did not smoke as much in the morning as he did in the afternoon. It also shows that in the afternoon Mr. A smoked at the same rate as Mr. B. It is quite possible, but also highly unlikely, that the observer happened to catch B between cigarettes (i.e., nonsmoking) at most of the morning observations. The next day's observations (again a baseline expressed in graph form) will immediately allow comparison between the two days' behaviors. The chance that a behavior would always be missed at the same time of day is negligible.

If after a few days of obtaining baselines, it is confirmed that B rarely smokes during mornings, several circumstances are now clear: (1) Even though both A and B smoke heavily, there are differences in when they smoke; (2) if smoking is to be used as a reinforcer with these persons, it must be used differently for A than for B.

Later chapters, especially Chapter 7, describe in more detail how cumulative records in simple graph form can be and are used to evaluate therapeutic progress in patients.

While cumulative records are widely employed in behavioral research, their use is still quite novel in mental hospitals where changes in behavior are a main concern. However, the effects of therapy should and do show clearly in cumulative records. One may suspect, therefore, that

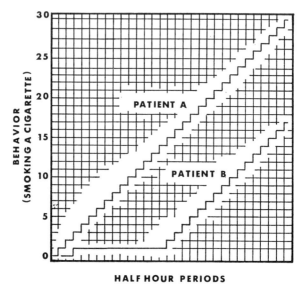

Fig. 6-8. Cumulative record of smoking activity of two patients.

such records will one day be as widely used in mental hospitals as temperature charts are today used in general hospitals.

EXERCISES, CHAPTER 6

1. Why are recods necessary in conducting behavioral therapy?
2. Prepare a summary report which presents the frequency of the following activities for a patient. (The summary should reflect the patient's behavior over the course of an entire seven day week.)

   Showering
   Getting up in the morning
   Eating meals
   Going outside the ward
   Tardiness for medications

3. How can the time sampling technique be employed to make observations on mealtime behavior? Suppose the ward psychiatrist wants to know how often three patients spill food. Will the time sampling technique aid you in obtaining frequency data in spite of the fact that you can only observe one patient at a time?
4. Nurse B has often stated that Carlos is always talking to himself. You find that you do not share this impression and wish to argue the point. Describe the procedures one would follow to back up your contention with empirical data.

5. What is the relationship between the mutually exclusive behavior categories and the apathy score used to assess a patient's behavior?

6. What is the main difference between data obtained using a time sampling technique and those obtained using a rating scale?

7. You have been assigned the task of taking each patient's temperature. You have taken ten readings and all of them are 104°F. Yet, each patient reports that he feels fine. Your previous experience with thermometers indicates that it is a _____ tool for measuring temperature. The one you are using must lack _____.

8. Give examples of the use of rates in our daily lives.

9. Construct for yourself cumulative records of your verbal responses in the course of a twenty-four-hour day, the quarter-hours you spent lying down in the course of a week, your cups of coffee drunk during a week. Along with each record, list possible control stimuli that were effective.

10. How could you use a typewriter to transcribe a cumulative record?

7

Record Keeping for Treatment Plans

Your study of this chapter should help you answer the following questions:

1. What is the importance of each of the elements that comprise a treatment plan?
2. How are data presented in each of the following ways?

   Performance records
   Graphs
   Cumulative records

3. How can treatment plans be made readily available for use by nursing personnel?

The terms listed below are introduced and defined in this chapter:

treatment plan
satiation
treatment schedule
performance forms
bar graph
scaling
line graph
cumulative records
shift surprises

ELEMENTS OF A TREATMENT PLAN

After baselines have been prepared, they must be evaluated. Exactly what is the patient to do? How is he to behave? What changes must be made? In order to answer these questions, and they must be both asked and answered many times in the course of behavioral therapy, a *treatment plan* is prepared. Treatment plans are schedules directed toward achieving specific terminal objectives for each behavior.

A treatment plan should contain the following basic descriptions.

1. Each initial and terminal behavior involved in therapy
2. Reinforcers effective for the patient undergoing therapy
3. Procedure to be used with respect to each behavior
4. Situations which serve as control stimuli

Each behavior for which treatment is planned must be clearly described. Any approximation of the undesired behavior must also be stated, as well as the desired terminal behavior. The descriptions must be highly specific so that each member of the nursing staff knows exactly how treatment is to begin and where it is to end.

The description must be stated in behavioral terminology because it is behavior which must change. This means using words which refer to characteristics of overt behavior such as "grab," "raise arms," "shake foot," and "eat with a spoon." Often nursing personnel have to construct a treatment plan for inner states of the patient. For example, suppose a psychiatrist recommends that a patient's self-esteem should be "enhanced." This request should prompt the question, "What must a patient do so that you can conclude he has gained in self-esteem?" The answer to this question can only be stated in behavioral terms. Self-esteem might involve behaviors like verbal statements of achievement or statements regarding positive feelings about oneself, or it might show itself in the patient no longer mingling with groups of lower status and seeking the company of higher-status groups. Once the behavioral meaning of concepts like self-esteem are clarified, nursing personnel can formulate plans because they now have direct access to a set of behaviors.

General terminology may be used when forming descriptions for a treatment plan but its meaning must be clearly specified. If a terminal goal is "good grooming" nursing personnel must describe which grooming habits need to be treated. Hair combing? Dressing? Selection of clothing?

Perhaps a desired behavior is that a patient appear more "feminine." Like all adjectives, this one has content meaning which seems quite clear until people are asked to give its definition. No two respondents will use exactly the same terms to describe what constitutes feminine appearance, but many will agree that femininity is associated with attempts to maintain personal appearance. "Attempts to maintain personal appearance" can and should be stated in behavioral terms such as the following.

Combing hair neatly
Wearing nonwrinkled clothing
Wearing well-fitting shoes
Asking about current fashions
Reading fashion magazines and discussing choice of color, length, and cut of dresses

In order to help a patient appear more "feminine," therefore, nursing personnel would selectively reinforce for behaviors such as those listed above.

Most frequently problems are presented in terms of something a patient does or does not do. For example, "the patient does not wear her dress correctly" or "the patient is always dirty." Nursing personnel must recognize that these are only partial descriptions of the problem. A behavioral analysis includes the patient's method of putting on a dress for the first example and detailed washing habits for the second.

One method for treatment of the problem leading to "does not wear her dress correctly" is to make a behavioral plan stating exactly how the patient might be taught to put on her dress so that she discriminates between "correct" and "incorrect" dress wearing.

An example of the behavioral portion of such a plan for a patient who might wear her dress backward is given in Table 7-1.

Table 7-1

Sample Treatment Plan for Inducing "Correct" Dress Wearing

Step	Patient must emit following behaviors
1.	Put right hand on one shoulder of the dress and left hand on the other shoulder of the dress.
2.	Grab dress shoulders which her hands are touching.
3.	Hold dress up at arms' length and look at it.
4.	Have patient tell if label (which normally appears on back neck of dress) is on side nearest her or farthest from her. If her answer is "farthest away," proceed to step 5. If her answer is "nearest," skip to step 9.
5.	Release dress with right hand and put shoulder of dress now held in left hand into right hand.
6.	Use left hand to grab shoulder of dress that was formlerly held by right hand. (This turns dress around)
7.	Hold dress up again at arms' length.
8.	Again have patient tell you whether label is on neck part nearest or farthest from her.
9.	Let go with right hand but hold on with left hand. Put right hand through hole at bottom of the dress until hand comes out of the armhole on her right side.
10.	Let go with left hand. Put it through hole at the bottom of the dress until hand comes out the armhole on her left side.
11.	Put dress over head by raising both arms in air. Poke head through the bottom opening of the dress until head comes out of the hole between her arms and at top of dress.
12.	Pull the dress down in position.

Of course it takes far longer to write (or read) a description of this kind than to execute it. But no step should be omitted in its preparation. In this example, suppose any of steps 5 through 8 had been left out! Only by accounting for all possibilities can the nurse be assured of reaching the desired terminal behavior.

Armed with adequate descriptions of the behaviors which contribute to complaints about the patient, nursing personnel can describe those behaviors which change the patient's condition. For example, if the patient is "always dirty," baseline information may provide the explanation. Perhaps the patient "does not shower correctly." In this case nursing personnel can reinstate behaviors which produce a clean body after showering. They may require that a reinforcer be withheld until the patient completes the following activities: (1) stands under water until thoroughly wet, (2) steps out of water and thoroughly soaps up using a washrag, (3) stands under water until all soap is rinsed off, and (4) vigorously dries all parts of the body.

The second element to be considered when making a treatment plan for a particular patient is a listing of the stimuli which function as reinforcers for that patient and thus can be used to strengthen behavior. One way an identification can be made is to tie a reinforcer to a behavior. If the frequency of the behavior *increases,* the stimulus is a positive reinforcer. In practice, this method, though highly reliable, is often overly time-consuming. Reinforcers can be tentatively identified in other ways. For example, interviews with patients often suggest stimuli which function as reinforcers. Questioning one patient indicated that her religious beliefs would not allow her to eat meat. She "preferred eggs as a protein supplement." Therefore, hard-boiled eggs were used as a reinforcer.

Premack has formulated a principle which is useful in detecting reinforcers. His work shows that if behavior X occurs more frequently than behavior Y, then behavior Y can be strengthened by making behavior X contingent upon Y. On the ward, if nursing personnel observe that a patient frequently interacts with members of the opposite sex, they might well conclude that this activity is reinforcing. If working is part of this patient's treatment plan, then a contingency can be arranged that requires the patient to work before she is allowed visits with men.

Nursing personnel can also review psychological literature to find new sources of reinforcers. Ayllon and Azin have analyzed the expenditure patterns of patients living in a token economy. They found that more tokens were spent for privacy than for commissary items. This information strongly suggests that behavior can be controlled by establishing contingencies using privacy as a reinforcer.

Despite America's huge annual consumption of sweets, candy is neither the only nor always the most effective reinforcer. Coffee, hot chocolate, brass tokens, and not surprisingly, art appreciation in the form of looking at pictures all can be effective reinforcers.

Prolonged use of a reinforcer can lead to *satiation*—the opposite of deprivation. In token economies this is of primary importance if the patient's treatment plan contains a number of individual behaviors. Under this condition it is possible for a patient to earn too many tokens for one behavior. This, of course, removes the state of deprivation necessary to make reinforcers effective, which in turn may make it impossible to reinforce other behaviors in his plan. Adjustment of the patient's cost of living provides the solution to this problem.

Immediate reinforcement is not always possible (and sometimes not desirable). Therefore, methods of bridging the gap between emission of a behavior and reinforcement must be found. Consider the following: One four-hour visit is scheduled to reinforce a patient after he has completed an entire week's work assignment satisfactorily. This plan may not be effective because of the seven-day delay between emission of the first response on day 1 and receipt of reinforcement on day 8. When this problem was encountered, we found special bank accounts an effective procedure. The patient received immediate reinforcement with tokens and could deposit these earnings in his special account. The account is special because he cannot spend the savings on anything but visits and staff members may not withdraw from it as a method of fining. The existence of the account provides the patient with a tangible representation of future reinforcement.

Once reinforcers have been listed, the procedure to be used with respect to each behavior is worked out as a schedule. A *treatment schedule* is the arrangement between the emission of a behavior and a reinforcer. A treatment schedule specifies the procedures that will be used to promote behavioral change in a patient. Because it describes treatment strategy, all nursing personnel must be thoroughly familiar with all its details. A concise schedule is the best way to guard against possible misunderstanding. Many schedules used in whole-ward behavioral therapy programs are similar to the one presented in Table 7-2.

An uncomplicated schedule of this sort directs nursing personnel to deliver a reinforcer each time they observe a particular behavior. After the behavior is well established, the schedule is changed so that reinforcement with tokens is used less frequently and social reinforcement more frequently.

Sometimes it is clear that the patient cannot perform the behaviors necessary for elimination of a problem. He may be brain damaged, severely regressed, or extremely retarded. In such cases the schedule must be changed to smaller steps. If necessary, the delivery of more than a single reinforcement for a given step might be considered.

Nursing personnel may be required to further refine behavioral descriptions and include additional points where a reinforcer should be delivered. Table 7-3 presents a plan for a patient who often put her dress on backward.

Formulation of this schedule assumes that the patient can follow verbal instructions and can identify the parts of a dress. The goal of any schedule, of course, is to provide the patient with a routine which brings about the desired terminal behavior—in this case, "dressing correctly."

Table 7-2

Sample Treatment Program Form

Treatment Program

Name   Steel

Date   June 1, 1967

Behavior	Reinforcer	Schedule	Control stimuli
Smiling	Tokens	Each time detected	As part of greeting
Talking to other patients	Tokens	Each time detected	
Sitting	Tokens	Each time detected	Patient must be with others; not alone
Reading (patient looking at printed material)	Tokens	Each time detected	Appropriate time and place; especially not in group meetings or at medications
Grooming—hair	Tokens or praise	Each time detected	Only when hair is not pulled tightly against head; prefer "feminine"
Completion of specific assignment	Tokens or free trip out-of-doors	Each time detected	Prior to reinforcement patient must say something positive about the job she completed

While most schedules initially call for close supervision, they should also include a method for relaxing support so that patients are eventually on their own. Every schedule should also be designed so that any member of the nursing staff after studying the schedule can use it to treat the patient for whom it was designed.

The final element which every treatment plan should contain is a description of situations which serve as control stimuli. When control stimuli are incorporated in a treatment plan, their relationship to the behavior and the reinforcement must be specifically described. Control stimuli operate in two ways. They can be used to give control, or they can be used to relax control. This means that nursing personnel need to describe exactly which reinforcers should be delivered and which ones withheld.

For example, suppose it has been decided that a withdrawn patient will be required to reply to a salutation. A nurse's "Good morning" should set the occasion for a similar response by the patient. The nurse is thereby giving control value to a stimulus. Or the treatment goal may involve eliminating the control function of a stimulus. At one time we noted that *denial* of any request made by a particular regressed patient set the occasion for belligerent behavior on her part. She would

Table 7-3

Possible Sequence of Steps in Shaping Correct Dressing

Sessions: Each morning when patient arises
After shower each day

Behavior	Reinforce
Phase One—Shaping	

Instruct patient to:

1. Put your right hand on one shoulder of the dress. Put your left hand on the other shoulder of the dress.	1 token upon completion.
2. Grab the shoulder your right hand is touching. Grab the shoulder your left hand is touching.	1 token upon completion. If patient drops dress do not reinforce; start again at step 1.
3. Hold the dress out at arms' length. Look at the dress. Can you see the little label on the part of the dress where your neck sticks through? (If yes, go on to step 4.) (If no, move to step 7.)	1 token upon completion. If patient drops dress do not reinforce; start again at step 1.
4. Grab the left shoulder with your right hand. Let go of the left shoulder with your left hand.	1 token upon completion. If patient drops dress do not reinforce; start again at step 1.
5. Grab the free shoulder with your left hand. (This turns the dress around.)	1 token upon completion. If patient drops dress do not reinforce; start again at step 1.
6. Hold the dress out at arms' length. Can you see the little label on the part of the dress where your neck sticks through? Patient should say "no."	1 token upon completion. If patient drops dress do not reinforce; start again at step 1.
7. Let go with your right hand but hold on with your left hand. Put your right hand through the bottom of the dress until hand comes out of the armhole on your right side.	1 token upon completion. If patient drops dress do not reinforce; start again at step 1.
8. Let go with your left hand. Put it through the bottom of the dress until hand comes out the armhole on your left side.	1 token upon completion. If patient removes dress do not reinforce; start again at step 1.
9. Raise both arms above your head. Poke your head through the bottom opening of the dress until it comes out of the hole between your arms. Can you finish by yourself?	1 token upon completion. If patient removes dress do not reinforce; start again at step 1.

Shaping phase completed when patient performs without error or follows complete set of instructions or anticipates each step in performance.

Table 7-3 (Continued)

Phase Two—Chaining, Part One

When patient:

1. Places her right hand on one shoulder of the dress and her left hand on the other shoulder of the dress. Grabs the shoulder her right hand is touching.
2. Grabs the shoulder her left hand is touching.

> 2 tokens upon completion· If patient drops dress do not reinforce; start again.

3. Holds the dress out at arms' length. Looks at dress. Indicates she can see the little label on the part of the dress where neck comes out. If so, she should go on to step 4. If not, skip to step 7.
4. Grabs left shoulder with her right hand. Lets go of the shoulder with her left hand.

> 2 tokens upon completion. If patient drops dress do not reinforce; start again at step 1.

5. Grasps the free shoulder with her left hand. (Dress is now turned around)
6. Holds the dress out at arms' length. Indicates if she can see the little label on the part of the dress where the neck should stick out. She should say "no."

> 2 tokens upon completion. If patient drops dress do not reinforce; start again at step 1.

7. Lets go with her right hand but holds on with her left hand. Puts her right hand through the bottom of the dress until it comes out of the armhole on her right side.

> 3 tokens upon completion. If patient removes dress do not reinforce; start again at step 1.

8. Lets go with her left hand. Puts it through the bottom of the dress until it comes out the armhole on her left side.

> 3 tokens upon completion. If patient removes dress do not reinforce; start again at step 1.

9. Raises both arms above her head. Pokes her head through the bottom hole of the dress until it comes out of the hole between her arms. She should finish on her own.

> 2 tokens upon completion. If patient removes dress do not reinforce; start again at step 1.

Phase completed when you perceive that patient always completes this routine with a minimum of verbal aid and/or anticipates future steps.

Phase Three—Chaining, Part Two

Gradually merge remaining portions of requirements relative to the amount of reinforcement. This continues until patient completes the whole routine and receives the total amount of reinforcement.

Phase Four—Removal of Direct Support

Start this portion of the routine as soon as the patient can perform the requirements of the plan with no verbal support. Continue training sessions but on occasion do not be present. If she completes routine on her own, lavishly reinforce her. Make your presence less and less frequent but be sure that she receives reinforcement when performance warrants. Throughout the course of the day patient should be reinforced by other personnel for having her dress on correctly.

strike out with her fists or use threatening language. Naturally, the treatment plan formulated for this patient included consideration of the use of stimuli which would relax and eventually extinguish belligerency in the face of denial.

PRESENTING DATA

A variety of means is available for presenting behavioral data so their information is quickly understandable. Three of the most common are the following.

Performance forms
Graphs
Cumulative records

Performance forms are nongraphic methods of organizing data. The term *form* refers to a structured outline which organizes the events recorded. Figure 7-1 represents one kind of performance form we have used to record patients' rising activities. (The activities themselves are fully described in Chapter 8.) General ward performance is quickly ascertained by examining the notations that follow the total. In this case, since five persons are involved the first seven days, a score of 5 shows immediately that all patients performed satisfactorily on a certain day. Any lesser score similarly indicates the deviation from "perfect."

UP AND AT 'EM PERFORMANCE RECORD

Month and Year ___*May 1967*___

Observer: Check each dormitory at 0630. If each of the patients listed meets all of the following criteria mark a plus (+) in the appropriate date column. Mark a (-) minus if you cannot score the patient plus.

Criteria: Patient is not in or on her bed
Patient is fully dressed
Bed is made

Name	1	2	3	4	5	6	7	8	9	10	11	12	13	14	15	16	17	18	19	20	21	22	23	24	25	26	27	28	29	30	31	total
Smith	+	+	+	+	+	+	+	+	+	+	+	+	+	+	+	+	+	+	+	+	+	+	+	+	+	+	+	+	+	+	+	31
Jones	+	+	+	-	-	+	+	+	+	+	+	+	+	-	-	-	-	-	-	-	-	-	-	-	-	-	-	-	-	-	-	12
Stone	+	+	+	+	+	+	+	+	+	+	+	+	+	+	-	-	+	+	+	+	+	-	+	-	-	+	+	-	-	+		24
Cruger	+	+	-	-	+	+	+	Discharged																								—
Piper	+	+	+	+	+	+	+	-	-	+	+	+	+	+	+	+	+	+	+	+	+	-	+	+	+	+	-	+	+	+	+	27
Total +'s	5	5	4	3	4	5	5	3	3	4	4	4	4	4	3	2	2	2	3	3	3	3	2	2	3	2	2	2	3	2	2 3	

Fig. 7-1. Sample performance record for patients's rising.

For the rest of the month, 4 would be "perfect" for the group. The total score is always interpreted in the light of the number of patients under observation. Each patient's performance is represented after his name and under the appropriate date. In this form, it is relatively easy to ascertain the periodicity of this behavior as well as its occurrence at all.

It would be a simple matter to use a single criterion for judging performance rather than the three that are required for a plus score in this example. However, any performance record form should make provision for at least the following information.

1. Identification of the behavior   (Up and at 'em)
2. Month and year   (May, 1967)
3. Specific instructions as to when observation is to be made and what notations are to be entered   (Observer: Check each dormitory . . . mark the patient plus.)
4. Criteria for evaluation   (Patient is not . . .)
5. Name of patient or patients   (Smith, Jones, . . .)
6. Calendar date   (1, 2, 3, . . .)
7. Summary   (Total)

Information regarding many other behaviors associated with ward routines can also be efficiently presented using performance records. Some that particularly lend themselves to this means are showering, eating, attendance at movies and dances, taking medication, response at group meetings, and seeing visitors.

Graphs are widely used for presenting statistical information which often lies buried among quantities of numerals, pluses, minuses, and other symbols. Unfortunately, many people find making a graph a formidable task. It need not be if you remember to follow a few simple rules.

Most graphs quickly show the relationship between two variables such as time and speed, growth and age, kind and size, or amount and source. However, when one of the variables involves two or more factors, a *bar graph* is often useful in making clear the relationship of this additional factor. For example, suppose you have obtained statistics concerning the number of tokens male and female patients spent for off-ward entertainment during the first three months of 1967. The two variables are months and number of tokens, and the additional factor is that both male and female spenders used the tokens. Ideally the data would have been recorded on a form already structured into the categories involved. If so, your first step, that of organizing the data into its components, has already been taken and you will have a listing such as the following.

Month—1967	Number of Tokens Used	
	Men	Women
January	550	500
February	50	425
March	125	450

If not, then you should list your data in some such fashion in order to have clearly in mind what it is you are attempting to show and to avoid confusion when transferring your figures to their proper locations on the graph.

All graphs have at least two axes—lines which intersect at a ninety-degree angle (see Fig. 7-2). Once these are drawn they should be labeled according to the two major variables of the information to be represented. Traditionally, any variable identified with time is assigned to the horizontal axis and any variable expressed numerically other than as a measure of time is assigned to the vertical axis. Hence, in the illustration, the horizontal axis is labeled "months" and the vertical axis "number of tokens."

In order to enter data, each of the axes of a graph must be scaled. *Scaling* is simply dividing an axis into units which correspond to levels or the range of a variable. For tokens-per-month data this means dividing the horizontal axis into three equal increments (since three months are involved) and the vertical axis into increments that range from 50 to

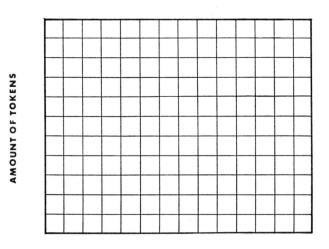

MONTHS

Fig. 7-2. First step in making graph of tokens spent during three month period.

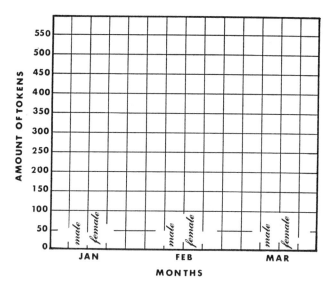

Fig. 7-3. Second step in making graph of tokens spent during three month period.

550. Consideration of this numerical spread makes a choice fairly simple—divisions by 100s or by 50s will be adequate.

Dividing the vertical axis by increments that represent 50 tokens each requires a total of 11 increments between the lowest number (50) and the highest number (550)—not an unwieldy total. To this one more should be added so that the measure can properly start at 0—the point of intersection with the other axis. In this case using 50 as a base instead of 100 also provides an opportunity to more accurately record the entries involving multiples of 25 midway between the 50-token steps.

Accordingly, three equal units are marked along the horizontal axis and twelve along the vertical with each appropriately labeled (see Fig. 7-3). In addition, light guidelines are drawn horizontally from each number marking and vertically from each month marking. Because two groups spent tokens each month, the month spaces were bisected by vertical guidelines. If standard graph paper were used, the guidelines would not need to be drawn since they would already exist.

For the next step refer to the data organized by categories as a first step in graph making. To show that 550 tokens were spent by men in January it is only necessary to locate the numeral 550 on the vertical axis and to find the place that the horizontal line intersects the two vertical lines extending upward from the space allotted to "men" for January. Then draw a heavy line from one of the vertical intersections to the other. Do the same along the projection of the numeral 500 to show women's expenditures for January. (See Fig. 7-4.) Similar entries should be made to represent the 50 and 425 tokens spent in February and

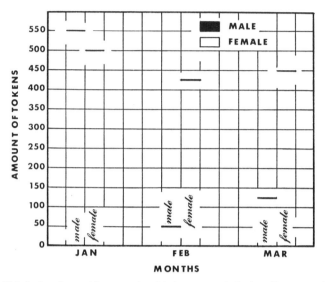

Fig. 7-4. Third step in making graph of tokens spent during three month period.

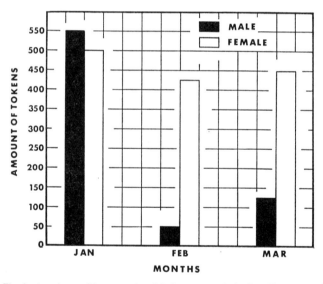

Fig. 7-5. Final step in making graph of tokens spent during three month period.

the 125 and 450 tokens spent in March. Because this is a bar graph, the vertical guidelines should be made heavier between the points of intersection and the points where they meet the horizontal axis. In addition, to give greater clarity in reading the graph, one set of bars should be differentiated in some way from the other and a key provided. At this point the bar graph will be complete. (See Fig. 7-5.)

Bar graphs can be made to run horizontally as well as vertically, and to present information with more than two factors of one major variable. Their effectiveness lies in the immediate contrast they provide for one or more groups performing the same behavior.

A very common graph used to present statistical information is like that on page 72 of this text. This is a simple *line graph* which, when properly done, makes instantly clear the relationship between two variables and any change that occurs in either one. In general the steps involved in making such a graph are the same as those for making any graph.

1-2. Compilation of data and organization by categories under two major variables
3. Drawing and labeling axes
4. Scaling
5. Locating intersecting points in area bounded by axes
6. Drawing connecting lines
7. Providing any key needed to clarify the elements represented

Unlike a line or a bar graph, which have entries at fixed intervals along a time scale, a *cumulative record* is a graph showing one response after another and the rate of occurrence over a continuous period of time.

Suppose a therapist wanted to know what use a patient was making of a cigarette vending machine. How many cigarettes were purchased? At what time of the day? Were they purchased all at the same time or one by one? A cumulative record of the patient's behavior at the cigarette machine would instantly provide this information. It could be procured manually by stationing a nurse at the machine and having him do nothing but observe and record the patient's behavior. It is infinitely more efficient to employ a simple recording device (called a cumulative recorder) consisting of a pen mounted so that its tip just rests on a continuously unwinding roll of graph paper. Such devices are readily obtainable through any scientific-instrument supply house.

A cumulative record indicates exactly when a response occurred, whether it was emitted more or less rapidly than the others being recorded (or at an identical rate), and the total number of responses at any time after the observation began.

Figure 7-6 represents the start of a record. As the paper slowly unrolls on a time control, the pen continuously makes a mark. Since no responses occurred in the first six minutes, the line is straight. In the next two minutes, three responses were emitted. Each of these is shown by a vertical line (*a*). The uniformity of the length of the markings for these responses shows they were made at a steady rate. The slant line at the end of the third response (*x*) signifies the occurrence of a reinforcer.

In the example of the cigarette machine, one might read from this cumulative graph that three responses were made (perhaps insertion of dimes) and that then a package of cigarettes was dispensed by the machine.

Following the slant line made by the pen, the graph next shows that no responses were made for approximately four minutes. (Note the horizontal line beinning at the first *x*.) Following this quiet period, however, six responses (*b*) were made in very quick succession and at a steady rate.

When the pen reaches the top of the paper it instantly drops to the bottom and continues right along with record making. Few cumulative graphs are scaled in the exaggerated way that the one in Figure 7-6 is. For laboratory records, most of which involve bar pressing and other extremely rapid manipulations, the mark made by a single response would not be easily identified because it would be too small.

The slope of the curve made by the accumulation of marks, however, is a valid indicator. Also, a scale can be applied which will give a fairly accurate measure of the time between responses and the total number of responses. These relationships are shown in the enlarged section of Figure 7-7.

Graphs are one of the most efficient means of presenting statistical data such as those accumulated in record keeping on a behavioral program because the relationship of the elements involved, as well as totals, can be so clearly portrayed.

MAKING TREATMENT PLANS AVAILABLE

No matter how significant data are, or in what form they have been presented, a tendency persists for nursing personnel to store information

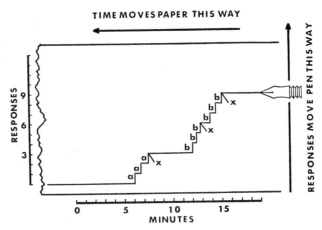

Fig. 7-6. Cumulative record.

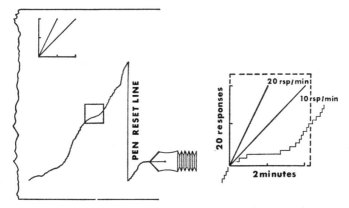

Fig. 7-7. Cumulative record showing use of rate scale.

in their heads and to pass on the specifics of procedures solely in verbal terms. While a certain amount of this is inevitable because of time factors, it is imperative that patients' programs be committed to a record which is readily accessible to all members of the behavioral staff at all times. The importance of this phase of record keeping became evident to nursing personnel of our program during an experience with a patient on the women's unit.

The patient was so exceptionally adroit in manipulating personnel that they soon became so accustomed to her manipulative tactics that no special procedures were used and staff members made their own individual adjustments to her behavior. Eventually, however, a specific treatment plan was formulated to change the undesirable behavior of this patient, but unfortunately, if any record was made of the plan, its availability was unknown, and nurses relied on their memories for treatment procedure. Within a week it became obvious that the patient's ways had not changed; she continually escaped contingencies which had presumably been established.

A follow-up study showed she had been obtaining reinforcers because another nurse "said it was all right." As soon as the patient's records were made available at all times, this inconsistency ceased and progress was made in the patient's treatment.

The circumstances of any particular treatment program will largely determine ways in which records can best be made accessible. The following methods have proved useful in different phases of our own behavioral program.

Notebooks
Card systems
Wall charts and open displays
Shift "surprises"

When using *notebooks* the record forms are punched to fit a large ring binder and filed alphabetically by patients' names. The accumulation of records for all patients are kept fastened together in the one binder. In order to remove a single form, the notebook must be opened, and the procedure must be repeated when the form is returned. The book itself should be kept on a prominent shelf or desk in a room used frequently by the staff. A drawback is that a notebook, even though it may be large and bulky, is easily relocated from one ward area to another. Constantly having to search for the book and the information it contains increases the likelihood that action will be taken without troubling to ascertain established procedure.

With *card systems* all cards containing information about the same patient are slipped into an open-ended envelope bearing the patient's name or into a pocket attached to a stiff backing and appropriately labeled. The entire collection of holders (envelopes or pockets) is then put in an open box or drawer in alphabetical order by patients' names. Such a system probably makes individual elements more subject to being misplaced than an entire notebook, but it also makes them easier to work with. If the forms are distinctive as to color and/or size they find their way back to the master file fairly readily. The size of the group for whom records are kept and the number of records nurses are expected to frequently refer to usually determine the relative advantages and disadvantages of notebook storage versus card storage.

Information displayed on *wall charts* in the dormitories, the eating areas, or wherever the patients involved are most likely to congregate provide maximum efficiency as far as accessibility and use are concerned. Since the record is always available both to staff members and patients, it is difficult for either to ignore the stimuli provided by such a constant reminder. Patients prone to attempt to manipulate the staff can always be immediately confronted with the elements of their programs and reminded to "see for yourself." An example of the kind of treatment program displayed on a wall chart is given in Figure 7-8.

Because nursing shifts change at regular intervals during the day and night but patient care goes on, most wards make use of some kind of running account of the day's events. Details which may influence decisions made by nurses taking over are recorded in a special journal. For reasons that are not altogether clear to us we have come to use the term *shift surprises* for this journal. Each staff member is required to read the day's "surprises" prior to going on duty so that she may ask questions and become thoroughly informed about any changes or special problems before interacting with patients. This record is kept in the ward office at all times.

Current Treatment Plan for : Helen

Behavior	Reinforces	Schedule	Control Stimulus
talking softly	tokens	each time	especially in groups
working	1 token per task	once each day	at 9:00 am
combed hair	1 cigarette	each hour	9:00 am to 9:00 pm

Fig. 7-8. Example of treatment program displayed as wall chart for quick reference.

In this day and age of ever-increasing amounts of forms and paperwork there is justified suspicion about "new forms that have to be filled out." But in behavioral therapy, records of the patient's behavior are the essential tools by which therapy is guided and by which its effectiveness is judged. Records, too, are one of the most effective ways, to prevent abuses of behavioral techniques: If a patient does not improve, his record will show this. Since the record also contains the prescriptions for treatment, they can then be scrutinized. Thus, records are a needed check in any program of behavioral therapy.

Last but not least, records are reinforcing to personnel because they can see a visual display of improvement resulting from a technique to which an individual nurse may have contributed much, perhaps all.

EXERCISES, CHAPTER 7

1. What are some of the methods employed to detect a patient's reinforcers?
2. Construct a line graph for the following set of data.

Day	Patient A	Patient B
1	100 responses	10 responses
2	50 responses	50 responses
3	53 responses	25 responses
4	22 responses	65 responses
5	10 responses	100 responses

3. Write a behavioral description of the separate responses involved in tying shoelaces.
4. What stimuli should control the behavior of shoe tying and be included in a treatment plan?
5. Construct a cumulative record for the data listed below. Use square-ruled paper and make a vertical excursion of the pen for "yes" entries and a horizontal for "no" entries.

Time	Entry
0600	yes
0700	yes
0800	no
0900	no
1000	yes
1100	no
1200	no
1300	no
1400	no
1500	no
1600	yes
1700	yes
1800	yes
1900	yes
2000	yes

6. Consulting your graph, answer the following questions:
    a. How many responses occurred between the hours of 0600 and 1300?
    b. Between what hours did the most continuously steady rate of "yes" entries occur?
    c. Between what hours did the most continuously steady rate of "no" entries occur?
    d. Suppose that each "yes" entry meant that a patient was observed talking to himself. At what time of the day would you be most likely to apply techniques which combat this behavior?
7. Show how the practice of keeping behavioral records most easily and surely prevents abuse of behavioral techniques.

Part IV

Clinical Applications of Behavioral Techniques

8

Behavioral Techniques and Ward Routine

Your study of this chapter should help you answer the following questions:

1. What behavioral techniques can be used to combat regression due to long-term hospitalization?
2. What behavioral techniques are useful when reinstating awareness and thinking?
3. What behavioral techniques can be used to induce patients to work?

The terms listed below are introduced and defined in this chapter:

regression
developing behavior—shaping
reinstating behavior
awareness
thinking
job description
fading
time card
terminal behavior

COMBATING REGRESSION DUE TO LONG-TERM HOSPITALIZATION

Prolonged hospitalization frequently results in severe behavioral regression for many patients. *Regression,* as used here, refers to an apparent loss of ability to take responsibility for such daily ward routines as rising and retiring, personal grooming, and arriving on time for meals and medicine. Sometimes nursing personnel unwittingly foster this seeming helplessness of patients by performing tasks for the patient which he could well do himself. This tendency is an undesirable accompaniment of the traditional attitude that no "sick" person should be expected to care for himself. The *apparent* ineptness of severely regressed psychotics in turn results in procedures which, as it were, instruct nursing personnel to reinforce regression. One training manual, for example, advises psychiatric attendants to do all they can to allow patients to work out compulsions by permitting them to engage in compulsive behaviors and offering no objections when such behaviors occur. Unfortunately, carrying out instructions of this kind all too often merely strengthens and maintains undesirable behavior.

In the Patton experiment various behavioral techniques were tried out to counteract regression due to prolonged hospitalization. Most of the procedures that were used concerned self-care activities in daily ward routine. Many others might have been used for the same purposes just as effectively and may even need to be employed when an environment differs markedly from ward life at Patton.

In this context, the distinction between developing new behavior and reinstating normal behavior must be kept in mind. *Developing a new behavior*—that is, *shaping*—calls for techniques by which a patient is expected to learn to do something he does not now do. It implies that the patient does not yet have a particular behavior in his repertoire. *Reinstating* a behavior assumes that at one time the patient emitted that behavior, but his performance now indicates that the behavior has very low strength or is not currently present. Developing (shaping) involves the piecing together of component responses. Reinstating refers to what is done to increase the strength of a behavior. In almost every case, the application of behavioral techniques to ward routines results in reinstating desired behaviors, not developing new ones.

The daily routines of hospital wards provide many occasions when the emission of desirable behaviors can result in reinforcement. Mental patients are required to get up each day, shower, and appear for ward activities. All these procedures can be structured in the form of reinforcement contingencies.

Early Morning Rising, or "Up and at 'em"

Getting up in the morning involves many individual acts. At Patton the colloquial phrase "Up and at 'em" identifies that the patient

1. Is on his feet
2. Is appropriately dressed
3. Has made his bed

For each of these behaviors the patient earns one token. In order to earn a three-token reinforcement, each patient must emit all these behaviors by six-thirty in the morning, when the night nurse makes rounds of all the dormitories on the ward before going off duty. Using a standard form (like the one on page 90) which lists each patient's name and the date, she checks for criteria 1, 2, and 3 mentioned above. If a patient meets all the criteria, the nurse marks a plus sign by his name and immediately hands over three tokens. If the patient has not met the criteria, the nurse enters a minus sign on the check sheet and does not deliver tokens.

When first instigated, this procedure resulted in less than 100 percent performance desired in each group. A modification which involved group pressure was then introduced. All patients in a dormitory that had less than 100 percent desired behavior in the "up and at 'em" routine were told that token reinforcement would be given only if all members of the group performed to criterion. When this technique was adopted, patients already emitting the desired behavior took it upon themselves to prod the malingerers into action. Procedures involving group pressure of this kind are used, however, only when at least 20 percent of a group are performing poorly and staff members do not have time to first work on an individual basis with recalcitrants.

Delivering reinforcement to patients for getting up by themselves can be integrated into the routine of most hospital wards. However, the reinforcement need not be tokens. Nor do patients have to be up, dressed, and with their beds made before receiving reinforcement. The mere act of getting up without being called might be reinforced for some patients with a sweet or a drink of juice. Getting up and to the dining area by a certain time could be reinforced with a cup of coffee. If the patient is suitably dressed, he might also be given a cigarette. Gradually both rising and dressing might be required (*chained*) before a patient were reinforced even with just coffee. If he has also made his bed he might be entitled to a cigarette as well. Other desired behaviors could be similarly chained by gradually increasing the required criteria.

It is interesting to note that immediate delivery of primary reinforcement approximates conditions which individuals outside the hospital provide themselves. It may be no accident that drinking a cup of coffee and smoking a cigarette is part of the morning behavioral repertoire of many "normal" people.

Showering

Most individuals who have had experience with the regressed psychotic patient are aware that on their own such patients bathe infrequently. Since most institutions have requirements regarding the number of baths patients must have per week, seeing that patients bathe sometimes becomes a full-time occupation for some of the nursing personnel. Since showering is a self-care activity which takes place at a specific location and usually at specified times, it is readily amenable to the application of behavioral techniques.

In the women's groups of the Patton program, shower rooms are opened three times each day: in the morning, in the afternoon, and in the evening. A continuous day-by-day record which notes the following activities for each patient is kept for the entire ward population.

1. Under shower
2. Soaped up completely
3. Rinsed off
4. Dried

The record is normally kept by a staff member who sits at the entrance to the shower room. When a patient finishes the last item (dries) reinforcement in the form of tokens is delivered. Each day's record provides an easy means for verifying performance by individual patients and for the ward as a whole.

The system used with the men's groups at Patton places an additional responsibility on the patient: It requires him to register as an indication that he has showered. With this procedure the shower room is open all day, so that patients can bathe at their own convenience. Upon completion of his shower, a patient registers at the ward office. Reinforcement can be delivered at that time or later at pay call using the register and subsequent detailed body inspection as the basis for payment. An aversive consequence in the form of a charge for not meeting inspection criteria or denial of a privilege can be attached for failure to shower or for neglect in registering.

This method has the disadvantage of lacking direct observation of a patient's behavior. There is less direct control and thus less detailed effect on behavior. For example, patients may consider it sufficient to spend a few seconds under the water without soaping or scrubbing. However, odor checks throughout the course of the day (for example, prior to entry into the dining room) can partially overcome this drawback.

Exercising

An unwillingness to exercise is also sometimes the result of lengthy hospitalization and calls for reinstatement of desired behaviors. Hospitals typically provide dances, swimming pools, miniature golf courses, and game areas for the purpose of exercise. However, frequently patients do not avail themselves of the facilities.

Getting patients to exercise can be accomplished through behavioral techniques just as rising and showering can. That is, patients emitting behaviors which are "satisfactory physical exercise" receive reinforcement. An exercise program which organizes the time and place of physical activities makes it easier to administer the delivery of reinforcers. A procedure used in the women's groups of the Patton program exemplifies one method of inducing patients to emit desired behavior. Every morning just before nine o'clock, a lounge area is cleared. Promptly at nine the television in that area automatically turns on to a currently popular program which is aimed at getting its viewers to exercise. The program is accompanied by music and the chatter of an amiable instructor. Patients earn three tokens if they do all the exercises shown on the program, two tokens for doing some of them, and one token for minimal performance. Of course, the criteria of reinforcement depend, as always, on the needs of individual patients and are therefore not always the same for everyone. When first organized, a staff member watched the entire session and delivered tokens while each patient was exercising. When this regular supervision could no longer be maintained, the patients themselves took over the procedure and kept track of their own performance. They used a check sheet and were "paid" at pay call on the basis of this record. Spot checks on the accuracy of the records were, of course, made periodically but surprisingly, the agreement between what patients actually do and what they say they do in such simple matters is very high. This veracity is the more puzzling in view of the discrepancy between fact and fancy so typical of schizophrenics in other matters.

Grooming

The bulk of additional self-care activities which may be brought under behavioral control fall under the general heading of *grooming*. Their importance stems from the immediate consequences personal appearance bring about outside the hospital. Sloppy appearance as well as bizarre behaviors can prompt a patient's return to the hospital. One of the hallmarks of the long-term-hospitalized schizophrenic is the obvious impoverishment of grooming habits in his behavioral repertoire.

As with any behavior, it is important to deliver reinforcers for desired grooming responses while these responses are being emitted. Reinforcement can also be made contingent upon evidence that the patient is groomed. But it may well happen that a patient does not make the connection between appearance and the behaviors that led to it. Thus compliments for neat appearance or disapproval for sloppiness may not in the least affect any related behavior. Neat hair, smooth face, clean hands, and fresh lipstick as well as combing hair, shaving, washing hands, and applying lipstick should bring prompt reinforcement.

The use of hospital-supported facilities greatly aid in the development of good grooming habits among patients. At Patton, extensive use is made of the beauty shop and barbering as a means of reinstating more personable appearance. Patients pay in tokens to have their hair cut, of course, but staff members are on the alert when the patient returns to the ward. The obvious improvement in personal appearance after a shampoo and set or a haircut is an occasion for lavish reinforcement by nursing personnel. The patient always earns more than he or she had to pay to get the haircut or whatever. It is also important to couple the delivery of reinforcers, such as tokens, with verbal statements of approval. Eventually, the patient must be brought to the point where positive social comment sustains such performance, and with personal appearance this does happen fairly automatically. The token is used here as a conditioned reinforcer for but a short while. Normal reinforcers which are in effect for all of us—admiring stares and wolf whistles for the girls, open or demure attention for boys, and generally respectful treatment for either—take over instantly and make it easy to "wean" the patient from the artificial token support.

Sometimes it is helpful to reinforce a patient directly while she is at the beauty shop and actually in the process of allowing someone to modify her personal appearance. In one instance when a patient in our program was extremely reluctant to have her hair done, staff members required her to pay tokens for the privilege of remaining on the ward. This procedure was sufficient to cause her to leave the ward to get her hair done but not subsequently to go again on her own accord. A change in tactics eventually brought about the desired behavior when the ward psychologist made it a practice to go to the beauty shop when he knew the patient was there and to reinforce her. After three occurrences of reinforcement under these conditions, the patient started to ask to have her hair done. It is now her practice to go to the beauty shop almost every week.

Resting and Sleeping

A striking feature of many mental hospital wards is the number of patients who may be found sleeping or resting during the day. In addition to using beds, patients sleep on chairs, benches, stairs, and sometimes on the floor. The behavioral techniques for modifying excessive sleeping or resting are simply to make the patient's livelihood dependent upon not sleeping or lying down except at night when all patients are expected to rest. To do this, nursing personnel must reinforce incompatible behavior (such as walking) or they might also make the undesirable behavior costly.

A woman patient spent approximately 80 percent of her time lying on her bed. Each staff member was instructed to reinforce the patient only when she was observed on her feet or sitting upright and awake in a chair. She received tokens for nothing else, yet had to pay for her bed, meals, and privileges just as before. Within two weeks she could always be found either sitting in a chair or strolling around the grounds, although she had previously rarely gone outdoors. She now pays to go outside where she sits or walks with other patients.

The technique of reinforcing behaviors incompatible with an undesirable response can be effective with many ward routines. Pacers may be reinforced for sitting, reticent patients for speaking, and incessant talkers for not speaking. Carried to what may at first seem an extreme, overly complacent patients may even be reinforced for angry or impolite behavior which can later be made to occur only under appropriate conditions through the use of proper control stimuli.

REINSTATING AWARENESS AND THINKING

Awareness is a quality possessed by a person who can reliably report events in his environment. He knows what is happening and shows that he does by actions and speech that correspond to what people expect in a given situation. When a mental patient's behavior increasingly conforms to what is expected, we say that his "awareness" has been increased.

In reinstating awareness in psychotics, the first step is to establish behaviors which bring the patient into contact with environmental stimuli that supply information. The next step is to design situations in which the information can be reported. A simple method is to make the relating of information about ward events valuable by pairing reports with the delivery of reinforcement. More regressed patients may also be reinforced for knowing the day, month, and year. Patients should be required to learn the names of all nursing personnel, the hospital superintendent, their psychiatrist, and their ward mates.

One patient in the Patton program who had been hospitalized for twenty years was severely regressed and spent most of his waking hours engaged in conversation with himself. Over the course of his commitment, this patient had developed the "habit" of referring to all employees as "Mr." or "Mrs. Patton." His behavior was maintained at high strength because usage of this name was sufficient for getting attention and help. This behavior was easily extinguished by witholding reinforcement through absolutely ignoring him whenever he addressed nursing personnel as Mr. (or Mrs.) Patton. At the same time, he was required to learn and use the names of the ward staff and to answer their frequent question, "What's my name?" Correct responses to this inquiry resulted in immediate reinforcement in the form of undivided attention. Once the names had been learned, attention was still withheld if the patient forgot or again used Mr. and Mrs. Patton. However, immediate reinforcement continued to be given for each use of a correct name. The patient now addresses all nursing personnel by their names and titles. Thus, this particular form of awareness was reinstated by supplanting an undesired behavior with a desirable one.

A wide variety of questions can be used to promote the development of awareness. Even if a patient cannot be reinforced for anything else, his answers giving information regarding the day's menus, times for medication, banking hours, and shift changes can provide opportunities for reinforcement. In addition, patients can and should be reinforced for behaviors involved in gathering such information. A patient observed reading the bulletin board or overheard asking questions about time schedules can be reinforced for his behavior and reinforced again if the information he gathers is passed on in substantially correct form. Patients can be reinforced for reading a newspaper and then again for a verbal news report of what they have read. In our program, one hour of television—the evening news hours—is provided "free" to all patients. (Other TV shows "cost" a token per minute.) Patients know that the next day at medication time, or during the ward meeting, they can earn tokens for reporting on world events.

Awareness is not difficult to assess, yet the question invariably arises, "How is it known that someone is really thinking?" But if awareness is inferred through someone's actions, the same inference can be made about *thinking*. Thoughts, like awareness, are invisible and private. But self-descriptive verbal reports about thoughts and actions on the basis of which the occurrence of thinking and awareness is inferred are public and visible. An individual acts as if he were thinking or as if he had previously been thinking, if and when he acts a certain way. Patients can be conditioned to behave as if such a process were going on and then reinforced for this action. Suppose, for example, that a patient saves tokens to go to a dance three days hence. Naturally this assumes that the patient "thinks ahead." Does it matter whether the patient saved his tokens by reinforcing him to hold onto tokens and not for having thought? To be sure, people are so used to believing that thinking precedes action that much conventional therapy tries to reinforce "right" thinking in the hope that action will then follow. Behavioral therapy reinforces the action regardless of its cause.

Practically, a situation may arise in which a patient has only enough tokens to purchase one privilege yet may also want another. Rather than make the decision regarding which privilege to buy, he wants someone else to make it for him. This sets the occasion for questions like, "What do you want to do?" or "What is more important to you?" If the patient answers he should be reinforced. Soon he will be asking such questions of himself and the support of further questioning can be withdrawn. If he follows through and his choice is consistent with the answer, he should receive reinforcement, either naturally through the privilege he now enjoys or, especially in early stages, through supportive reinforcers that are commonly used with him. In short, a good practice to follow when reinstating thinking is to engage a patient in a conversation which presents alternatives so that he makes a choice. The staff member can also ask a patient to state the consequences of the various choices. When he does so he should, of course, be reinforced because listing consequences is said to show thinking.

Situations in which the patient can be induced to think arise constantly on any ward. It does not help the patient if nursing personnel insist on doing his thinking for him. Depositing tokens in the ward bank is a common situation in our program. Frequently the patient wants the banker to indicate how many he should deposit or withdraw. This can be an occasion to reinforce thinking by such replies as, "How many will you need for the rest of the day?" or "What are your needs going to be?" Sometimes a patient attempts to avoid the thinking required to answer by merely depositing all his tokens. This should be followed by questions such as, "Now will you have enough tokens for dinner?" or "Won't you need some of those tokens for cigarettes?" Such inquiries will usually force the patient to think as desired. But suppose he does not. Suppose he simply walks away. The wise behaviorist will now say nothing. Let the environment take care of things now. Dinner time will come and the patient will have no money to pay for his dinner. Chances are that the bank will be closed then. It is not the nurse who must learn to think, but the patient. Only the consequences of thinking will accomplish this—not admonishment, threats, advice, prodding, and certainly not thinking *for* the patient.

Certain routine procedures used on many wards must be totally eliminated if patients are indeed to think for themselves. For example, patients should not be called for daily medication. Medication can be given at standard times and in standard places. If that is done patients can be expected to—and do—appear without prompting beyond a first time or two during orientation. Other ward routines that lend themselves to reinstating thinking are

Meals
Pay calls
Showering
Grooming
Regular group meetings
Regular work assignments
Store or snack bar
Rising and retiring

Few patients miss more than one meal or one chance to get cigarettes, clothing, or some piece of equipment they want from a facility that is open only during certain hours of the day. Those who ignore medication, group meetings, acceptable grooming, etc., can be made to pay (in tokens or whatever medium of exchange is used) for the privilege of *not* doing something. Alert nursing personnel can soon determine the price a patient is unwilling to pay and charge accordingly so that the desired behavior is elicited.

Putting patients on their own responsibility to meet ward routines not only makes for greater efficiency, but is one of the most effective ways in which behavioral techniques can be applied to reinstate desirable behaviors such as awareness and thinking.

ESTABLISHING A WORK PROGRAM

Almost all mental hospitals use patients for housekeeping tasks. In addition to helping solve critical manpower shortages, work assignments are considered beneficial for any patient physically able to move about freely. This emphasis is not surprising in view of the value society places upon work. Most adults work to earn their livelihood or the respect of the community and usually expect similar behavior from others. Belief in the virtue of an honest day's labor is so strong that the subsequent conditioning engaged in to promote this belief results in little tolerance for the person who behaves differently.

Still another factor enters any consideration given to a work program for mental patients. Upon release patients will be expected to work. In truth, a factor favoring the patient's discharge is that he has demonstrated he is willing and able to work. In view of this, behaviors that lead to acceptable work habits should be reinstated.

In their article "The Measurement and Reinforcement of Behavior in Psychotics," T. Ayllon and N. H. Azrin have recommended that two conditions be met when setting up a work program for the chronic schizophrenic: (1) The results of the patient's work should produce a relatively enduring change in the environment, and (2) the time for work should be closely scheduled by making the necessary equipment available only during specific hours. Establishing these criteria makes it possible to know exactly what is being reinforced. The quality of a patient's work can easily be assessed when it involves an obvious change in environment; making equipment available only at specified times circumvents the patient's ability to claim he did the work earlier or later. If these provisions were not met, it would be quite difficult to make reinforcement contingent upon a specific level of performance.

Hospital work assignments break down into two broad classifications: on-ward assignments and off-ward assignments.

On-ward Work Assignments

On-ward work assignments for patients listed below are used in a typical women's unit of a hospital for the mentally ill.

Office worker	Vacant rooms cleaner
Job monitor	Cigarette roller
Exercise monitor	Token sorter
Back section cleaner	Game room monitor
Office cleaner	Clothes room helper
Door monitor	Nurse's section cleaner
Yard worker	Entry halls cleaner
Bed board cleaner	Kitchen worker
Laundry helper	Kitchen supervisor
East dorm cleaner	Dayhall cleaner
Recreation room cleaner	Dust mopper
Halls sweeper	Broom closet orderly
Stairways sweeper	Employee's coffee room orderly
Medicine cups cleaner	Shower room supervisor
Table setter—Diet room	Shower checker
Clean laundry sorter	Chair washer
Wastepaper basket emptier	Wall washer
Window washer	Mopper-waxer
Screens cleaner	Wash chairs in therapy room
Ironer	Porch cleaner
Fire escapes cleaner	Tokens cleaner
Inside vending machine cleaner	Drinking fountain cleaning
Light fixtures cleaner	Errand doer

Other lists have been developed elsewhere. Ayllon and Azrin, for example, have developed an interesting list which includes accurate descriptions of the behaviors involved in each assignment. Nursing personnel or reliable patients check all jobs as soon as the work is completed. Since most of the tasks result in some kind of a change in the environment, the quality of work is easily assessed. If the floor was dusted, no dust should be on the floor; if papers were stapled, a pile of stapled papers is the criterion. After checking, the nurse signs a list which is handed over to the banker who pays the amount called for.

Many patients who are considered "poor workers" and those who have developed an extensive repertoire of responses to successfully avoid work can be brought to perform by establishing contingencies between working and the necessities of ward life. The procedures specified here have proven to be quite effective. However, there are always patients, such as those with physical limitations or severe regression, for whom special techniques may have to be developed.

The first step is to announce the work assignments. Each patient must be given highly specific information regarding what is expected of him. This information should include an accurate description of each task involved in the assignment, as well as the time interval in which the task is to be completed. It is useful to arrange for certain work assignments in the morning and others at bedtime. This is merely a matter of convenience. Both on getting up in the morning and toward evening, ward life causes patients to be "in step" as it were; that is, it is easier at these times to work on tasks that are similar for many of the patients. An exact specification of each job's requirements is important so that the patient has no outlet for excuse making or otherwise manipulating nursing personnel. For example, many patients wish to perform work tasks "when they feel like it." If this is allowed, the inevitable result is poor performance or claims that work was performed when it actually was not.

Figure 8-1 is an example of a *Work Description* card which is very useful in the initial stages of reinstating work behavior. The requirements as presented on the card are explained verbally to the patient just prior to the first exposure to the job. In some cases, a staff member stays with the patient to ensure that the procedures are carried out and to direct adequate performance. During these sessions, the staff member

---

Job Dorm cleaner	**Time** 9:00–9:30 a.m.

Equipment

1 Dust mop
1 Dust rag
1 Dust pan
1 Cleaning rag
1 Pail of water

Requirements

1. Pick up equipment at 9:00
2. Dust all ledges, partitions and sills (every day)
3. Dust-mop entire dorm floor except area under beds
4. Shake out dust rag and dust mop outside behin the ward
5. Empty and clean water pail
6. Rinse out cleaning rag
7. Turn in all equipment at 9:30 or before
8. Wash insides of all dorm windows (each Saturday)

Fig. 8-1. Job description of dorm cleaner during early phase.

Job Dorm Cleaner	**Time** 9:00–9:30 a.m.

Equipment	1 Dust mop
	1 ___ ___
	1 Dust ___
	1 Cleaning rag
	1 ___ of water

Requirements

1. Pick up at ___ o'clock
2. Dust all partitions, ledges and ___
3. ___ ___ ___ ___ ___ ___ ___ ___ ___
   ___ ___
4. Shake out dust rag and dust mop outside behind the ward
5. Empty and ___ ___ ___
6. Rinse out ___ rag
7. Turn in all equipment at about ___
8. Wash insides of all dorm windows (each ___)

Fig. 8-2. Job description of dorm cleaner during later phase.

immediately reinforces the patient's behavior upon the completion of each step. After the patient's level of performance increases and stabilizes, the card itself takes the place of the support given by the staff member's presence. Once this stage is attained, the patient is required to have the card with him during the performance of the job. If the patient does not have the card, he must demonstrate that he knows each requirement specified. If he cannot meet either of these tests, various consequences may be attached either in the form of nonpayment or in terms of a reduction in pay. If the terminal behavior has been properly paced by taking the patient a step at a time through the performance of the assignment, instances of this undesirable consequence will be infrequent.

When the patient performs adequately and with great regularity, the information the card provides must be faded so that the patient increasingly performs on his own. Fading may be accomplished by gradually eliminating the information on the card over a period of time. Figure 8-2 presents the card approximately half faded.

Once fading is begun, the patient should be tested fairly regularly for his knowledge of the information on the card. Nursing personnel can do this by asking the patient to state what items should be on his card or by observing the performance of tasks to see if all are performed. Adequate performance should be consistently reinforced so that the desired terminal behavior is obtained—that is, so that the patient knows all the information on the card and regularly performs each item satisfactorily.

Payment for on-ward work assignments may be made either at the time work is performed as in the instance cited above or at a regular ward paycall. Regardless of the pay system used, it is wise to avoid lengthy delays in reinforcement especially in the initial stages of reinstating any behavior.

Terminal behaviors, that is, those behaviors which in the initial staff meeting were set as desirable goals for the patient, are most efficiently reinstated when reinforcement for work performed is scaled to the level of performance. By using a work description card, different amounts for reinforcement can be delivered in terms of the number of tasks performed, for example, one token per item completed. It is also useful to make provisions for bonus payments. For example, a bonus might be given when a patient completes all items on the card in the time specified or when exceptionally good performance occurs. While tokens afford the most convenient way to function as conditioned reinforcers, any other object that has reinforcing value may, of course, be used, staff time permitting. For example, if the patient performs well, a bonus of additional minutes out-of-doors might be given.

A work description card system has the advantage that performance can be assessed in terms of a patient's individual capabilities. Card usage also allows staff members to set clear-cut objectives and pace requirements so the patient may change at his own rate. Naturally, for patients whose degree of contact with reality is near normal, the procedure described here is not necessary. However, usage of the card is indicated in all instances until it is firmly established that the patient is aware of exactly what is required on a particular work assignment. In other words, there is nothing magical in this procedure. When a patient can simply be told to work and he performs adequately, there is no need to take small steps.

Once the patient is functioning on his own and it is apparent that as much progress has been made as possible, the procedure should be repeated on another assignment. This can continue until the patient's work behavior resembles that of individuals in the community performing similar functions. As the patient progresses through different and more complex jobs, it can be expected that he will learn faster and may rapidly reach a point where the support given earlier is no longer necessary.

Off-ward Work Assignments

On off-ward work assignments, patients work in areas of the hospital other than their ward. Many patients can learn or already possess skills which the hospital may require. In addition, the patient is rarely busy throughout the day, and it is considered beneficial for patients to be kept occupied. Some off-ward work assignments involve highly responsible tasks while others, in and of themselves, are only meaningful in the sense that they give the patient something to do. Off-ward assignments give patients an opportunity to temporarily escape the contingencies established on a behaviorally oriented ward. In such a situation the stimulus complex which is the ward then rapidly becomes a control stimulus that hinders generalization to the outside world of the newly formed behaviors. This problem can be circumvented, however, when a behavioral program does not exist as an isolated entity within the hospital. By establishing friendly and cooperative relations with other areas of the hospital a behavioral program can be extended beyond the confines of its own wards. However, behavioral procedures may tax the patience of many supervisory personnel, and friendly relations are necessary in order to obtain the desired ends of a treatment program.

A female patient in our program had been working in the ward kitchen for approximately six months. Nursing personnel then decided it was time to give her the responsibility of learning to function without the close support found on the ward. The patient was extremely resistive and returned to the ward after only five or ten minutes. Naturally, she was immediately sent back to her assignment, only to return an hour later. This tug of war went on for approximately ten days, sometimes half a dozen times per day. During this time a major problem was to convince her off-ward supervisor that there was rhyme and reason to all this. He naturally felt that he could not depend upon the number of hours she would work, and he found it extremely frustrating to have the patient leave in the middle of a task. However, the patient, who was paid by the hour, was not earning many tokens under his regimen, and in time the consequences of this behavior caught up with her. She eventually adopted more consistent work patterns, reported to work on time, and remained throughout the work period. Without the cooperation of her off-ward supervisor, the insistence on the part of the behavioral personnel that she return to work could not have been feasible.

Supervisory personnel who are not directly involved with a behavioral project can aid in other ways. In another case, the patient would report for work but refused to perform adequately. That he appreciated the value of tokens was evidenced by his spending patterns on the ward. A conversation with his off-ward supervisor revealed the latter's willingness to institute a period of on-the-spot reinforcement during working hours. He subsequently reinforced the patient with tokens whenever performance warranted. Consistent application of this procedure reinstated the behavior desired of the patient.

Surveilance of patients during off-ward assignments is just as necessary as during on-ward assignments. In exchange for their work, patients receive reinforcement commensurate with its quantity and quality just as most workers do who are not patients. Therefore, supervisory personnel must have some means of grading performance. Figure 8-3 represents a time card used for individual off-ward workers in the Patton program. It shows arrival and departure times and the total number of hours worked. When his card is turned in, the patient is paid at an hourly rate. The rate of pay is usually 90 percent of the total number of tokens the patient needs per day. It can be set at a higher or lower percentage depending on the patient's opportunity to earn from other sources, such as pay for grooming, rising, and being on time. Unless working is the focus of treatment, payment should not exceed 100 percent of the patient's daily needs for tokens.

The patient is responsible for maintaining his work record on the time card. This means it is his responsibility to obtain the signature of his supervisor upon arrival and departure from work. The card is set up so that wages are paid once a week or once every two weeks. This procedure approximates conditions outside the hospital. If necessary for hospital purposes, however, patients can be paid on a daily basis according to the entries on their cards. Increasing the time gaps between

TIME CARD

Name _____   Pay Period

Job _____

Month _____   Weekly _____   Bi-weekly _____

                                       Location_____

Employer: Please initial all enteries.

Day	In	Out	In	Out	Pay Rate	Hours Worked	Total Pay
SUN							
MON							
TUES							
WED							
THUR							
FRI							
SAT							
SUN							
MON							
TUES							
WED							
THUR							
FRI							
SAT							

Comments:

Fig. 8-3. Sample timecard for work assignments.

pay periods is part of the method used in the Patton program to wean patients from dependence on immediate reinforcement.

The time card system isn't totally adequate for the purpose for which it is used in a behavioral treatment program since it fails to provide a method for detailed assessment of work performed. In other words, scaling of wages according to poor, standard, or exceptional performance cannot be made. In a way, it is an all-or-none kind of record. It does, however, ensure that patients on off-ward assignments perform to some level of acceptance on their assignments. And it places in the hands of the patient responsibility for his own behavior, which, after all, is the terminal behavior desired from the use of behavioral techniques with all ward routines.

EXERCISES, CHAPTER 8

1. The fading technique used in connection with working is a useful method of removing artificial response support. What other situations might set the occasion for fading out stimuli?
2. Describe some of the methods used to induce awareness and thinking in patients? Make up a treatment plan for a patient who is a heavy smoker and who rarely is aware of ward events.
3. John is a severely regressed psychotic patient. He rarely gets out of bed, shaves, or engages in any physical labor. Your ward psychiatrist wants John to perform an on-ward job. Select a job which may be performed on the ward, and prepare a treatment program which induces John to work.
4. Mary is habitually late for medications. Mary is very fond of the out-of-doors. How can Mary be induced to be prompt for medications?
5. Describe some of the routines of your daily life. What reinforcement contingencies are involved?
6. Discuss some of the routine procedures which foster the patients' dependence on the hospital.
7. Make a list of the behaviors that you believe a chronically ill patient should be expected to perform without help from nursing personnel.
8. Smitty was observed to have dirty feet on 80 percent of all direct observations conducted for a two-week period. The baseline data also revealed that Smitty could be found painting pictures four times each day. Arrange a contingency to increase the frequency of clean feet observations. Be specific.
9. Many believe that the mental hospital should be a refuge, a place where the patient can escape the stress of community living. In view of this attitude, justify the use of a work program.
10. List as many behaviors as you can which lead us to the inference that patients are aware of their environment.
11. Make a similar list for thinking.
12. Outline five reinforcement contingencies involving behaviors which patients are expected to emit each day on the ward.

9

Treating Odd Behaviors—I

Your study of this chapter should help
you answer the following questions:

1. How is manipulation of the staff by
   patients interpreted in a program
   of behavioral therapy?
2. When is ignoring a behavior sufficient for its extinction?
3. How and when is the formation of
   incompatible behaviors used to
   eliminate odd behaviors?

INTERPRETATION OF PATIENTS' ATTEMPTS AT STAFF MANIPULATION

When nurses are asked which problems are most prevalent in dealing
with mentally ill persons, they invariably refer to patients who attempt
to "manipulate the staff and the existing rules." By their answers, nurses
imply that patients are doing something which, because of existing hospital regulations or ingrained beliefs, effectively controls the behavior
of the staff in a way detrimental to both patient and staff. There may
be, for example, a hospital rule stating that if a patient faints, the physician on duty must be called instantly. A patient who has been in
the hospital for a long time may know of this rule and quite patently
use wanton fainting to force the nursing staff to call a doctor. Or a
patient may realize that with a shortage of personnel, nurses have little
opportunity to exchange information. With this knowledge, it is a simple
matter to tell a nurse that a certain privilege should be granted, a token
paid, a headache pill given, or a door opened, because some other
nurse—typically one who just went off duty—said so. Even without
such knowledge of rules and procedures, a patient may manipulate the

staff by verbal or other behavior which, in our society, effectively controls others. The patient, for example, may threaten suicide. Or he may simply defecate on the floor.

In effect, the patient who does these things is a skillful behavioral engineer, whether he knows it or not. He uses control stimuli to his own immediate advantage. Through his manipulations, the patient also escapes the beneficial therapeutic influences of the ward environment. The nurse knows this but is caught between the horns of a dilemma: On the one hand the patient's threat or act may be real. He may indeed have a headache, a fainting spell, an intent to commit suicide, a weakness of the bowels, or a loss of memory. In that case the nurse should, of course, be controlled by the stimuli the patient's behavior presents. On the other hand, from experience or simply intuition, the nurse may feel sure that the patient is faking. In this case, naturally, she should not let these stimuli control her in the conventional way. A patient who has just seen the doctor and who merely likes to chat with him a little longer should not be able to use a fainting spell to regain the doctor's attention. Yet, to suspect that this is the purpose of a fainting spell and to know for sure are two different matters. What is the nurse to do?

Fortunately, in behaviorally oriented treatment these problems can be dealt with on a factual basis. The key lies in the behavioral baselines that have been obtained and the records of progress that are constantly being maintained. Obviously, the need for close medical supervision of any treatment program becomes evident here. It must be clear without any doubt that there are no physical reasons for a given behavior which might be used in staff manipulation.

Odd behavior which is used to manipulate the staff or the reinforcement schedule designed for a patient may be dealt with through three main approaches:

1. Disregard for the behavior in question
2. Attachment of consequences which affect a patient's other activities
3. Establishment of new desirable behaviors which are incompatible with (and prevent from emerging) the undesirable manipulatory behavior.

These approaches will be discussed in the examples that follow. Their application presupposes an existing behavioral therapy approach on the unit or ward where they are to be used.

One necessary limitation of the effectiveness of any of the techniques to be described must be recognized. Upon the patient's release, the cultural background of the community outside the hospital very likely will again effectively reinforce the manipulatory behaviors which were extinguished by the behavioral therapy program. The hospital practicing behavioral therapy, therefore, is a discriminatory stimulus complex which allows the formation of the discrimination: inside hospital–outside hospital. Inside the hospital manipulatory behavior is not reinforced, outside it is; inside the hospital manipulatory behavior is not successful, outside it is.

Now, if one by-product of this discrimination is that at the slightest sign of difficulty in getting along outside the discharged patient avoids getting himself back into the hospital, then at least some good has been served. But the root of the problem is, of course, the general public's lack of knowledge about behavior. In time, knowledge in this field will spread in the same way new knowledge about mental illness itself is beginning to spread. Still, misconceptions exist and thus demand from a behavioral therapy program not merely the extinction of manipulatory behavior, but in all cases, the establishment of new behaviors which make the manipulations unnecessary.

Hunger Strikes

A strong stimulus available to control the nursing staff is the hunger strike. Even the threat of going on a hunger strike is enough to elicit some response from listeners and thus receives some reinforcement.

Only by completely disregarding such threats can those responsible change this behavior. Withholding social reinforcement while the response (saying, "I'm going on a hunger strike") is being emitted extinguishes the response. The patient's threat should, of course, be discussed with the total nursing staff as soon as possible so that all members are prepared for the behavior which is then likely to occur. After having extinguished talking about a hunger strike, the patient will now probably commence an actual one. A behaviorally trained staff simply ignores the patient's absence from the dining room. In effect the patient has again set up a schedule under which a behavior is not reinforced. The staff keeps track of the meals that are being missed, but neither mentions them to the patient nor in any way shows concern to other patients that anything unusual has been noticed.

In theory the staff should be prepared to give the patient food supplements at the time of regular medication call and without special attention. But in practice it never will be necessary to do so. In our experience no patient who tried to manipulate the staff through an actual hunger strike missed more than five meals. In fact, the more frequent pattern is that the patient misses a single meal and then returns to eat normally.

This regimen is successful, of course, only if the staff is sufficiently trained in behavioral techniques to appreciate the problem and to treat the patient accordingly. The longer a hunger strike lasts, the more difficult it may become to prevent ingrained staff behaviors from interfering with the progress of the treatment. "Pity," "compassion," or by whatever other names these behaviors are called have a long history of reinforcement and may not be as well under the control of therapy as they should be. In such cases the charge nurse must decide which is more difficult: to maintain the staff's appropriate behavior or to utilize additional techniques which will hasten the break of the strike. With an untrained staff the second alternative is usually more easily accomplished. In either case, however, the patient will be helped. Additional techniques which can be used involve arranging reinforcers contingent on the patient's eating. Heavy smokers, for example, can readily be induced to eat if the availability of cigarettes hinges on having eaten a meal.

Getting a patient to eat again does not end treatment. The environmental conditions which brought a patient to announce or actually engage in a hunger strike must, of course, be explored. The daily staff meeting is the normal occasion for this. With behavioral baselines on hand, it is usually not difficult to determine why the behavior occurred and what should be done about it.

As an example, a patient may have exhausted various other means to escape a behavioral program which calls for being on time when medication is given. He may have feigned illness, overslept, or stated outright he did not care for medication. All this is contained in his record. What strong behavior can he still marshall to escape the prescribed medication? It is not difficult to predict that he might go on a hunger strike.

From joint meetings, the staff can learn to recognize that sometimes the emission of a strong behavior, such as going on a hunger strike, is a welcome sign that a given therapeutic program is taking hold. In many instances, in order to escape the contingencies which have been established for him, the patient has simply exhausted more common behaviors and is now attempting to bring stronger behaviors into play. Thus, depending on the details, a hunger strike sometimes signals that improvement will now be rapid because there are few ways left by which the patient can continue to avoid the contingencies of the therapy program designed for him.

Suicide Threats

Everything that has been said about hunger strikes is equally valid for suicide threats, and in principle the same techniques for control are applicable. The hold which the threat of suicide has over members of our culture is, however, infinitely greater than that of a hunger strike. Furthermore, after suicide has been threatened, there is no telling whether action will or will not follow. And since, unlike a hunger strike, action may be instantly fatal, a moral issue is raised for all persons in contact with the patient at the time of the threat. If the patient were to make good his threat and lose his life, those in whose presence the threat was made might be blamed by society or by themselves for having failed to prevent death.

Like sex, suicide has been a taboo topic in our culture for centuries. Only recently has there been a concerted effort to determine under what conditions people will actually commit suicide. Results so far show that it is difficult to predict when somebody threatens suicide as a manipulatory device, and when not. Personal success or failure apparently have little to do with suicide. Self-destruction occurs over issues that may seem trivial to anyone but the person whose life is lost. Written or spoken announcements of intent precede some suicides but by no means all.

It is probably impossible to prevent a person who seriously wants to kill himself from doing so. There are, however, a few simple rules which should be followed when a patient announces suicide.

1. **The patient should not be left alone.**
   In effect this is a deprivation schedule: The patient is deprived of privacy. Privacy thus becomes a strong reinforcer which can be used for the shaping of behaviors, including verbal behavior indicating an interest in living, long-range goals and plans, and hopes for the future. The person(s) who stay with the patient need not do anything special. Their presence is merely to prevent bodily harm or to call for help if harm has been inflicted.
2. **Tools with which the patient can bring on sudden death should be removed from his environment.**
   This means razor blades, glassware, knives, screw drivers, and ice picks. Belts, ties, and shoelaces are permissible. It takes much too long to use these items effectively for self-destruction if the first precaution, that of not leaving the patient alone, is followed.

The restrictions should be lifted as soon as the patient's interest in constructive activities and also his own statement make it evident that he no longer is interested in killing himself. The common technique of separately treating every patient whose record mentions that he is suicidal is unrealistic. Whether thoughtlessly or with real feeling, probably every human being at one time or another says, "I wish I were dead." If the remark is overheard and recorded in a patient's medical record, that patient's entire future can be governed by this incident. In staff meetings the importance of such entries should be carefully weighed. No action should be taken, however, in defiance or circumvention of what the existing rules demand in connection with a medical record. But, if the entry "suicidal" is patently wrong, then the record should be changed accordingly. Often the patient's long-term behavior so clearly refutes the record that little discussion is needed to authorize the change.

We had two such examples. In one, a male patient considered suicidal had for twenty years been daily "debugged," for razor blades. Nearly every day blades were found on his person, but not once had he used (or threatened to use) them to injure himself. It became clear to the behaviorist who worked with this patient that the latter greatly enjoyed the enhanced reputation which daily merited special attention from the nursing staff. When inspection was discontinued, the blades lost their reinforcing value and the patient stopped hoarding them on his person.

In another instance a woman patient—not suicidal according to her medical record—interrupted a staff meeting with the announcement that she was going to the roof to jump down. There was strong conviction on the part of the treating psychiatrist and the nursing staff that she was incapable of making good her threat. Their response, therefore, was simply to tell her not to interrupt the meeting. She left, but as she left they heard her run up the stairs to the second-story balcony. The next moments were agonizing. Student nurses, whose classroom was across the street, had their recess and noticed the patient on the roof. When they came running to report what they saw, they were instructed to stop looking at the roof and to act unconcerned. It was difficult not to reinforce the weeping patient when she came down the stairs exactly twelve minutes after making her threat. However, this patient never made another suicide threat, nor was the matter ever discussed with her. It is probable that treatment of this case had a strong effect on the other patients, too. Unreinforced behavior is not imitated. To know that no reinforcing consequence is attached to a behavior extinguishes thinking about the behavior as well as its emission.

Fainting

Nineteenth-century females were expected to faint easily, thus showing that they were indeed "ladies." The use of coarse language, the sight of blood or violence, a strange odor, too much heat or cold, a piece of good music or bad, all could and frequently did serve as stimuli for fainting which in turn was reinforced by attention and respect. Society still tends to reinforce such behavior in women although probably not as lavishly as Victorian society once did. To treat manipulative fainting, it is first necessary to have medical assurance that there is no physical cause. Given such assurance, the behavior can and should be completely ignored. If a patient faints in the middle of a passageway, nurses should matter-of-factly arrange for traffic to flow around the patient. Since the behavior most probably had been on a schedule of continuous reinforcement, it extinguishes swiftly.

Excessive Office Visits

Much of the beneficial affect which nurses can have in the general therapeutic effort rests in the fact that they are available virtually without limitation twenty-four hours per day. But invariably some patients abuse this availability of nursing personnel and beleaguer the staff office from morning until night. They ask trivial questions or merely want to chat. Like any other behavior in a behaviorally oriented unit, this prediliction is made part of the general therapeutic plan. A patient who is withdrawn will be reinforced for talking to nurses and for coming to the office with problems or mere comments about the weather. But the patient who uses visits with the nursing staff as the sole source of social interaction should receive the opposite treatment—no reinforcement.

Friendly discouragement has little effect on most patients in extinguishing excessive office visits. This is not surprising, since the friendly manner in which a patient is told not to bother the nurses in many cases constitutes an effective reinforcer which sustains the patient's behavior. Complete disregard of the behavior is called for to effect extinction.

This technique of ignoring behavior works equally well with the mentally retarded who are believed too "dumb" to understand what is being said to them. Ayllon and Michael report the case of Lucille, a mentally retarded adult. The nurses felt that Lucille's frequent visits to the office would simply have to be tolerated since she obviously could not understand instructions to the contrary. In studying the problem, the data presented graphically in Figure 9-1 tell the story.

Prior to treatment, baseline data were obtained on the frequency with which Lucille visited the office. The behavioral treatment consisted very simply in completely disregarding Lucille's visits. As the cumulative record in Figure 9-1 shows, the behavior occurred at a stable and high rate. As treatment progresses the slope of the curve becomes less and less steep. The curve's slope is finally near parallel with the horizontal axis of the graph, which means that the behavior is only rarely emitted.

Ignoring a behavior requires a good deal of self-control especially because indifference is normally equated quite correctly with "not caring." In a behavioral program, however, nurses care very much. This is, in fact, precisely why they employ the technique of ignoring something or other—in this case the patient who comes to the office just to visit. It takes some practice, but not much, to carry out ignoring without at the same time giving the impression of being angry (which, of course, would defeat the whole purpose, since anger in this case is a response which the patient's behavior controls). It is equally important neither to deliberately look away from the patient to be ignored,

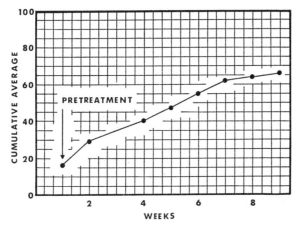

Fig. 9-1. Cumulative record of office visits during extinction. (*After Ayllon and Michael.*)

nor to studiously look at him. A simple trick is to select a series of objects in the room and on the patient's person and look at them in turn. If one is already doing something that requires full attention, the best method is to continue as if the patient were not there at all.

It frequently turns out that demands on nurses' time are a useful indicator of behavioral changes. In staff meetings, time and again it becomes evident that frequency curves (cumulative records) of patients' requests and interactions with nurses reveal much that can be of benefit in designing schedules of reinforcement and in evaluating existing ones. To make the measure of a patient's demand on nurses' time even more meaningful, the following procedure is used. A basic price is attached for all patient interactions with staff members. Even therapists who are not behaviorally oriented understand and have found empirically that successful therapy sessions must cost money. Free advice is seldom appreciated and hardly ever followed. It is little trouble to decide in the daily staff meeting to set a price for consultations for a patient who visits excessively and to raise the price until control of frequency is achieved.

Getting around Nursing Personnel

Another condition which requires considerable self-control exists when a patient finds a nurse who is a "soft touch" and alternately uses the subtlest and coarsest forms of flattery to manipulate this staff member. Flattery is universally used as a reinforcer and is often effective even with persons who fully know they are being flattered. That flattery can be so effective with nursing personnel demonstrates to the behaviorist the state of deprivation which widely exists for even simple recognition of a job well done. In our culture it is common to punish failure, but to take adequate performance for granted. Hence, the surest way to combat a staff member's susceptibility to flattery is a consistent system of recognition for good work. This can take place informally during the daily staff meeting, but also formally, when superiors evaluate the performance of subordinates.

Patients in behavioral programs well know that tokens must be paid to obtain necessities of ward life. This fact makes mealtime a particularly susceptible occasion for attempting to obtain tokens from a nurse who is considered a "soft touch." Only recently a Patton patient who regularly sought to escape work discovered the "soft" side of a staff member. Prior to mealtime the patient made a great show of cleaning the top of the water fountain located just outside the dining room door. She then reported to the nurse, "I did my job. I cleaned the water fountain." This invariably prompted a delivery of tokens which in turn provided the patient with a meal at an output of some thirty-seconds labor!

Quite naturally, such a staff member is predisposed to allow access to food if only the patient does something. The behavior that a patient emits under the necessity of earning tokens for meals is often of limited quality, but calculated to meet the standards of the "soft touch." Admittedly the ingenuity and endeavor of such a patient are laudable. However, by gradually reinforcing those behaviors other than at mealtime, the patient could and should be weaned from using them for manipulation.

Patients often give lengthy and numerous plausible but phony reasons why they should be reinforced. An effective way to combat these tactics is to make sure all nursing personnel are familiar with the conditions prevailing for reinforcement. If at any particular moment someone is not sure about a contingency, the patient should wait until a determination can be made from records or from a better-informed staff member. For whatever reasons, if a particular patient is extremely adroit at getting around nurses, his program of reinforcement should be gone over and its requirements tightened and clearly specified. Control of reinforcers is a serious responsibility because of their clear connection with behavior. Delivery of reinforcers to a patient must occur under conditions which promote desirable behavior. Reinforcing manipulatory behaviors such as those used to get around nursing personnel is clearly not desirable.

Under a behavioral program, members of the staff are directly reinforced by their patient's improvement. Since behavioral procedures are often not only carried out by the nursing staff, but are actually planned and designed by them, a patient's recovery is a reinforcer for the particular nurse responsible for the change in behavior. But it takes time for this reinforcer to become effective. In a behavioral program self-control is required at all times and should be strengthened in frequent training meetings during which the effects of leniency are discussed.

Temper Tantrums

A temper tantrum is a display of anger by kicking, slamming, screaming, and similar evidences of extreme agitation. In dealing with outbursts of this kind a distinction must be made between patients for whom this is a common behavior (that is, it has been part of the patient's behavioral repertoire for as long as he has been in the hospital) and patients who employ temper tantrums only as a means of escaping the contingencies of a behavioral program. The distinction is necessary because a choice of techniques is required depending on whether the behavior is an old behavior on a variable ratio schedule, or is either a new behavior or an old one acquired under a schedule of continuous reinforcement. The common reinforcer for the temper tantrum is, of course, that an individual by this behavior gets his way. If, in the past, this was successful some of the time, extinction is bound to be slow. If it was successful all the time, extinction will be swift.

For patients with a history of hospitalization before transfer to a behavioral unit, the schedules that prevailed, and whether or not tantrums occurred, can be ascertained through records and interviews. With newly admitted patients, a discussion with relatives or spouse usually yields the same information quite readily.

If the patient has never before indulged in tantrums, or comes from an environment where his temper tantrums were habitually reinforced, the course of treatment is simply to ignore the behavior. Typically in such cases, failing to reinforce even a single tantrum will be sufficient to extinguish the behavior. Of course, subsequent reasonable actions should be lavishly reinforced.

On the other hand, if the behavior has been strengthened under a schedule of variable ratio reinforcement, it would be too time-consuming to employ a simple extinction procedure. Also, the continued interference with the general ward program would become intolerable.

A standard procedure is to place the patient in a seclusion room without comment and with as little fuss as possible. Such a room need not be a padded cell or have any special attributes. Its purpose is merely to remove the patient from the general ward environment while he throws his tantrum. Nursing personnel communicate with the confined patient only during periods of calm behavior. If a service is rendered, such as water given or a bed pan brought and the patient begins to show signs of renewed agitation, the service is immediately terminated. As soon as the patient has remained quiet for a period of time, the door is unlocked and the patient is released and reinforced for his reasonable behavior. The quiet time required depends on many factors. To begin with, a period as short as five minutes may be sufficient. But if the behavior recurs, the time of calmness before release should be extended even to as much as one or two hours.

Placing the patient in seclusion eliminates the possibility that the tantrum can elicit reinforcement. Suppose a patient throws a tantrum because he is refused a cigarette until a particular work assignment is completed. Even if the staff member does not, another patient might provide the reinforcer.

Aside from extinguishing the response by withdrawing its reinforcer, isolating a patient involves the use of aversive control; few patients find seclusion to their liking. The behavioral principle involved is reinforcement using a negative reinforcer. Remaining quiet (the behavior to be strengthened) allows release from seclusion (terminates the aversive stimulus). This technique has been used by Montrose M. Wolf, Todd Risley, and Hayden Mees in an experiment with an autistic child.

It is rare that withdrawal of reinforcement and/or aversive consequences produce immediate reduction in the frequency of tantrums for patients who have been on a variable ratio schedule. Such patients ordinarily must experience several applications of these techniques before a marked change in behavior takes place.

Public Defecation, Incontinence, Enuresis

Public defecation is most clearly a behavior that can be used to manipulate the staff. In common with all odd behaviors discussed in this chapter, it may also signal a state of deprivation for some unrelated reinforcer. Incontinence and enuresis do not as obviously fall into this category and may, indeed, not be such behaviors. The key to an understanding of the differences lies in a behavioral analysis of the relevant environmental variables.

A thorough medical examination must precede any behavioral modification of improper voiding habits. Only if there is assurance that so-called "psychological" forces are solely responsible, should the problem be treated behaviorally. The first step, naturally, is to obtain baselines with special emphasis on time of occurrence. For retarded patients, a complete toilet training program may have to be undertaken (see Chapter 13).

If the behavioral baseline shows that elimination of urine occurs only at night, it will be necessary to establish discriminative stimuli for the patient to awaken him (or her) when the bladder is full. Ian Wickes describes such a procedure involving the use of a special sheet which triggers an alarm when even slightly moistened. The alarm wakens the patient at a time when control stimuli which his body produces are still sufficiently strong to be heeded. The difficulty with this technique is that the alarm rings only when urination has already begun; hence, it is not completely successful. In his experiment Wickes had 65 percent success in 100 cases.

Nevertheless, from a behavioral standpoint this technique makes more sense than the oft heard advice to keep liquids from the enuretic before retiring and to awake him every few hours. This way of proceeding cannot possibly be successful (other than perhaps by chance) because the behavior of getting up in response to control stimuli from the bladder is not emitted. To change a behavior and to influence the conditions under which it predictably will be emitted requires the presence of the relevant stimuli. In other words, the bladder must be full when the patient awakens and subsequently goes to the bathroom. Wickes's technique approximates this condition.

It may be useful to encourage a patient to give self-descriptive reports whenever the need to urinate is felt. The nurse should accompany the patient to the toilet and during that time ask for a description of bodily sensations. The answers necessarily make reference to and bring into focus those control stimuli which are of importance for recognizing a full bladder and consequently awakening at night when the same stimuli are present.

If the baseline shows that urination occurs into clothing during the day as well as in the bed at night, the procedures mentioned for the enuretic should be combined with schedules of reinforcement for proper urination (if such occurs) and the introduction of slightly aversive consequences following each wetting. In no case should the nurse completely clean up without the patient's involvement. Much of this will depend on the patient's degree of contact with reality, but even the most regressed patient should be required at least to help.

Defecation is treated in the same manner except when it is clearly used as a manipulative device to get attention or to escape a schedule of reinforcement. A patient who uses defecation for these purposes should be treated in much the same way as is the patient who throws a temper tantrum: After having him clean up the area where he defecated, he should be given a short time in seclusion. In addition, his privileges should be severely curtailed by raising their price to a point where he can pay only with difficulty. Proper elimination behavior during this regimen should, of course, be generously reinforced.

Cursing

Foul language, screams, and threats should by and large be treated much like temper tantrums. However, a satiation technique which sets aside a separate room where the patient is actually reinforced for emitting this behavior has also proven an effective means of changing undesired behavior. Unexpectedly being reinforced (with cigarettes, tokens, or any suitable reinforcer) for a behavior which in the past was maintained by altogether different reinforcers is apparently so shocking to some patients that after only a single reinforcement the behavior ceases. When this is not successful, a condition may be introduced whereby after each reinforcement the volume of sound must be increased to bring on the reinforcers. We have used this technique effectively under the following schedule.

1. One minute of cursing or screaming   1 cigarette,
   in the isolation room   token, etc.
2. Two additional minutes of continuous   2 cigarettes,
   louder cursing   tokens, etc.

The patient will often cease cursing or screaming after this event. Quiet weeping typically follows. This behavior should be reinforced by immediately releasing the patient from seclusion. In the absence of sufficient staff, the procedures described for temper tantrums—a period of calm required before release—is simpler, of course.

Breaking and Throwing

Frequently patients adopt the tactic of breaking and throwing objects as a means of manipulating nursing personnel. These behaviors signal that the patient does not like the treatment he is receiving. They warn that it may become even more extreme. Naturally, if a patient's violence is such that the immediate environment is being ravaged or the patient's safety endangered, simply ignoring it, although behaviorally the best means to weaken such violence, is not feasible. Other measures must be taken in order to protect the patient and hospital property.

However, patients frequently break or throw personal possessions. In such cases, a patient should experience the consequences of his undesirable behavior. Nursing personnel should not immediately replace damaged or lost articles. For example, one of our patients threw her glasses whenever she could not have her own way. Immediate replacement would keep her from the consequences of her childish behavior; therefore, no immediate action was taken to provide her with new glasses.

Another situation which makes patients face the consequences of their acts is token throwing. Patients sometimes appear for meals with insufficient tokens and are not admitted to the dining room. This can elicit the response "token throwing." The patient usually throws the tokens to the floor and leaves in disgust. When this occurs a staff member merely collects the tokens and pockets them, making no comment nor any effort to return them. Without fail the patient returns requesting a "refund." If, under these circumstances the nurse returned the tokens, the patient would be prevented from experiencing the consequences of his behavior. Therefore, thrown tokens are not returned.

The same procedure applies for other forms of breaking or throwing. If a patient rips off clothing, no replacement is provided by the staff. It becomes the patient's responsibility to find other clothing to wear; this usually involves waiting for the clothes room to open. In the interim, no special action is taken.

Nursing personnel are often tempted to reinforce a patient's careful attempts to fix an article broken during this kind of behavior. This might be acceptable were it not for the possibility that the destructive behavior might also be reinforced. The rule applied in this case involves the time interval between the destructive act and the act of repairing the object. If it is a lengthy interval, perhaps the patient may be reinforced; for a short period of time, it might not be wise to reinforce. If the patient has never before offered to repair a damaged item, naturally reinforcement is warranted.

Fighting

Occasional disturbances caused by minor frictions inevitably associated with ward life should also be treated like temper tantrums—the patient quietly removed to an isolated room and released after an appropriate period of calm. But there is also the bully who starts fights at the slightest provocation, or even without any, and who loudly and continually criticizes others. For such a person a more elaborate treatment program is required. The behavior is strong because it carries its own reinforcement. The reinforcer may be getting one's way, dominating others, being kingpin, and last but not least, attracting staff attention. These reinforcers, with the exception of the last, are available only if, in some important way, the partner in a fight is weaker than the patient. To avoid the availability of the reinforcer, it is desirable to locate the patient in a dormitory together with stronger patients. But even that does not remove the attention the patient gets when he picks a fight and himself gets beaten.

Successful therapy for the habitual fighter should establish behaviors which are incompatible with fighting. For example, the patient should be reinforced for taking part in daily calisthenics sessions. In addition, if there are sports teams on the hospital grounds and the patient's condition is such that he can participate, he should be reinforced for doing so. An extensive program of education in "getting along with others" should be introduced. This is achieved most quickly by reinforcing the patient for reading passages from "how to win friends"-type books. The patient should be required to report in writing on what he has read. This technique has proved effective no matter how regressed the patient is, as long as he can read and write. Obviously, no perfect essay or book report should be required. A severely regressed patient might be reinforced, for example, for copying an important word on the first page of the book he is given. Then he might be reinforced for selecting and writing down the most frequently mentioned word in the first ten pages. After that he might be asked to prepare written answers to questions about the book. The purpose of this is to strengthen reading which is a behavior incompatible with the kind of social interaction that leads to fighting. But the contents of the reading matter should strengthen behaviors which earn the reinforcers which are so important in paying for necessities on the ward. Thus, there are three objectives: draining excess energy through physical exercise, reinforcing behaviors incompatible with fighting, and establishing new behaviors which result in some of the same reinforcers as does fighting.

When there is evidence that excessive fighting among patients is caused by institutional conditions, these rather than the disposition of the patient should be modified. Ward arrangements, for example, where juveniles are arbitrarily located near or with geriatric patients inevitably lead to difficulty. Such arrangements reflect poor hospital management rather than shortcomings of the patients. (Juveniles can, of course, be used in constructive ways with geriatric patients and vice versa. It is only the housing arrangement which is being criticized here.) A judicious amount of social activity diminishes fighting among patients, and all major hospitals have such programs. Under behavioral therapy, access to social activities (dances, movies, trips, baseball games) is naturally made contingent on proper behavior. Thus, by its nature, social activity not only reduces fighting, but can be effective as a therapeutic tool.

Absenting Oneself without Permission (AWOL)

A program of behavioral therapy can only be as strong as the degree of control it exercises. If patients can escape this control, the program may do more harm than good. If, for example, the patient who absents himself from such a program without permission is upon return routinely accepted by another unit, he successfully avoids the therapeutic contingencies designed for him. Other patients will learn of this and, of course, if avoidance of the contingencies is reinforcing for them, will use the same tactic. Hence, it is important to arrange with the administration that returned AWOL patients be placed without delay back in the program. This may require special procedures on the behavioral unit, such as physical checkups for contagious diseases or pregnancies. But these additional burdens are well worth such inconvenience. If returned, the patient gains nothing by his "escape." Nor is he punished in any way. Since behavior that goes unreinforced eventually extinguishes, AWOL does, too, under this regimen. What is more, other patients may see the futility of AWOL and thus not emit the behavior themselves.

Still, there are invariably some patients who are so regressed that they absent themselves not to escape contingencies on the ward but simply because once near control stimuli outside the ward they are more influenced by them than by those on the ward. Such patients traditionally are kept on locked units and simply are never exposed to the control of outside stimuli. But such a regimen is not really useful in changing the importance of these stimuli for the patient, although it does, of course, keep the patient from AWOL.

Taking such a patient for daily walks on the grounds and pointing out landmarks to him which are to act as control stimuli for returning to the unit is a much better technique. In first exploring this procedure a staff member should conduct such walks. But there is no reason not to let other patients (for whom such landmarks are already functional) come along and finally conduct them themselves. At Patton we have added a subtle twist to this procedure. If patient companions are used with severely regressed patients, we call them "guides" and they are provided by the staff free of charge. If we wish to attach a slightly aversive touch to the presence of the companion, we call them "baby-sitters" and the patient pays for their services at an hourly rate commensurate with his general earning capacity.

A patient's going AWOL may occur just prior to release, apparently as a means of ensuring the security of continued hospitalization. When this is the case, the patient is told that such behavior will not obtain the desired result. This threat is often sufficient to terminate any further attempt at escape. In other cases, the patient may persist and nursing personnel must look for those elements of the environment that are functionally related to the behavior. For example, close observation and counseling revealed that a patient who continually went AWOL at the time of release did not want to be placed in a certain setting. All that was necessary to alter his behavior was to find a more acceptable placement for him outside the hospital.

EXERCISES, CHAPTER 9

1. The cumulative record in Figure 9-2 shows Alice's and Lisa's work on the unit. Lisa is a good worker. What does the record suggest about Alice's work performance? Which example from the chapter does Alice's record correspond with?
2. Describe five ways in which patients can take advantage of nursing personnel's gullibility.
3. A favorite manipulative tactic used by patients is to claim unfairness. All patients are, of course, on different treatment plans. Suppose patient A has restricted access to cigarettes while patient B smokes freely. Patient A claims this is unjust. "We're all equal," is his plea. What is your reply?
4. Just prior to each work period Peggy reports that she is ill. The ward physician cannot find any medical reason for Peggy's behavior. Yet,

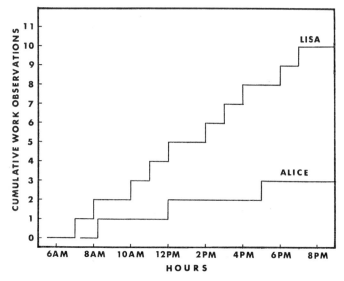

Fig. 9-2. Cumulative record of work performance of two patients.

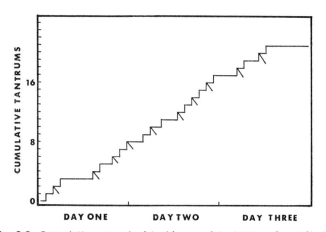

Fig. 9-3. Cumulative record of incidence of tantrums of a patient.

from a therapeutic point of view working is considered beneficial for her. What steps would you take?

5. The cumulative record in Figure 9-3 is of tantrums emitted by Stan. The hatch marks indicate occasions when the tantrums caused a staff member to leave him alone with his voices.

    a. Assuming that "being left alone" reinforcers tantrums, what kind of a schedule is described by the record?

    b. How should Stan's problem be dealt with?

6. Under what conditions should a patient's manipulatory behavior actually be reinforced as a therapeutic measure?

7. Mary used fainting to control the behavior of her husband. Under behavioral therapy this behavior has been completely eliminated and Mary is to be discharged. Without cooperation of the husband what will happen after the discharge? How should the staff utilize the willingness of the husband to cooperate to keep Mary out of the hospital?

8. An overweight patient starts a hunger strike on a Saturday morning. There will not be a staff meeting until Monday. The nurse in charge decided to ignore the patient's absence from meals. How does the nurse justify her course of action?

9. As with all taboo topics there is much misinformation about suicide. List some facts about suicide.

10. How do facts about suicide affect the behavioral therapy of suicidal threats?

11. What do excessive visits to the nurses' office indicate? How can the indicative value of these visits be sharpened?

12. What is meant by "self-control" in a program of behavioral therapy? How is this behavior strengthened? How is it a self-reinforcing behavior in an extended program of behavioral therapy?

13. Johnny, a juvenile patient, has a long history of having thrown temper tantrums. His mother worked and did not always have sufficient time to attend to Johnny. Most of the time she said that she coped with his tantrums and did not let him get away with it. But sometimes she was so hurried in getting to her job that she gave in and let him have his way. What course of action does this knowledge about the past history of reinforcement dictate to the therapeutic staff?

14. A patient is transferred to the behavioral therapy ward because of incontinence. Ten days later the referring psychiatrist asks for success of therapy. What should be explained to him about the necessity of obtaining baselines on such behavior?

15. What needs to be discussed in staff meetings regarding a course of action for treatment of patients who persist in going AWOL?

10

Treating Odd Behaviors—II

Your study of this chapter should help you answer the following questions:

1. How are tics treated with behavioral therapy? Why is mechanical equipment sometimes necessary in the treatment of tics?
2. How can delusions be brought under stimulus control?
3. What behavioral techniques are effective with hallucinations?

The terms listed below are introduced and defined in this chapter:

conversion reactions
hysterical conversion
delusion
stimulus substitution
hallucination

Tics

Doubtless because of their obviousness, nervous tics, together with complete loss of movement of part of the body, are usually the first psychoneuroses to receive attention. They are considered *conversion reactions* (conversion hysterias) because according to the mentalistic model they are manifestations of conflicts of ideas in symbolic but visible form. A mental concept, in other words, is converted into a significant body symptom. Thus, by way of advising caution in business affairs, the mind may say, "Look before you leap"; the body then causes the head to bend forward, the eyes to bulge, and the head to jerk right and left as if to say, "Watch how I'm looking before I leap."

To the behavioral therapist, hysterias of this type are behaviors. Behaviors, possibly, with highly unusual sources of strength, but following the same laws as any other behaviors follow, provided it has been established that disease of the brain itself, such as encephalitis, is not the cause of the difficulty. In short, thorough medical examination is required, and only after it has been determined that there is no organic basis for the hysterical movement (or lack of movement), behavioral therapy can be undertaken.

As usual, baselines are required to establish the frequency and circumstances under which the behavior occurs. If the tic is one of high frequency such as a gross blinking of the eye, short observation (which may include interaction with the patient) is useful. For example, the observer might utilize a telephone timer which is set for intervals of perhaps one to three minutes. He needs such a signal to know when to terminate an observation period. During observation he simply counts the number of times the tic occurs. For this he might utilize a mechanical counter that can easily be concealed in a hand and depressed every time a tic occurs. The total number registered on the counter divided by the number of minutes for which the observation was made yields the rate per minute of the response. In some instances this rate will be extremely stable for different observers and under different conditions and times. It may also become evident that behavior is obviously stimulus controlled. For example, a comparison between the rate of eye blinks obtained by a female and a male nurse will show such a discrepancy that the sex of the conversation partner is clearly a relevant stimulus.

Because of the high frequency with which tics are typically emitted, and because of the need to attach consequences immediately, it is wise to utilize electrical or mechanical equipment in the treatment. The treatment itself most typically involves the use of continuous reinforcement terminated for limited periods by the emission of the tic.

Beatrice Barrett, an experimental psychologist, used this approach with a thirty-eight-year-old male whose multiple tics were of fourteen years standing. The man emitted major body movement including contractions of neck, shoulder, chest, and abdominal muscles; eye blinks; and openings of the mouth. As a reinforcer, Dr. Barrett used taped music of the patient's own selection. During the experimental sessions the patient was seated in a chair especially equipped to pick up gross body movements, in this case tics. The patient listened through earphones to the music he had selected. Each response picked up by the specially equipped chair caused the music to terminate for one and a half seconds. In addition, the patient could restart the music only by *not* emitting a tic for one and a half seconds. Initially the patient emitted tics as frequently as one per second. By the fifth half-hour session this rate was down to fifteen tics per minute, and by the eighth session the patient was able to sit quietly for as long as fifteen minutes. This patient, whose tics had been refractory to extensive psychological and pharmacological therapies, had not been aware of the occurrence of the tics during the last few years he had emitted the behavior.

Barrett's method shows the desirability for mechanical or electromechanical devices in the treatment of such behavior. But even where such equipment is not available, an attempt can be made to selectively reinforce a patient for not exhibiting undesired behavior. When interacting with the patient the nurse sets a time-alarm device for as short a period as she knows the tic is not normally emitted. When the alarm rings, the nurse immediately reinforces the patient for not emitting tics. Gradually she increases the time period required to obtain reinforcement. This method avoids the subjectivity of reinforcing at the end of a sentence or some other stimulus controlled moment when the connection between being reinforced and not emitting the tic might not be made as strongly. Patients are usually quick to recognize that the alarm signals that no tic has occurred for a certain length of time.

In experimenting with this approach we found that the tic readily comes under stimulus control with the nurse being the control stimulus. In her presence the behavior disappears, but in her absence it is back in full force. In one particular case we made an agreement with the patient that he would pay a token every time the behavior (sideways turning of the head) was observed by any staff member. There was a marked reduction of the behavior but not complete extinction.

Satiation techniques may be attempted, too. Here the patient is paid for emitting the tic at an ever-increasing rate. Since most patients who have tics want to see the behavior eliminated, they show surprise at being paid to do something they do not like to see happening. In such instances it is definitely called for to explain that learning to emit a behavior on command is equivalent to controlling the behavior.

Successful use of still another technique for controlling tics is reported by A. A. Rafi who worked with a patient suffering from a right-foot-tapping tic with a rate of nearly ninety taps per minute. Rafi built a treadle on which the patient could place her foot. Either forward or backward movement of the treadle caused the sounding of a buzzer. This highly motivated patient was, in effect, being reinforced by the newly acquired skill of balancing the treadle so that neither the forward nor the backward buzzer sounded. Figure 10-1 shows the effect of this regimen.

Perhaps more than with any other behavior, tics tempt people to regard the behavior as a symptom which is bound to disappear as soon as the underlying (mental) cause is removed. This happens because the patient often wants to rid himself of the behavior and is seemingly not reinforced in any reasonable way for emitting the behavior. As the examples show, however, tics operate under the laws which govern behavior in general. Since every tic is different physically, however, and even similar ones may be under different behavioral control, the ingenuity of the therapist is taxed to the utmost in their treatment.

More readily accessible to reinforcement techniques is the nonuse of muscles as an *hysterical conversion*. Here the mind presumably holds

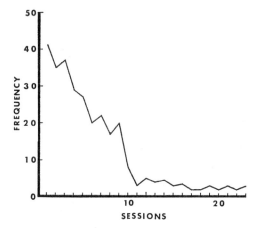

Fig. 10-1. Extinction of a tic through Rafi technique.

a strong resolve not to do something, such as killing father or drinking alcohol, and the body converts this resolve in the obvious symbolism of being unable to move hands or arms. What is called for is simple reinforcement of movements, however small, which in gradual steps can lead to reinforcement of the total movement.

Sometimes prolonged disuse of muscles has led to atrophy, and then the steps which are initially to be reinforced must be so small as to seem irrelevant. In this process the selection of the proper reinforcer is of particular importance since there is need for parceling it out in small quantities. This is necessary to assure proper exercise of any muscles which may have atrophied. For the first response, however insignificant it may seem, there must be strong reinforcement. But gradually the practice of this movement must be reinforced by relatively small portions of whatever reinforcer is being used. This can be accomplished by increasing the ratio of responses required for a single token, for example. Single puffs on a cigarette are also useful. Even if the unused muscles are those involved in speech, behavioral therapy can be applied. Lovaas has shown its application even with autistic children.

Delusions

A delusion is "a false belief maintained despite experiences and evidence to the contrary" [12]. On what basis can you conclude that a person has a delusion? You can reach this conclusion when a person persists in making statements which are not true. For example, a patient may continually ask, "Why are you trying to kill me?" when there is absolutely no evidence that anyone has this intention. The apprehension is simply based on a false belief. Yet the patient acts as if it were true and no amount of rational argument can dissuade him.

The basis for treating such a patient is that had he never said a word about his belief, no one would ever have suspected that there was a delusion. His continuous verbalization marks him. If the frequency of his seemingly unfounded comments could be reduced, he might be considered less delusional; if the patient never again verbalized in this way, he would be considered "cured" and members of the outside community would not reject him because of delusions. Thus, therapy for delusions aims at arranging conditions so that the frequency of "delusional questions" can be reduced.

We applied this principle to the treatment of a delusional adult female for whom social interaction was a strong reinforcer. After baseline observation, nursing personnel concluded that the attention her questions brought controlled her reference to delusions. An extinction schedule was arranged in which talking did not bring attention when it contained reference to her delusions. All nursing personnel were instructed to terminate social interaction as soon as the patient asked a "crazy" question. They were to act as if the patient weren't there and, on subsequent contacts, were not to answer questions as to why they had ignored her or in any way to discuss the delusion. However, especially close attention was to be given and tokens awarded whenever a "good conversation" occurred.

The procedure resulted in a sharp decrease in the number of times the patient asked a delusional question. This success was limited, however, to her interaction with ward nursing personnel. She continued to talk about her delusions with other patients and generally with people not on the ward. Yet it was clear that some control had been acquired and that the patient had made a discrimination between those who would and those would not listen.

Another experience with a delusional patient reveals the high degree of control maintained when members of the nursing personnel become control stimuli which inhibit expression. The patient was a thirty-eight-year-old female diagnosed schizophrenic reaction, paranoid type. She had been hospitalized because of a series of letters she had written to various state and local officials about a marihuana ring operating in the backyard and attic of her apartment, although there was no evidence of such a ring.

Upon transfer to the behavioral ward, she stated that nothing was wrong with her and that she really was not a patient but an agent for hospital supervisory personnel and she was there to write reports concerning "the goings on around here" as part of her job. She freely expressed the circumstances of her commitment since she was "right" and everyone else was wrong.

To deal with her frequent delusional statements, such descriptions were made a costly behavior. Each time her conversation included delusional material, she was assessed as many as twenty-five tokens. This resulted in complete cessation of such talk. As the patient explained, "Well, what's the use? You don't believe me anyway and it just isn't worth it."

Extinction was initially accompanied by signs of frustration. That is, the patient became angry the first few times she had to pay for her delusions. Following this phase, however, she gave up willingly and seemingly harbored no resentment. Proof of the fact that nursing personnel had become strong control stimuli inhibiting the patient's expression of her delusions came about during a course offered psychiatric residents at the hospital. As part of their studies the residents attended interviews with patients exhibiting a symptom formation considered "classical."

The interview in the case of the delusional patient was conducted by an experienced psychiatrist who was well acquainted with the patient's behavior. Two nurses from the behavioral ward where the patient lived were also present. After approximately fifteen minutes of questioning it was quite clear that the patient would not volunteer any information regarding her delusions. Finally the patient said, "I know what you want me to say, but I'm not going to unless those nurses guarantee that it's okay." Permission was granted, and the patient immediately described her delusions. However, now details of the delusion were strikingly altered. It was as if, through lack of practice, the patient had forgotten much of the original delusional system and had to restructure. In other words, while suppressing verbal references may not eliminate delusions per se, these references are nevertheless strong maintainers of a delusion. Deprived of verbal self-descriptive support, delusions seem to slowly die away.

Behaviorally this makes good sense if delusions are viewed as thoughts which must be reinforced, just as much as any behavior, in order to maintain strength. Once support of the evidence of delusional thinking is withdrawn, provided there are no other reinforcers to maintain thinking, delusions should naturally weaken and even extinguish.

Stimulus substitution, a technique aimed at substituting a stimulus which is more acceptable for one that is not considered acceptable, can also be used to extinguish delusional behavior. After ten years of hospitalization, a forty-year-old male still believed that as long as he kept chewing a number of small rocks which he held in his mouth, "the rays" could not harm him.

Treatment began by requiring payment for chewing rocks. The price was set rather high which rapidly terminated rock chewing on the ward without, however, having any effect on the patient's behavior as a member of an off-ward garden crew.

During a discussion of their limited success, one of the nurses suggested that the patient be given some other means of warding off the rays that he obviously believed in. If rocks had this capacity, perhaps something more acceptable could be substituted. The device chosen was a transistor radio.

The patient was reassigned to the ward clothing room, given a radio, and told that he could listen to it if he wanted. But, he still had to pay for chewing rocks. Because he refused to listen to the radio, a new contingency was designed. In order to obtain payment for his work in the clothing room, his radio had to be on. Over a period of time he could reliably be found working and apparently listening to the radio. However, at this point he still had problems with rays.

The next contingency was to have him carry the radio on his person. Tokens were delivered whenever he was observed listening to it. Nursing personnel also frequently hinted that listening to a radio was a much better behavior than chewing rocks. If he agreed, he was given tokens. Now his behavior began to change. Close checking with other patients and hospital employees who frequently interacted with him revealed that he no longer chewed rocks and that he had become an avid radio fan. When interviewed for release he was questioned about his former behavior. Much to everyone's surprise, he was reluctant to discuss that he had ever chewed rocks. Furthermore, he denied knowing anything about the rays. "What do you think I am, crazy?" he asked.

These three cases demonstrate that regardless of whatever prompts individuals to engage in delusions, more acceptable behavior can be brought about through behavioral therapy.

Hallucinations

Hallucinations represent another challenge to the practice of behavioral therapy because of their high frequency among hospitalized mentally ill. Coleman defines hallucination as "a sense perception for which there is no appropriate external stimulus" [13]. The question is, how does a therapist know that a person hallucinates? Again the answer is based on the behavior of the patient. Coleman's definition terms the hallucination a sense perception which, as such, is invisible. What *is* visible is a possible reaction which may follow a sense perception. A sound, a light, a touch are stimuli which can be perceived and usually, though not always, cause visible reactions. A person who hallucinates apparently reacts to stimuli which others can't perceive. This does not mean that the hallucinator does not hear, or see, or feel as he responds, any more than it is doubted that a person can dream or imagine. To the behaviorist, hearing, seeing, and feeling are behaviors which follow the same laws as those valid for overt acts commonly considered behaviors.

This entirely novel way of regarding perception and sensation was first proposed by B. F. Skinner on the basis of his own experimental work leading to the original formulations of operant conditioning. Behaviors are normally emitted in the presence of stimuli in the environment. The verbal community cannot, of course, see the behavior which takes place inside a person who sees, perhaps, a green patch. Thus people cannot selectively reinforce others for "correct" seeing. That is to say, there can be no discrimination learning for the behavior itself. But what people can and do selectively reinforce are the self-descriptive comments made by the one who sees a green patch.

Members of any culture learn when self-descriptive reports of what is seen, heard, or felt are appropriate and when they are not. Upon awakening, for example, it is entirely acceptable to talk about little black men chasing red cows over a green meadow even though the audience knows full well that the recounter of dreams never left his bed and there are no black men, red cows, or green pastures anywhere near. What is not tolerated in our culture are reports about seeing little black men, red cows, and green pastures when the audience perceives nothing to account for them.

To extinguish such behavior, self-descriptive reports should, of course, be completely ignored. But this is not typically what happens. In our culture, references to voices or visions usually bring forth alarm and concern. For the person who desires to escape the realities of a given environment—a marriage, a job, an unpleasant task—an opportunity to manipulate an audience in such fashion is most welcome. The behavior becomes strengthened because it is reinforced through the manipulation it makes possible.

Just how much hallucinatory content is under listener control was demonstrated through an experiment involving a thirty-six-year-old schizophrenic female who continually reported being in communication with famous personalities. Three student assistants assumed the roles of listeners during daily twenty-minute visits with the patient. One of the male students wore sandals, a beard, open collar, loose jacket and a SNCC button. Another presented the picture of a clean-cut young man with military bearing who carried a Rockwell anti-Semite and anti-Negro pamphlet quite visible to the patient. The third, a friendly girl, tried to appear nondescript in both dress and demeanor. As predicted, the patient reported to the student who emulated a freedom fighter that she was in communication with Martin Luther King and similar notables. To the student whom she apparently identified as a Nazi party member, she said she was not really a Negro but a Latin and that she hated Negroes for their filthy ways. She claimed that many of the rallies Rockwell conducted had actually resulted from conversations she had had with him in which he sought her advice. To the girl, her hallucinatory references were at first about religious figures, then movie stars. All the students had merely greeted the patient and explained in one sentence that they were "summer students here to make patients more comfortable." During the conversations they only agreed with whatever the patient said by nodding and/or murmuring "yes."

From this evidence it was obvious that the patient had learned to discriminate among audiences. Equally clearly, the audiences controlled the contents of her hallucinations.

Behavioral treatment for this problem is two-pronged. One, the patient who excitedly tells about voices he hears should be calmly told that everyone hears voices. A useful statement might be as follows.

> When I go to the store and see a new dress I usually hear two voices. One tells me, "Go ahead, buy the dress. You'll like it!" The other counters, "But you have to meet your budget. You can't afford to buy the dress!" And sometimes these voices argue. Of course, I listen to them and then follow one or the other or neither one. That is what you should do with your voices, too. There is no need to tell everyone about them.

Such a statement should be followed by disregarding any further references to voices. Being equated with everyone else is sufficient to weaken the hallucinatory behavior of some patients for whom being different through hearing voices and having visions is a reinforcer.

Two, simply attach a prohibitive price to verbal or other behavior which indicates the presence of hallucinations. Hallucinatory activity is easily identifiable. Frequently the hallucinator quietly talks aloud with his voices while pacing, or sits with eyes closed, rocking himself back and forth. Although contingencies cannot be arranged between what the patient hears and sees at such times, consequences can be attached to undesirable behaviors which occur during hallucinatory episodes.

Reinforcement for incompatible behavior and charging for behaviors signifying hallucinatory activity are procedures which lead to a reduction of such responses.

Beth, a forty-two-year-old patient, with a diagnosis of schizophrenic reaction, chronic undifferentiated, could frequently be found rocking back and forth whispering in a low voice. When questioned about this behavior she asserted, "I don't do that and I don't hear voices." Treatment began by telling her that for each time she was observed rocking back and forth with her eyes closed and murmuring to herself she would have to pay ten tokens at the end of the day. For each time she was observed not acting this way she would receive tokens.

Initially the patient lost tokens almost every day, but within approximately two weeks hallucinatory behavior was observed less and less frequently. Beth's bank account soared to 800 tokens! She became more cooperative and volunteered information regarding the content of her hallucinations. She reported that visitations from her "soul people" and her sister's "inner being" were less and less frequent.

The information received from Beth was useful in strengthening the procedure. For example, she indicated that she always hallucinated when strange men came on the ward. This set the occasion for close observation of her behavior when visitors were present, and lavish reinforcement when no hallucinatory behavior was emitted at such times. Beth's cooperation was surprising but actually not too unusual in such cases. Apparently close association between nursing personnel and a functioning reinforcer, or perhaps the specific definition of the procedures used, prompted her to divulge previously private information.

In treating Julie, a different procedure was followed. Reinforcement was contingent upon Julie's providing information regarding the content of her hallucinations. This information was used to help her control her problem behavior. Julie would seclude herself on her bed, close her eyes, smile, and in general look as if she were out of contact with the real world. If she could not find seclusion she would simply adopt a "far away" expression wherever she was and become oblivious to her environment.

Her disturbance also involved grooming habits. She would forget to shower and change clothing. Her makeup was often bizarre in appearance and she invariably piled her hair high on her head with little or no combing. Furthermore, there seemed to be a correlation between the occurrence of hallucinations and her going AWOL.

Since Julie did not voluntarily talk about her hallucinations, the therapist put her on a program of reinforcement for providing information. The treatment proceeded in three steps.

1. Reinforcement with tokens for reporting that hallucination had occurred
2. Reinforcement for tangential information such as duration and details of what she heard and saw
3. Reinforcement for volunteering the information

In order to prevent cheating she was assured—not altogether incorrectly —that by and large the nursing staff knew when she engaged in hallucinations which they confirmed by catching her in the act on several occasions.

Our step-by-step procedures resulted in obtaining the following information. Julie harbored a well-developed hallucinatory system and it was her voices, God, and the devil who told her to go AWOL. Therefore she was told, "Whenever your voices tell you to go AWOL and you resist, you can earn tokens. Whenever you go AWOL, it will cost you tokens."

During the initial stages of the procedure the patient had difficulty resisting temptation and told the nurses, "God and the devil say they will blow up my stomach if I don't do as they say." She adopted the tactic of coming to her counselor during episodes and asking to be locked up but was told that she had to learn to resist the temptation itself. Putting Julie on her own in this manner and making her pay for the consequences of her acts eventually cured her of going AWOL.

Persons not familiar with behavioral techniques may justifiably wonder whether these procedures merely cause patients to hide their symptoms. Since the only way of determining the presence of behaviors such as delusions and hallucinations is through the patients' actions, if patients can be brought to the point where they no longer engaged in the behaviors, what reason is there to conclude that they still suffer from a disease signaled by a symptom now gone?

Another concern might well be that use of specific contingencies may somehow make the patient worse. We have not had a single instance in which the application of behavioral procedure was followed by a change which permanently intensified an expression of psychotic behavior. Admittedly, there have been occasions when a given approach has not resulted in change at all, or where sloppy application of technique resulted in the appearance of new problems. In the first instance, the patient is no worse off than before, and the nursing staff always discovered a procedure which ultimately induced positive change. When application of technique brought on new problems, prompt termination of the procedure was always followed by a return to the status quo.

Of course when procedures are begun, patients often resist and may appear to feel unduly the pressure of new demands. Initially there may be considerable upheaval and emotional reactions are sometimes present. But in themselves, these are signs of impending change. Then, too, behavioral therapy often involves the use of extinction procedures. Research has demonstrated that the initial course of extinction always involves signs of emotionality. Provoking reactions, therefore, seems to be a natural outcome of applying behavioral techniques. Perhaps further explorations will reveal methods for alleviating the occurrence of outbursts. Until they do, behavioral therapists must be willing to face up to patients' restiveness with the knowledge that the patient is capable of changing but does not always react to change gratefully.

EXERCISES, CHAPTER 10

1. Examination of Scotty's record indicates that his pronounced limp has been diagnosed as a conversion reaction. What does this mean?

2. At times John emits a gross body movement. This response seems to be most pronounced on days when his relatives visit him. You have been supplied the following data based on systematic observation.

Visitation Record	Response Rate per Minute prior to Visit	Response Rate per Minute during Visit	Response Rate per Minute after Visit
1-10-67 Mother	0.354	25.5	9.3
1-31-67 Brother	0.320	0.323	0.256
2-4-67 Mother	0.106	31.6	0.416
2-28-67 Father	1.91	0.305	0.555

   a. How do the data support the hypothesis that John's tic is most pronounced on visiting day?
   b. What stimulus seems to set the occasion for high frequency of the behavior?
   c. The notes accompanying the observation sheet indicate that John's mother "babies" him during visits. What does this suggest in the way of treatment?
   d. Prepare a treatment plan for John based upon your conclusions.
3. All of us, at one time or another, have believed that some other person was "out to get us." What makes these experiences different from delusions?
4. Which examples given in the chapter suggest that hallucinations are under the control of the environment?

11

Treating Odd Behaviors—III

Your study of this chapter should help you answer the following questions:

1. How can crazy talk and mutism as part of patients' behavioral repertoire be extinguished?
2. Why is public undressing a relatively easy behavior to control? How can it be controlled?
3. How can the technique of satiation be used to control hoarding?

The terms listed below are introduced and defined in this chapter:

mutism
hoarding

Crazy Talk

Human talking is almost wholly under the control of listener attention. Listening to oneself talk is, of course, reinforcing, but there is usually a very special condition such as learning a new language or practicing a poem by heart, which sets the occasion for listening. Even at such times people do not talk just to hear themselves. It is the attention of a listener which reinforces and thereby sustains talking.

This behavioral explanation of why people talk provides insight as to how society reinforces some forms of talking which should really not be reinforced. An example is stuttering as pointed out by I. Goldiamond who has studied this behavior extensively. Even in the noisiest cocktail-hour conversation, silence and rapt attention instantly prevail while a stutterer tries to speak.

For nonsense talk the situation is similar. That humans must at all times attempt to understand what someone has to say has become an unwritten law prescribed by our feelings for "humanness." Often the more incoherent and nonsensical the verbal output, the more interested seems the audience. Such interest is, of course, justified only if it were true that by some means or other it is possible to make sense of what is being said. Traditional therapeutic procedure assumes that listening is extremely important for in this way the therapist can solve the patient's verbal code and thus gain insight into the patient's problem. But this is a highly questionable assumption since attentive listening reinforces the use of "crazy talk." Clearly, a much simpler assumption about nonsense talk is that it simply does not make sense and should not be reinforced by attentive listening.

This latter assumption underlies behavioral treatment of crazy talk in mental institutions. Ayllon and Michael conducted experimentation which explored the effect of withholding reinforcement for crazy talk. Their data show that such behavior is under the control of listener attention and can be extinguished by withholding attention.

Extinction of psychotic talk should not be expected to take place within a matter of days. It is not always easy to discriminate between normal, reasonable content of sentences, and psychotic content. Thus there will be occasional reinforcement (through listening) to crazy talk. Nevertheless, considering that some patients have indulged in such behavior for a quarter of a century, it is remarkable that within three months such behavior can at least be reduced substantially. In Ayllon's and Michael's experiment, baselines for one patient showed that over 90 percent of her talk with nurses had psychotic content. By withdrawing attention whenever the patient talked crazy and giving attention whenever the patient talked sense, within twelve weeks the proportion was reduced to 25 percent nonsensical references.

We found a slight modification which improved the effectiveness of the approach used by Ayllon and Michael. Whenever a nurse discovered nonsense talk during a conversation, rather than abruptly turning away without comment she would say, "That's crazy talk and I'm not listening to crazy talk," and then leave. This method has the advantage of giving the nurse a self-emitted control stimulus to change her behavior from listening to nonlistening. The transition between the two behaviors is thereby more clearly marked and avoids such traps as her walking away smiling, frowning, or plain embarrassed because of the unusual behavior she is expected to emit. In addition, a verbal label is attached to the patient's behavior which should serve as another stimulus to help in learning the discrimination between normal (acceptable) talk and crazy talk.

On the other hand, it is of no advantage, and is perhaps even detrimental, to accompany reasonable talking on the part of the patient with statements like, "That's nice reasonable talking." This sounds, and is, condescending and might well have an aversive effect. The attention of a listener, his agreement or disagreement with what he hears, and his answering and elaborating are the reinforcers that sustain reasonable talk for all human beings including mental patients.

The selective reinforcement for crazy talk that takes place in a hospital ward does not automatically generalize to the environment outside the hospital. Visitors almost invariably constitute a new stimulus in the presence of which the behavior has not yet been established.

Visitors who come to the ward, official or otherwise, should be informed concerning patients who are on special schedules of reinforcement for verbal behavior. Visitors provide a link with the world outside, and their selective reinforcement goes a long way toward generalizing extinction for crazy talk. Ogden Lindsley has a means of dealing with this situation. A big sign over the entrance to his behavioral therapy program at Parsons (Kansas) State Hospital advises visitors to attend only to desirable behavior.

A version of crazy talk which requires a different approach is the mumbling of a series of meaningless speech sounds some of which, however, are acceptable words. If this behavior is emitted frequently, daily treatment sessions are in order, during which the patient is reinforced first for words and then for sentences. An unusual case of this type involved a patient for whom previous experience had convinced us that only the strongest reinforcer could bring about the desired change in behavior. For this patient, a woman, beer was such a reinforcer.

At the first session the therapist sat beside her holding a small cup into which he poured about 1 ounce of beer. He told her she could have beer for each word she spoke. As soon as she uttered a word, she was given the beer to drink. The cup was refilled each time she spoke another word. At the end of the twenty minutes, she had used thirty-two words and treatment was suspended.

The emission of desirable verbal behavior was now under the control of sips of beer which in turn the nurse controlled. On the following day he reinforced her only for each noun she spoke. Before receiving 32 ounces of beer (a limit which the therapist set as maximum for any one session), the woman had spoken more than a hundred words.

During the third session she was required to combine nouns and verbs, thus making simple sentences. Even though talking went on constantly, at this session the patient used only enough noun-verb combinations to make eight sentences, but the regimen continued on a daily basis for a week. At that time a new refinement was introduced. From then on, whenever the patient emitted nonsense words or interposed nonsense into simple sentences, the therapist poured the ready ounce of beer into the sink instead of giving it to the patient. In effect this was a "time out" from the reinforcement contingency since the supply of beer was seemingly unlimited and the next reinforcer was available at the utterance of a meaningful sentence. The experiment continued toward more complex sentences. By then the entire nursing staff was instructed to selectively reinforce sentences spoken by the patient with tokens at any time throughout the day, but to totally disregard such utterances as "Joe Palooka—world—mine—food—shoe—swimming." In the course of a summer the patient resumed acceptable speech habits. Also by summer's end, reinforcers other than the experimenter-controlled sips of beer became effective so that there was no need for special weaning from the support of the artificial reinforcer.

The technique of setting aside a special room in which crazy talk is tolerated is also useful. Under this procedure the patient can buy time in a private room to talk nonsense and, for an additional fee, can have his conversation recorded and played back. We believe that this technique may even be useful for reinforcing aspects of nonsense talk. By such aspects we mean the kind of reinforcing value which lies in some of Gertrude Stein's writing or nonsense poems and literature which are part of our cultural heritage. It is quite conceivable that in a society which demands reasonable speech, there is a state of deprivation for nonsense speech. In other words, nonsense speech may well become reinforcing. But it is important to set proper conditions for its emission. Lewis Carroll's "Twas brillig and the slithy toves . . ." is delightful partly for its onomatopoetics and its alliterations, but also (probably) because it allows us to hear words for their own sake and not because of their meaning.

Mutism

Behavioral procedures are equally useful in reinstating speech for patients who refuse to talk or whose degree of verbal interaction is minimal. The following example shows how Isaacs, Thomas, and Goldiamond used operant shaping techniques to reinstate speech in a "mute" psychotic male.

A session in group therapy revealed that sticks of chewing gum accidentally dropped from someone's pocket attracted the interest of a forty-year-old catatonic patient classified as completely mute. The procedure and results of using gum as a reinforcer are given in Figure 11-1. From the time of the session at which the patient first answered questions, he would thereafter reliably answer additional questions for the therapist. However, he would not verbalize for anyone else. In order to generalize the response, a nurse was asked to be present during sessions with the therapist and patient. After a month the patient began answering her questions, too. It later became apparent that the patient would make verbal requests if nursing personnel would respond to his requests. This set the stage for all nursing personnel to respond only to verbal requests rather than to continue to interpret and act upon his gestures. The authors reported, however, that the patient makes verbal requests only when no other form of communication results in reinforcement.

Week	Procedure	Reinforcement	Result
1–2	Gum held before patient's face	Gum given when patient's eyes moved toward it	Patient regularly looked at gum as it was presented
3–4	Gum held before patient's face	Gum given when patient's eyes moved toward it and lips moved as though to speak	Patient regularly looked at gum and moved lips
5–6	Gum held before patient's face and therapist commanded, "Say 'Gum. Gum.'"	Gum given when patient made sounds approximating word "gum"	Patient suddenly said, "Gum, please," then answered questions about his name and age

Fig. 11-1. Steps in reinforcement therapy for a case of mutism. (*After Issacs et al.*)

For example, he does not talk to other patients or members of the hospital-at-large since they still interpret nonverbal requests.

The process of *shaping* (successive approximation) is exemplified in treatment used with this mute patient. The therapist did not demand that the subject talk to him during the first session even though there was strong evidence that the patient had talked before hospitalization. A particular kind of reinforcer was used, one which the patient's own behavior identified. The therapist simply delivered reinforcement step by step as the patient approached the terminal behavior desired of him.

The study also exemplifies the principle of *stimulus control* as various procedures had to be used to get the response to generalize from therapist to a single nurse to all nursing personnel. Success with other patients and members of the hospital-at-large was never achieved because these environments were beyond the control of the therapist.

Total mutism is not frequently encountered among the patient population of a mental hospital, but a number of patients fail to interact on a verbal level with their ward mates. A study conducted at Patton used the daily pay call to reinstate this kind of socializing.

One particular patient had been hospitalized for twelve years and was diagnosed schizophrenic reaction, chronic undifferentiated. On the basis of casual observation, verified by daily objective records, it became known that the patient failed to socialize with other patients. She would talk to nursing personnel, but even these interactions were limited to very brief requests of a practical nature. Because she was a compulsive worker, the staff required her to pay whenever she worked beyond her regular assignment. This left the patient with a great deal of free time. To encourage her to interact with her ward mates, the patient was informed that she would have to earn most of her tokens by socializing. At pay call each day she was required to name the people (other than nursing personnel) with whom she had talked. She was also expected to give a brief summary of the topics covered in these conversations. The nursing staff would listen to her report and note the number of individuals and the number of different topics, then deliver reinforcement according to the following schedule.

Requirement	Reinforcement
Talk with one to three ward mates	1 token
Talk with four or more ward mates	4 tokens

The patient was not provided with information regarding the contingency other than what was contained in the relationship between performance and reinforcement. Still, she rapidly caught on to this schedule and began giving reports such as, "I talked to Mary and told her I'm thirty-eight years old," or, "I talked to Helen and I told her I'm not married." For twenty-five days per performance was perfect relative to the schedule of reinforcement. Observation throughout the day, however, revealed that the patient held these conversations on the run. She would approach her audience and make the statement literally in passing. While this procedure induced her to interact with other patients, it was certainly lacking in the total desired behavior. Therefore, her schedule of reinforcement was modified as follows.

Requirement	Reinforcement
One person—must talk about at least four different topics	4 tokens
Two persons—must talk about at least eight different topics	6 tokens
Three persons—must talk about at least twelve different topics	8 tokens
Four persons—must talk about at least sixteen different topics	12 tokens

Initially, the patient did not do well under this schedule. She typically failed to cover enough different topics for the number of individuals whom she engaged in conversation. After two weeks, however, she dramatically increased the number of topics per person and began obtaining maximum or nearly maximum reinforcement according to the schedule. Obviously she was no longer able to breeze by her intended audience but had to stop in order to cover the number of topics needed to meet the criterion for reinforcement. In addition, the kinds of topics she covered took on a different character. Instead of making statements about her age or marital status she might say, "Don't you think the lights on the Christmas tree are beautiful?" or "My mother brought me a pair of red slippers the last time she visited me."

In short, behavioral therapy is not a magic procedure that once applied will yield magic results, nor is it a cut-and-dried procedure. Behavioral therapy requires flexibility and constant analysis of behavior as it is being shaped. At any time the direction of behavioral therapy is as much determined by what the patient does as by what the therapist wants to achieve. Even if it were possible to make rules to fit each and every case, an understanding of the principles of behavior makes for flexibility, not the blind application of rules.

Public Undressing

Not infrequently female patients take off their clothes at what seem to be most inappropriate times. In reality, however, these times are those most likely to sustain the behavior because there is invariably an audience whose attention reinforces the behavior. Undressing of this kind is not to be confused with the exhibitionism of males with sex-behavior problems. Exhibitionism is a low-frequency behavior, but the kind of undressing discussed here is typically of high frequency and occurs under predictable environmental conditions.

Of all odd behaviors, this one is probably the most easily dealt with, assuming the hospital administration agrees to the treatment program required. Since from prior observation it is almost always already known when and where the patient will do her undressing, as many as possible of the potential viewers should be asked to ignore the behavior. Also the nursing staff should have available a highly effective reinforcer.

One undresser was a heavy smoker. On the first day of treatment the nurse showed her a plastic case containing forty cigarettes. As anticipated, during the early morning hours when maintenance crews passed on their way to work, the patient ran out on the lawn and began to strip. Without comment the nurse walked up to her and held the case of cigarettes so that it was plainly visible. She removed three of the cigarettes, crumbled them in her fingers, and scattered them on the ground, but did nothing to stop the patient from undressing. As the skirt came off, another three cigarettes were destroyed. Still the patient continued her behavior. After destroying another three cigarettes the nurse went away and left the patient alone. By then the work crew had gone by and the patient reclothed herself. About half an hour later the entire procedure was repeated. On that day the patient smoked five cigarettes instead of her usual forty. On the next day there were thirty-one cigarettes for her, and on the third day all forty [14]. The

behavior had ceased. In effect, the patient had been reinforced for behaving properly but, at the same time, had experienced that the magni-
tude of reinforcement was limited by the presence of the undesirable
behaviors.

Undressing, as well as provocative dressing, is strictly a manipulative
behavior and should be treated as such. Selective reinforcement for
proper dress is the main technique to use. As is so common in our
culture, proper behavior is taken for granted and improper behavior
is to be controlled through punishment, which is clearly seen to be
ineffective everywhere. It is true that the patient, once the behavior
has been changed, will be discharged into an environment which does
not overtly seem to reinforce proper dress, but the patient can be weaned
from the support of the artificial reinforcers used in therapy by using
whatever natural reinforcers exist. Society treats a properly dressed
woman more courteously than a sloppily dressed one. A decently dressed
man will have a better chance at getting a job than one dressed like
a bum. On the ward these desirable differences can be reinforced by
those who understand behavioral principles.

Hoarding

Another behavior believed to be indicative of a deranged mind is
the hoarding of trivial items. As with many behaviors, this is a relative
matter. The philatelist who collects old and used stamps is not considered mad, but the patient in a mental hospital who collects tiny
squares of paper is. Hoarding is admired in the squirrel, but despised
in the miser. Before embarking on a program to weaken hoarding behavior, it should, therefore, be asked without prejudice just how injurious
the hoarding really is. If it is merely something that disturbs the patient's
relatives, perhaps their tolerance of a minor foible should be changed
rather than the patient's behavior.

On the other hand, hoarding can be disruptive and reach proportions
which are not tolerated by either the hospital or the community within
which the patient is to live.

Objects which we have found to be attractive to hoarders are scraps
of paper, rags, stones, magazines, and, much to the concern of nursing
personnel, razor blades! Hoarding takes on a bizarre character when
the amount of material hoarded obtains enormous proportions relative
to the size of its storage area. In addition, such a collection becomes
a problem on a ward since any "pile of junk" is not viewed as desirable
by hospital administrators.

Stimulus satiation is an effective technique for controlling hoarding.
When an organism is in continuous commerce with some stimulus, it
can be assumed that the stimulus functions as a reinforcer. One functional relationship between reinforcers and behavior is that a stimulus

may temporarily lose its ability to reinforce once the organism has had its fill. This relationship is termed *satiation* and is the opposite of deprivation.

Ayllon used this relationship between stimulus and response as the basis for treatment of hoarding. The patient under study collected large numbers of towels and stored them in her room. This behavior had been a part of her repertoire for at least nine years of hospitalization. On the basis of objective observation, the patient could be expected to have approximately twenty towels in her room on any given day. Ayllon reports that many efforts had been made to discourage hoarding with no permanent result.

In an effort to control this behavior, nursing personnel ceased removing towels from the patient's room. In addition, at varying time intervals throughout the day a staff member would take a towel to the patient's room and give it to her or in her absence simply leave it there. During the first week this procedure took place seven times per day. By the third week of treatment, the number of towels brought daily increased to sixty. When the hoard of towels reached 625, the patient began to find them aversive. She said to the staff, "Take them towels away!"

From this behavior, satiation was assumed and no more towels were provided. But neither were any removed by the nurses. During the next ten weeks the patient disposed of her towels until at any given inspection no more than five could be found. Ayllon's report states that throughout the following year the patient never resumed towel hoarding. In addition, and contrary to the expectation that some other symptom would emerge to show the "inner need for security" of which hoarding is taken as proof, the patient showed no tendency to adopt other forms of undesirable behavior to replace the symptom "hoarding."

Other behavioral techniques may, of course, be used. Ayllon reports in the same context the case of a patient for whom food reinforcement was made contingent on wearing a proper amount of clothing instead of the bulk she was normally hoarding on her person. The procedure simply required initial determination of the patient's normal body weight. Her entrance to the dining room was then made contingent on her weighing in, and weighing no more than her normal weight plus a specified amount for clothing. As always, the initial steps required were small: Only two pounds less than the twenty-five which the bulk of her hoarded stockings, skirts, blouses, shawls, and sweaters usually weighed was required to give access to the dining room. Gradually the requirement was tightened, and by the end of a fourteen-week treatment period the weight of her clothing allowance had shrunk to a normal three pounds.

In the course of treatment the patient did display emotional behavior. She cried or burst out in anger when she didn't meet the weight criterion set and had to remove excess clothing in order to do so. The staff was well trained to disregard such behavior, and therefore the patient's reactions were not a problem. For the first time in nine years her parents again took her out on a visit because, in their words, "she no longer looked like a circus freak."

EXERCISES, CHAPTER 11

1. Claire, a very attractive patient, sometimes dresses in a most provocative manner. Close observation revealed that whenever she did not earn enough tokens she would purposely dress and behave so as to attract attention from male staff members and patients alike. Several incidents with male patients made this method dangerous; however, it was successful on most occasions. (She obtained cigarettes, candy, etc., without paying in tokens.)

   a. What should male staff members do when Claire flirts?

   b. How can Claire's behavior be controlled?

   c. How can incompatible behaviors play a role in treatment?

2. Fred insisted on collecting snails from the garden. While from one point of view his biological expeditions were admirable, he insisted upon carrying his snails in his pockets and refused to use more acceptable containers. Figure 11-2 describes the course of treatment.

   A is the baseline period.

   B represents the effects of satiation.

   At *B'* Fred said he hated snails.

   C is a test period measuring the effect of satiation.

   At panel *D* Fred was not allowed in dining room unless he removed a progressively greater number of snails from his pockets.

   a. What information is provided in panel *A* of the figure?

   b. Was satiation effective? How does the graph indicate this?

   c. Which technique was effective?

   d. How would you have dealt with this problem?

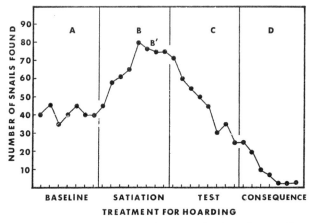

Fig. 11-2. Course of Fred's treatment for hoarding snails.

3. The chapter presented a method for reinstating social verbalization (socializing) in a female patient. What behavioral technique was used? Why did nursing personnel allow the patient to use such brief conversations?

4. Mary refuses to wear her shoes correctly. Rather than place her whole foot into the shoe she crushes the heel and wears them like heelless slippers. Since this contributes to the rapid wear of the shoes, you have been requested to change this habit. What can you do?

5. John has been walking backward for the past five years. On several occasions this method of ambulation has led to serious accidents. He engages in this behavior whenever he goes anywhere. He paces around the ward walking backward, stands in lines backward, and walks the five blocks to his job backward. He has been referred to you with the purpose of eliminating this behavior. The only information regarding possible reinforcers that you have obtained is that John is a big eater. How can you reinstate proper ambulation for John?

6. Myrna can be found lying on the floor watching television during her entire waking hours. You have been called in to consult with ward nursing personnel in an effort to get Myrna to at least sit and watch television. How can you solve their problem using a behavioral approach?

7. Marty insists that he must collect string and carry it with him at all times. A weekly shakedown reveals that he carries as much as 1,000 yards of string at a time. What behavioral technique might be used to eliminate this behavior? Be specific and spell out the procedure you would use if confronted with the problem and planning a program for Marty.

8. Stella has the disconcerting habit of raising her dress out of-doors whenever a nice looking gentleman passes the ward. Because of this habit, Stella is kept indoors for months at a time. Stella is a chain smoker. You have previously reinstated working, using cigarettes as a reinforcer. How can you eliminate Stella's problem using cigarettes as the reinforcer?

12

Treating Odd Behaviors—IV

Your study of this chapter should help
you answer the following questions:

1. What are some of the eating behaviors commonly considered "odd
   behaviors" when emitted by mental
   patients?
2. What are some of the ways the following can be used to change undesirable eating behaviors?

> control stimuli
> satiation
> negative reinforcers
> extinction
> discrimination
> aversive stimulation

TREATING UNDESIRABLE EATING BEHAVIORS

Many odd behaviors encountered in a mental hospital are associated
with eating. It is not unusual to see patients gulp an entire dinner
in little more than three minutes, grab quantities of food they do not
need, or spill food and beverages on clothing and tables. In some instances, obesity is a problem which may require special food limitations;
in others, an increase in food intake is necessary in order to preserve
health or even life itself. Occasionally, changing undesirable eating behaviors calls for elaborate procedures before acceptable responses are
attained. At other times, only a slight modification in normal routine
is needed to establish contingencies which bring about the desired
behaviors.

Food Throwing and Food Stealing

It is not likely that all food throwing is supported by the same reinforcers for every patient nor that the same reinforcer is always effective

for one person. But food throwing like any other response under the control of the environment is accompanied by consequences which reinforce and sustain it.

To change an eating behavior that is considered a problem, the first step, as always, is to obtain baselines on the frequency and conditions under which this behavior occurs. Impressionistic reports that a patient "always throws food" are to be mistrusted. The baseline for food throwing should be formally obtained over at least a two-week period. During this period the patient should be treated exactly as he had been. If he has been admonished not to throw food, the admonitions should continue, even though a behaviorally trained staff knows full well that their admonitions will have little if any effect on the patient's behavior. Indeed, if such behavior is controlled by attention, then admonitions regardless of their contents could be reinforcing.

In addition to noting occurrences of food throwing, the report should show as many extraneous circumstances that prevail at a meal as possible. What other patients sat at the same table? Was food late or early? Was the weather outside good or bad? Was the food sufficient? Did it contain meat or fish? Was the patient well dressed or sloppy? Many of these environmental stimuli may be completely irrelevant when the baseline data are analyzed, but all should be recorded for there is no telling what may later be of significance.

In the most fortunate circumstances, baselines will show that some environmental stimulus was present whenever food throwing occurred. Sometimes the data may contain only a hint of this. In that event a sequence of fifteen meals is arranged over five days, during which the control stimulus is deliberately introduced seven times and completely avoided the remaining eight times. If food throwing occurs only when the control stimulus is present, its identification is certain and a program of reinforcement for competitive behavior can be started.

During the Patton experiment we identified the sitting together of two other patients, one of whom was a friend of a food thrower, as such a control stimulus. This case is the more remarkable in that some twenty other variables which had been carefully listed over a ten-day baseline period had yielded nothing that could be connected with food throwing. When the baseline record was discussed, however, a particularly observant nurse mentioned that at least once she saw the food thrower's friend sitting with another patient. On the hunch that this might be the control stimulus, we arranged for its deliberate introduction and removal. By the end of the second day there was no doubt: Every time the food thrower's friend sat with this other patient, food throwing took place. Interestingly, she threw food at whoever was near her, never at her friend or the friend's companion.

Treatment was now simple. The patient was a heavy smoker and cigarettes were used directly as reinforcers for not throwing food when the stimulus which normally controlled food throwing was present. At first cigarettes were given if no food had been thrown within two minutes after entering the dining room and in two minute intervals thereafter. At the next meal the interval was extended to three minutes, which yielded the patient four cigarettes.

This regimen was maintained for one week. By then it became evident that another behavior was being reinforced: dawdling over food. The patient became the last to leave the dining room and during the last session earned ten cigarettes for not having thrown food for thirty minutes. It was then decided to lengthen the period to five minutes and to introduce the control stimulus only irregularly.

During the following week the control stimulus was present at five meals only. From the beginning of the treatment period the patient had not once thrown food. This resulted in the appearance of another reinforcer for not throwing food. Patients who had dreaded to sit near the food thrower now became more friendly. After the second week the regimen was completely abandoned and normal dining room behavior was apparently maintained even without cigarette reinforcement. Not once during this entire period was the control stimulus identified to the patient, and there is doubt that she could have verbalized the relationships that had been arranged between her behavior, her friend's location, and cigarettes.

But cases where a control stimulus can be identified are probably rare. Over a three-year period this example is the only one that came to our attention in a program involving both male and female patients. When no control stimulus can be identified, the possible reinforcers for the behavior in question should be listed and details about the behavior should be asked.

Does the patient throw the food against the wall or on the floor?
Does he throw food at other patients?
Does he throw food at nurses?
What kind of food does he throw?
Specifically, what does the patient do after he throws the food?
What do others do after food has been thrown?

Most frequently attention is the most powerful reinforcer for food throwing. If this behavior were not so disruptive, the simplest technique would be to ignore it. But this clearly cannot be done when other patients are involved. One procedure which proved useful with a female (but not with a male) patient consisted in letting each patient eat in a room by himself. This was in a ward with an established token economy; therefore, we raised the price for the meal in the private room to three times that of the meal in the ward dining room. In addition, no knife and fork were provided, only a spoon. If the patients ate without toying with the food and without dropping it (both of these patients previously threw food by dropping it on the floor), some of the tokens were refunded and a knife and fork provided for the next meal. Within two days both patients were again allowed to purchase meals in the dining room. The female patient did not throw food and was paid the meal price for having been "good." She was kept on that schedule for a month and then put on variable ratio schedules until her release from the hospital. The male patient promptly dropped food when he resumed eating in the dining room and was returned to the private room for subsequent meals. In the private room he again ate without dropping food. It turned out that he was in the hospital solely for his unacceptable eating habits and that eating in privacy was a highly self-reinforcing behavior for him. Arrangements were made with a family care home for the patient to eat alone. He has been out of the hospital for over two years at the time of this writing.

Even if such procedures fail, a technique described first by Teodoro Ayllon has proven reliable in cases of this type. Nursing personnel reported that an overweight female patient continually stole food from dining tables even when she had just eaten a full meal. At the time of their report, the patient had been hospitalized for nine years as a chronic schizophrenic. Neither coaxing nor admonishment extinguished her undesirable behavior, and she also failed to heed the medical reasons for restricting food intake.

Baseline data substantiated the nurses' original report: The patient stole food two-thirds of the time. Ayllon reasoned that having access to the meals itself possibly constituted a reinforcer which maintained the strength of this particular behavior. Hence, a schedule was begun which terminated the meal every time the patient stole or, indeed, made a move to steal. The latter was easily identified by placing the patient at a table separate from other patients. As soon as she moved toward another table she was removed from the dining room so that further reinforcement of eating no longer followed the attempt to steal. The basic behavioral law applicable here is that a response is weakened if it no longer results in reinforcement. Ayllon reports that in two weeks the patient extinguished successfully on this behavior. When we applied the same technique in our own program it was equally successful with another male food thrower who had not responded to the private dining room method.

It is safe to say that establishing a routine for dealing with food throwers, food droppers, and food stealers goes a long way toward coping with these problems. Attention is probably the strongest reinforcer for this behavior and its programmed occurrence provides an effective means of controlling behavior.

Noisy and Messy Eating

Sloppy eating patterns are directly engendered by the barracks environment which prevails in some ward dining rooms. Patients are prone to belch and break wind throughout a meal, mash their food in one mess, and eat with the wrong end of a spoon. In short, sometimes a general uncouthness prevails which shocks the unprepared observer. Such eating habits are more common with men, although they are found occasionally with women. Naturally they must be corrected before discharge since the community outside the hospital regards such behavior as a sign that the patient is still mentally ill.

For some patients the hospital becomes a welcome refuge, and undesirable eating habits afford an easy way to impress the staff that they are too mentally sick to be discharged. Any appeals which stress the uncouthness of this behavior merely reinforce it. The patient eats sloppily to stay in the hospital, and any confirmation that he is, indeed, eating sloppily reinforces his behavior and permits him to effectively control his environment.

In such cases we have found the following technique useful, although, there are doubtless others which will work equally well. To begin with, we tell the patient that he eats sloppily and that, as far as we are concerned, that is his privilege. As all privileges, though, this one also has its price. Before each meal the patient is asked whether he is going to want to eat "his way" or like other people. A meal eaten "his way" costs twice or several times more than the price of a meal eaten normally. If the patient pays the extra amount, and some do, it is mandatory that the nurse in charge does not take him to task or berate him for his sloppy habits. Most patients, however, will choose to pay the lesser amount. If they still indulge in their idiosyncrasies, the meal is terminated on the grounds that they did not pay for the privilege. (If a patient, for reasons of health needs the food, he is given the choice of paying for the privilege at that time.) This regimen is extremely effective, and soon the patient eats normally as a matter of course.

Some patients may simply have fallen into sloppy habits because no one seems to mind or because no one tells them not to eat that way. A nurse on the men's unit at Patton developed a technique which takes the following course. She first tells the patient that he eats sloppily and spells out in detail what should be changed. With some patients this is all that is required; with others it is of no avail. She then sits with the patient at mealtime and says, "We'll play a little game. Here are five tokens for you. Every time you burp (or whatever the undesired behavior is), you are to pay me one of these tokens. Every time I think you eat particularly nicely, I'll pay you a token in addition to those you already have." If the patient loses all his tokens and still owes the nurse, he is given a bib to wear during the next meal. Since a bib serves as a powerful aversive stimulus, the patient rapidly improves his eating habits. To wean a patient from the token reinforcer, fewer and fewer tokens are given until finally none are needed.

A general procedure is also most useful here. Many of the sloppy eating habits, both men's and women's, are clearly due to the absence of control stimuli for proper eating—one of which we have found to be members of the opposite sex. The results of introducing five female patients into a dining room where for years only sixty male patients had eaten is a most convincing testimony to the power of control stimuli. To begin with, the women selected to eat with the men were given this task as a privilege. They had to pay the staff for being permitted to go there. This assured that motivation to mingle with the men was high and resulted also in extensive sprucing up for the occasion. The men had not been forewarned. When the women appeared in the dining room they were directed to five different tables. Men who had slouched over their plates suddenly rose and adjusted chairs for the ladies. Polite conversation ensued. Most patients, even "proper" eaters changed their table manners instantly for the better. We kept records of the total time taken to complete the meal, the amount of interaction between patients, and the incidence of sloppy eating with some of the patients.

The results were impressive. For these men the total time previously taken to complete the evening meal averaged around five minutes. Now it took twenty minutes. Talk among patients during the meal had been almost zero, now there was lively and polite conversation throughout the meal. The average number of objectionable eating responses for four men had been 6.25 incidences; now it was down to 1.25 (caused by one man who slurped and used a spoon throughout the meal).

As this evening meal regimen continued, the original improvement did not entirely remain. Apparently the men became used to the women and reverted to sloppy behavior. But some never again departed from good manners in the presence of the women, and no patient let himself go quite as much as he had prior to their introduction. In wards where men and women habitually eat together their intermingling probably already produces relatively fewer sloppy eating habits.

Eating an Unbalanced Diet

Preferences for only certain foods sometimes seriously interferes with patients' physical health or are so unusual as to be thought unacceptable behavior. For example, we treated a patient who sprinkled pepper on his vanilla ice cream. A behaviorally trained nurse avoids concluding that such behavior is a sure manifestation of mental illness. Pepper on ice cream may not be to everyone's taste, but for other than a mental patient it might be considered no more than an eccentricity. Nevertheless, if unusual or unhealthy food preferences are to be changed, several techniques make this possible.

We were asked, for example, to deal with a patient who ate only white foods: Milk, vanilla ice cream, mashed potatoes, vichysoisse (chives carefully removed) and boiled potatoes. This patient also dressed in light-colored clothing, preferably white. To her the color white meant purity, niceness, heaven, and godliness. Black meant sin, pubic hair, devils, and badness. To begin with, we used a schedule of satiation. At breakfast she was served four large glasses of milk—no toast, no bacon, no eggs. For lunch she was given a large serving of mashed potatoes and four more glasses of milk. She was told that she would be paid for requesting and eating bacon, but she declined. With this food regimen, we also took her light clothing away and substituted regular hospital garb. She was a generally apathetic patient, but on first being handed dark clothing, she ripped the blouse in anger. About two hours later she asked for and instantly received needle and thread (the nurses had completely disregarded her tantrum). She was also given a white scarf as a reinforcer for the constructive act of mending the torn blouse.

Yet during this satiation period her eating habits did not change. We then began to increase the price for the milk and at the same time increased potential pay if she were to eat bacon or anything dark. Until then the price of all her meals had been the minimum price paid by all patients. A dramatic event then occurred at a Sunday lunch. On the last day on which medical prudence allowed the satiation technique, roast beef with a tasty sauce was being served, and the patient was given her usual white diet. During the meal the patient suddenly screamed loudly, reached for a tureen with sauce, and poured the contents over her head.

The nurse fortunately resisted the impulse to ask for assistance to put this patient into restraint and isolation. Instead she calmly took the patient aside and led her to the bathroom. There the patient said, "I've been a fool, forgive me for doing this, I won't do it again." The nurse helped the patient clean up, wrote her report, but took no further action. On Sunday evening the patient ate her first balanced meal in over six months of hospitalization.

Satiation can be a risky technique medically since a patient may be on a satiation diet too long without satiating. A nurse on the men's unit in the Patton program developed a technique which uses preferred foods as reinforcers. They are given only when the patient has eaten something he normally does not eat. This requires personal attention as do most behavioral techniques. But once the patient eats what he normally would not touch, there is usually no difficulty. The nurse sits with such a patient and presents him with whatever he should be eating. Within sight of the patient she also holds whatever she knows is appropriate as a reinforcer. This she determined from making a behavioral baseline. If the patient completely refuses to eat whatever he should, he misses the entire meal. If, however, he takes so much as a bite of the nonpreferred food, especially in the beginning of the regimen, she reinforces him with a bit of the preferred food.

In most hospitals there is little control over what patients eat. Hence, missing a meal is a minor problem compared to the dietary deficiencies which occur through unreasonable food preferences. Sitting with a patient during meals also assures that the nurse is quite aware of his exact intake and allows judicious supplementation with vitamins whenever needed.

As mentioned previously, odd food combinations—such as pepper on ice cream, pickled herring with chocolate pudding, or sugar on beef stew—should never be unquestioningly taken as evidence of a patient's mental illness. They may well be genuine, although unusual, preferences. On the other hand, they may be odd behaviors calculated to elicit sympathy and attention and thus are, indeed, those which bring the patient to the hospital. If they are the latter, they will emerge only in the presence of an audience, not when the patient eats alone. An observer, as it were, is the control stimulus for odd behavior of this kind. To check whether the behavior is merely a bid for attention, it is only necessary to observe the patient without his knowledge while he eats by himself. If the odd behavior does not occur, it is nearly certain that it is under the control of an observer. In such a case extinction can be achieved by consistently ignoring the behavior. Only patients who do not react to his odd behavior should be at the same table with him. The entire staff must cooperate in this extinction procedure. To generalize the effect of this schedule, any visitor who comes to the ward at mealtime should be told of the schedule the patient is on and asked to cooperate. Under such a regimen we have extinguished such behavior within two months, even though the behavior had apparently been on continuous or near continuous reinforcement for twelve years.

Eating Too Much

A belief exists in our society that mental conditions such as frustration, dejection, and depression can cause obesity. This is not so. Depending on how they are defined, these conditions might cause extensive eating, but it is eating alone that causes obesity. Some mental patients are admittedly fat. Often the source of their overweight condition is believed by them to reside in invisible forces. Is it any wonder that short of enforced diets, nothing seems to help such patients?

Eating is a behavior and as such can be brought under the control of stimuli which apparently function for people who are not fat. C. B. Ferster has brilliantly described control stimuli and contingencies which are of interest in this context. It is on the basis of his experimental work that we dealt with overeating on the Patton project.

Ferster's work shows that in the course of a day a fat person will bend his elbow and bring food to his mouth more often than a person of normal weight. This is a behavior which can be brought under stimulus control. However, before attempting to shape new eating behaviors for an obese patient, the following are needed.

1. A complete medical examination and a guide to the patient's normal caloric and supplementary needs when not overweight.
2. A baseline showing under what conditions the patient eats other than at mealtimes.
3. Familiarity with what reinforcers are effective for the patient.

When these items have been covered and a schedule of reinforcement has been prepared, a nurse should plan to eat with the patient and be ready to reinforce for (1) eating more slowly and (2) discriminating between acceptable and unacceptable food.

To achieve the first objective, the nurse may require that the patient speak a complete sentence between each spoonful of food. As the patient does this the nurse reinforces him. The most striking result perceptible to the patient will be that it takes "forever" to eat. Furthermore, toward the end the food will be cold.

This allows the nurse to selectively reinforce for eating warm food (acceptable) and not to reinforce for eating cold food (unacceptable), This is, of course, a simple discrimination schedule which can be highly refined. For example, when prime rib is being served, the nurse can use a color chart and show the patient how the outer layers of the meat look too brown to eat and how there is fat between outer layers that is utterly *polysaturated* (a word which must be uttered with extreme disgust). The pink and rosy inner parts, on the other hand, are "good" to eat and the patient gets paid for eating them.

To include further control stimuli, the patient is constantly asked how the food tastes, and descriptions of pleasant sensations in the mouth as well as unpleasant ones are reinforced. The unpleasant sensations are further tied to "unacceptable" aspects of the food and the pleasant ones to desirable aspects.

Poking at food to inspect it critically, even toying with food is reinforced. Contrary to common belief, fat people seldom care or even know what they are eating. By becoming selective, the patient is being reinforced for emulating the behavior of a gourmet, a person who eats only that which meets high critical standards.

The extinction of indiscriminate eating at the table is relatively easy to accomplish. Eating between meals is much more difficult to control. The entire staff—and, if possible, patients who can appreciate the problem—must be informed and must cooperate. Whenever the patient refrains from snacking, reinforcement must be given. If at all possible, no mention should be made of eating or of food so that no verbal control stimulus is introduced which might defeat the effect of the reinforcer. Stimuli which control eating for this patient must be identified and either removed from the environment of the patient or tied to noneating instead of eating.

It would be worthless to deprive the patient of the sources of snacks. However effective for reducing weight, this would not change behavior. Extinction requires the emission of a response without a reinforcer following that response. Similarly, if candy is a control stimulus for eating, it will become ineffective as a control stimulus only if it is present during noneating. Consequently, sources of candy are not curtailed, but reinforcement is given for not eating while the candy is readily available.

Fortunately, there are few fat people for whom being overweight is a reinforcer. For most fat people the results of losing weight are themselves strong reinforcers. Favorable comments by the staff and other patients, in addition to the patient's own pleasure, reinforce the noneating behaviors which lead to loss of weight.

In time, other reinforcers which sustain the necessary amount of noneating will become effective. Greater attraction to the opposite sex, greater agility in self-care, better fitting suits and dresses, and the patient's increased sense of well-being eventually serve as control stimuli.

If personnel shortages preclude individual attention at mealtime, arrangements should be made for obese patients to eat in a separate room or in a separate section of the regular dining room. At Patton we have used the separate room technique for as many as nine patients at a time. The nurse in charge reinforced for slow eating and also for leaving food on the plate. All patients in this group lost weight.

Paradoxically this often left the successful patients with more tokens than were required for the meal in the first place. Still, the fact that some patients could not be reinforced often enough or not in small enough steps under this procedure makes it of less value than an individual approach.

A nurse on the women's unit at Patton conducted another group study of eating behavior. She informed four overweight women that tokens could be earned for every ounce of food left on their plates. In addition, tokens earned in this manner were exchangeable for privileges such as visits home, new dresses, or trips downtown. Before deciding on the schedules of reinforcement, however, ten-meal baselines were prepared which showed that the women had been consuming 28 ounces of food per meal and 8 ounces of milk, which was obviously too much since the women did not lose weight with these amounts.

The initial step made it easy for the four patients to earn tokens since the same portions were served that they had been eating. Over a period of a week, however, the servings were reduced to 16 ounces of food and no milk. These amounts made it gradually more difficult to leave food. However, each patient continued to leave a small amount on her plate after each meal. On rare occasions, a patient reported for the meal but turned in her full plate in exchange for tokens. The contingency was maintained for two months during which time each of the patients lost weight as shown in Table 12-1. To determine whether

Table 12-1
Results of Two Months Conditioning for Weight Loss

Overweight Patient	Weight before Conditioning, Pounds	Weight after Conditioning, Pounds
Patient 1	205	195
Patient 2	190	175
Patient 3	229	208
Patient 4	176	157

new reinforcers had become established through this program, all four patients were thereafter no longer reinforced with tokens. However, the amount of food left on the plates continued to be weighed. Two of the patients (3 and 4) went on leaving food, but the others reverted to their former behavior of cleaning their plates. The two patients who continued to leave food had lost proportionately more weight. It seems quite plausible that for them more and stronger reinforcers had come into play which made the token support unnecessary.

Arranging the environment to control food intake can also be accomplished by using aversive control. As Dr. Ferster points out, dieting is difficult because the undesirable consequences of overeating are experienced so long after the behaviors responsible for them have been emitted. People notice that their clothes are tight or that their abdomens are enlarged only after a fairly prolonged period of indulgence. Ferster suggested, therefore, that dieters manipulate ultimate aversive consequences so as to bring such consequences closer to the behaviors that caused them.

Applying this technique to their own dieting problem, two employees on the Patton program arranged their environment so that consequences would quickly be attached to eating habits—i.e., weight gain. Each day they weighed in on the ward scale. The weighing took place publicly. If their present weight was one pound over the previous day's weight or if at the end of a seven-day period they individually had not lost at least one pound, their fellow staff members enforced the contingency agreed upon: to wear for four hours a sign announcing

> I AM A BIG FAT SLOB

The aversiveness of the sign was enhanced by having both it and its letters large! To further ensure the effectiveness of the sign as a negative reinforcer, it had to be worn in front rather than in back. Upon seeing the sign, the staff and cooperating patients made disparaging remarks about fat people. When the sign was not being worn, the dieter received reinforcement by way of positive verbal comments. During the experiment, both employees not infrequently had to wear the sign, yet both eventually lost weight. Also, the aversive consequences of sign wearing extended beyond the limits of the ward for the sign was reported "on the minds" of the subjects whenever they were confronted with tempting food.

Eating Too Little

Throughout man's history he has been plagued by lack of food. Literally millions of people have perished within a single year in the course of a famine. The terror with which the surviving members of an entire population remember the horror of such an experience is passed on from one generation to the next at first through tales and warnings. Later the details fade and what remains are the behaviors which avoided starvation for the survivors and their descendants. Is it any wonder that with this cultural heritage man views the signs of starvation with utter alarm? Powerful stimuli goad him into action, attention, and concern. And it is equally understandable that he who starves himself arouses alarm in his fellowman, receives attention, causes concern—in short, controls the behavior of others.

There are some physical conditions of the body which cause starvation. But there are also some individuals for whom the concern, the attention, and the love from others are such powerful reinforcers that, having failed through other behaviors to obtain these, they overcome their fear of starvation and stop eating. These are the *anorexic* patients who have no known physical problem causing malnutrition. Men who believe they control the respect of no one, women who think there is nobody who cares—as soon as they stop eating, the community takes notice of them. A wife who might not respect her husband any more than she ever did, now calls the doctor and asks, "What's wrong?" She then demonstrates her concern with attention and care. But even if she were to tell her husband, "Go ahead and starve yourself. I can't stop you!" the husband knows that society won't let her carry out her threat. For society refuses to tolerate deliberate starvation.

Ironically, the very fear of starvation which goads man to prevent hunger is also the powerful reinforcer which brings the anorexic patient to the brink of death. The behavioral approach to treatment is to let the patient experience that noneating fails to bring the responses (the caring, the concern, the sympathy) so drastically sought. As with any behavior that no longer is reinforced, there will then be extinction.

But even though such a regimen makes sense, society does not readily accept it as a means to control undesirable behavior. Fortunately, Arthur J. Bachrach and his coworkers documented a pure application of this principle [15]. Their work confirmed the predicted results and cured a patient who though thirty-seven years old and 5 foot 4 inches tall weighed only 47 pounds. These investigators rearranged the contingencies which normally follow starvation (not eating → care, sympathy . . .) and made a wide variety of reinforcers contingent upon eating. The course of treatment is summarized in Table 12-2.

At first the investigators observed the patient's current environment and determined which reinforcers might be available (antecedent observations). Then they structured a special environment for the patient which allowed them to establish contingencies between the desired behavior (eating) and reinforcers (changes prior to treatment). In addition, they formulated a treatment plan which successively strengthened the component behaviors of eating. Examination of the data shows that by introducing new situations and people the investigators made sure the behavior generalized to other stimuli.

Figure 12-1 shows the patient's progress in terms of weight gain from the beginning of treatment until discharge from the hospital. The graph, which is based on data presented by Bachrach et al., demonstrates the effectiveness of the treatment program. By concentrating on eating, the investigators were able to arrest the patient's weight loss and eventually reverse many of the physical effects resulting from the patient's self-enforced starvation.

Non-self-feeding

Occasionally a patient seeks to assure continued attention and sympathy by refusing to feed himself. Ward environments in which the patient is considered an invalid quickly lends itself to reinforcement of

Table 12-2

Procedures Used in Treating a Case of Anorexia*

1. *Antecedent Observations*
   a. Patient had attractive hospital room with flowers, pictures, pleasant view
   b. Visitors freely permitted—letters and gifts received
   c. Radio, records, phonograph, and TV provided and operated for patient—books and magazines brought and read to her
2. *Changes Made prior to Treatment*
   a. Patient moved to private room on another ward—plain and unattractive—no view of grounds
   b. No visitors allowed and ward personnel instructed to perform routine duties with minimum of comment
   c. Patient denied personal mail, use of radio, books, magazines, records, TV
3. *Treatment*

Phases and Behavior	*Consequences*
a. Movements associated with eating	
Lifted fork	
Lifted fork to obtain food	
Lifted fork, speared food, lifted food to mouth	
Lifted fork, speared food, lifted food to mouth, and chewed	Pleasant talk from experimenter
Lifted fork, speared food, lifted food to mouth, and chewed and swallowed	
b. Amount of food consumed	
Any amount	Radio, TV, phonograph
Incremental increase in amount	Radio, TV, phonograph, mail, visitors, hair-care
c. Generalization	
Eating specified amount of food and showing weight gain	Could eat with other patients in solarium and outside the hospital, had choice of menu, walk on grounds, visit with family and friends
d. Plateau occuring at 63 pounds	
Patient believed to be vomiting meals in sink	
Weight gain as well as eating required	Access to all reinforcers

* From work of Bachrach et al.

this behavior. Traditionally, nurses have been expected to spoon-feed such patients. Refusals of this kind are not to be confused with anorexia where the patient will not eat at all or only very little. The non-self-feeder says he is hungry but that he is too feeble or shakes too much or is too uncoordinated to be able to feed himself.

For such cases, Ayllon and Michael developed a technique using a negative reinforcer. Their subjects were two women who had been observed to be fastidious concerning the neatness and appearance of their clothing. They had also apparently completely adjusted to being spoon-

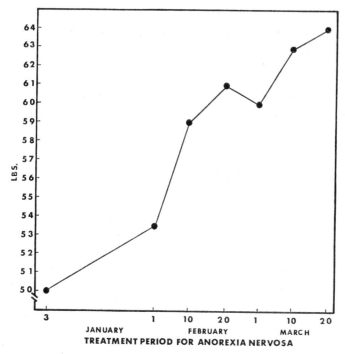

Fig. 12-1. Weight change of an anorexic patient reinforced for eating. (*From data by A. J. Bachrach et al.*)

fed. Treatment for one of the women began with the following instructions to the nurses.

> Continue spoonfeeding the patient; but from now on, do it in such a careless way that the patient will have a few drops of food fall on her dress. Be sure not to overdo the food dropping, since what we want to convey to the patient is that it is difficult to spoonfeed a grown-up person and not that we are mean to her. What we expect is that the patient will find it difficult to depend on your skill to feed her. You will still be feeding her, but you will simply be less efficient in doing a good job of it. As the patient likes having her clothes clean, she will have to choose between feeding herself and keeping her clothes clean, or being fed by others and risking getting her clothes soiled. Whenever she eats on her own, be sure to stay with her for a while (three minutes is enough), talking to her or simply being seated with her. We do this to reinforce her eating on her own. In the experience of the patient, people become nicer when she eats on her own [16].

In other words, the spilled food was a negative reinforcer which could be eliminated by one response: holding the spoon and feeding oneself.

The method resulted in the discharge of both patients since hospital admission had been based on former undesirable eating behavior.

Significantly, the negative reinforcer was effective for these patients. Other patients might not find this same event aversive. To establish what stimulus will serve as a negative reinforcer, it is only necessary to test what behavior a patient will emit in order to escape or avoid experience with that stimulus.

Summary

Not every possible eating problem that occurs has been described, but the preceding examples and procedures show the general attitude toward such problems and also the general direction in dealing with them through behavioral means. The way in which a person eats, or that he eats too much or not enough, greatly concerns members of our society. Because of this, it is easy for the mental patient to use unusual eating habits to show his peers that there is something wrong with him. The tragedy of our society is that this signaling by the patient gets reinforced and thus, when the problem which caused such signaling may no longer be there, a new problem has been established.

The behavioral approach takes eating for what it is—a behavior. If eating behaviors signal some other environmental condition under which the patient does not get properly reinforced, a thorough behavioral analysis will discover this. In the meantime, however, the unusual eating patterns should not themselves be reinforced and thereby made into a problem. If they have already been made into a problem and the original difficulty which caused the patient to use this handy signaling device is already remedied, then the establishment of normal eating behaviors will consitute the whole cure (as it did in the case of Ayllon's two non-self-feeders).

EXERCISES, CHAPTER 12

1. Construct a treatment program for an overweight patient which aims at teaching the caloric content of various foods. When formulating the plan keep the following questions in mind. How can I be sure that the patient knows the caloric content of foods? How can I arrange the patient's environment so this knowledge will be applied?

2. Make a set of systematic observations on someone's eating behavior by enumerating the different behaviors emitted by your subject. If possible, your subject should be a patient; however, observations can be made in restaurants, college cafeterias, or even the dining room of your own home. Select the highest-frequency behavior emitted. Give a value to each of the behaviors observed and construct a plan for changing the highest-frequency undesirable behavior.

3. Dianne, a chronic schizophrenic, eats rapidly. On several occasions the speed of eating has resulted in severe attacks of indigestion. Your ward physician wants you to arrange a program which will slow Dianne's eating pace. Prepare a program which accomplishes this result.

4. Describe the relationship between refusal to eat and the control it normally exerts on behavior of others. Why is it cruel to allow this tactic to control us?

5. Carl is a very regressed patient who has been hospitalized for fifteen years. He does not like to eat the kind of foods necessary to maintain good health. At mealtimes he barely touches his meat and vegetables but immediately consumes his milk and dessert. Describe a procedure to reinstate eating. The ward physician has indicated that it is crucial that Carl start eating a balanced diet. Formulate a plan using positive reinforcers which might induce Carl to eat a balanced diet.

6. Describe two examples in which behavior is controlled through usage of aversive stimuli or ultimate aversive consequences. Use examples which contain these elements from real life.

7. One method of controlling eating behavior is to arrange the environment so that the ultimate aversive consequences for eating occur in close proximity to eating behavior. This chapter gave one example of how this was accomplished. Name three other ways that dieters can arrange their environment using this method.

8. In conditioning experiments with lower organisms a time-out from reinforcement often occurs when the animal makes an error. The time period representing time-out is normally very short (five seconds). How can this procedure be used to reinstate acceptable table manners?

13

Retardates, Psychotic Children, and Geriatric Patients

Your study of this chapter should help you answer the following questions:

1. What are some of the ways behavioral techniques can be used to help the mentally retarded?
2. How can a behavioral approach be used to treat the psychotic child?
3. How does behavioral therapy affect geriatric patients?

The terms listed below are introduced and defined in this chapter:

light box
labeling
geriatric

TREATING THE MENTALLY RETARDED

The retarded, the psychotic child, and the geriatric patient are vastly different from the adult chronic schizophrenic in factors such as mental age, physiological makeup, apparent capabilities, and expectations. Yet the behavioral therapist does not allow these factors to alter significantly his attitude toward the patient. The patient is, above all, an individual who presents problems in behavior. He either does or does not do something that others believe he should or should not do. It is the therapist's task to formulate a treatment plan which helps to change the patient's behavior to a desired way. The fact that the patient represents a particular diagnostic category does not change the therapist's basic procedure. He identifies the problem, looks for reinforcers, and formulates a schedule.

According to wide belief, the prognosis for the mentally retarded is generally pessimistic. This lack of hope is typified in A. F. Tredgold's "Mental Deficiency" [17], a classical work in the field of mental retardation, which expresses the view that retardates are almost beyond clinical aid. Except for borderline cases, expectation of significant improvement following traditional procedures is ordinarily minimal.

However, reports covering behavioral therapy with retardates do not substantiate this view. In fact, they permit a positive attitude. Most generally the behavioral approach to treating retardates is based on the same principles of behavior as those used with schizophrenics and applies the same variety of techniques as those described in this text. The areas of application, however, and sometimes the emphasis are considerably different. With adult schizophrenics a great part of treatment lies in extinguishing undesirable behaviors and reinstating desirable ones. With retardates, the entire program is almost always a matter of developing new behaviors, many of which are incompatible with those already existing.

Considerable emphasis is placed on educating retardates to read, write, and do arithmetic. These are important skills which the retarded needs if he is to function at all normally in a community outside the hospital. For the same reason, emphasis is placed on the development of such self-care skills as dressing and toileting, skills which enhance the social acceptability of all human beings. With the profoundly retarded—those individuals whose IQ cannot be established—the obvious emphasis has been to condition simple responses before working on complex responses. For example, a child would be taught to hold a spoon before being taught to eat with such a utensil.

Most modern hospitals treating the retarded have some kind of education program. The main difference between traditional programs and those structured along behavioral lines is that the latter systematically maintain reinforcement contingencies between student behaviors and functioning reinforcers. The former demand little or nothing in the way of performance on the part of the patient.

The program at Rainier Hospital, Buckley, Washington, is an example of how behavioral procedures are used in an educational setting in a mental institution [18]. The children in this program know that they can earn marks during class. A mark is simply a line drawn on a piece of graph paper; it functions as a conditioned reinforcer. If, in the course of a single class session, a child has a full page of marks, his achievement can be traded for trinkets, candy, or toys.

The behaviors desired of each child are programmed individually, and only a small increment of learning is expected from step to step. For example, when working on spelling a child matches letters to a model. The teacher presents a word on a card and the child is expected to move printed letters on the cards on his desk until he thinks he has matched the letters in the model. Upon completion of his task, he raises his hand and the teacher inspects his work. At that time she delivers reinforcers (marks) if the work warrants it. If not, the student continues moving the letters until he is satisfied he has the correct spelling.

After each satisfactory completion a new model word is presented and the child continues manipulating the letters in front of him. The steps the child is asked to take recognize that spelling is largely a matching task and they are designed to provide him with practice in this skill.

The writing program at Rainier is another example of how behavioral techniques are used in educating retardates. In the first phases of this program [19] the child is asked to trace a letter. To make the work easier, the child's paper, with a model underneath, is placed on a light box. (A *light box* is simply a glass face-plate serving as one side of a box which contains a low-watt electric bulb. The light shining through the two pieces of paper makes the model quite distinct. The same effect can be attained by holding two pieces of paper up to a window glass.) As the child traces what he sees, he develops the motor skills needed for writing.

Once he becomes proficient in tracing, he is asked to trace and copy. In this step he first traces a letter using the light box. Then the light is turned off and he is asked to make the same letter only from what he sees or from memory.

From tracing and copying the child moves to straight copying of a model letter and then to writing the letter just from memory. At first the child is given only single letters to trace or copy. After these become part of his repertoire he goes on to combinations of letters, then short words, longer words, combinations of a few words that may or may not make a sentence, and finally sentences.

Reading comprehension is also part of the program at Rainier. After reading a sentence aloud, such as "The cat walked three steps and then meowed," the child is expected to duplicate the cat's action. If he can, his comprehension of what he read is assumed. Children are also given simple instructions to read and appropriate objects to demonstrate comprehension. For example, suppose the instructions read, "Place two red cars and three toy lemons in box 6." If he can perform these responses without help, the teacher assumes that he has comprehended what he read and reinforces his success.

In addition to using behavioral techniques for teaching skills that are part of the curriculum of all normal grade school classrooms, retardates are helped to greater social acceptability. For example, a child who can dress himself and remain reasonably clean through a day is more easily integrated into a community setting outside the hospital than one who cannot perform such simple self-help tasks.

The Mimosa [20] program, described in a report from Parsons

(Kansas) State Hospital, includes details concerning their work with personal help skills.

The residents in this program were on a token economy and earned tokens with reference to the following desired terminal behaviors.

Grooming and self-care:	Combing hair, brushing teeth, bathing, using deodorant, polishing shoes, getting clothes out for next day, taking care of clothes
Work assignments:	Cottage cleaning, cleaning bins and drawers, putting laundry away
Deportment:	Using "please" and "thank you," playing radio and TV quietly, sitting appropriately and eating neatly, speaking quietly on telephone
Cooperation:	Helping others with dressing, following directions willingly, sewing, writing letters for others
Volunteering:	For demonstrations, for running errands, for taking younger children to assignments, for putting away sewing, games
Special activities:	Playing games, ironing, sewing, speech and music programs, research activities

In turn, behaviors such as the following had to be paid for.

Negligent in self-care:	Dirty or torn clothing, unmade bed, poor grooming, messy bins and dresser drawers
Rowdiness:	Running, throwing objects, fighting or unreasonable arguing, yelling, teasing
Disrespect:	Addressing adults inappropriately, not minding, lying, stealing, refusing to work
Inappropriate behavior:	Sitting on floor with legs sprawled, sitting on sidewalks, lying on furniture other than beds, hanging on to nursing personnel, changing clothes other than privately
Breaking rules:	Going inside forbidden areas, leaving without permission, not putting away materials

As in any token economy the residents in the Mimosa experiment pay for all privileges as well as the necessities of ward life. The following are typical of the privileges that required varying amount of payment.

Cottage activities:	Phone calls, parties, home movies, watching TV, private talks with adults, record player, use of crayons and scissors, walking to meals unescorted
Regularly scheduled hospital activities:	Movies, canteen visits, swimming, dances, sports activities (other than required). . . .
Special hospital activities:	Working at another cottage, walks on grounds, assisting in class, field trips, beauty shop, holiday parties. . . .

Obviously a careful study of reinforcers within the hospital environment had been made by the nursing staff, for highly individual stimuli are listed such as "use of crayons," "walking to meals unescorted," and "private talks with adults."

Not all retardates have the same capabilities any more than schizophrenics. Nursing personnel working with profoundly retarded patients often face what at first seem insurmountable problems. However, an experiment conducted by P. R. Fuller [21] points out that even the most regressed human being is capable of some degree of learning. His patient was an eighteen-year-old male whose repertoire was extremely restricted. He spent his days and nights lying on his back since he could not roll over by himself. Attendants reported that he did not move his trunk or legs, and they could not recall any instances of his speaking. He could, however, open his mouth, blink his eyes, and move his arms, head, and shoulders. Because he had been in this condition his entire life, it was assumed by those who cared for him that he was incapable of learning.

Fuller undertook to determine whether a vegetative human organism such as this young man was amenable to conditioning procedures. For a reinforcer he selected a warm sugar-milk solution and arranged to deliver drops into the patient's mouth through a large syringe. The response he sought was "raising the right arm until it was in a vertical plane." Reinforcement was delivered only when the patient emitted this single behavior.

By the end of four sessions the patient was raising his arm at the rate of three responses per minute without any accompanying shoulder or head movements. Thus the strict reinforcement contingency had resulted in response differentiation. Fuller states that additional responses might have been developed had the project continued. In any event, his work demonstrates the power of operant techniques in reaching human beings exhibiting mostly vegetative qualities of life. While the responses developed were fairly simple, they represented a substantial therapeutic gain for this particular patient. In this case the power of behavioral technique stemmed from its ability to modify behavior in the complete absence of a means of communicating instructions of any kind to the patient. The only information present was the relationship between a discrete response and the delivery of reinforcement.

Not all profoundly retarded are as incapable of helping themselves as was the patient Fuller chose for his experiment. Yet in many hospitals nursing personnel spend an inordinate amount of time simply dressing, undressing, feeding, and toileting their charges. T. S. Ball working at Pacific State Hospital (Pomona, California) developed a behavioral program aimed at teaching self-help skills to retarded children.

Chaining was one of the procedures used in the instruction program. That is, each response in the sequence served as a discriminative stimulus for the next response. The procedure is like that employed in learning a poem by heart. The word "Mary" is at once a response and a control stimulus. It evokes the response "had" which in turn is a control stimulus for the response "a" which controls "little," and so on.

Undressing is more easily done than dressing and so, in Ball's experiment, children were taught to remove clothing in an orderly fashion before they were taught to put clothes on. In describing the steps in teaching undressing skills, Ball wrote as follows.

> A good garment to begin with is a somewhat oversized T-shirt. You start with the shirt almost off except for one arm, so that it is more or less dangling from one shoulder and arm. Tell the child, "Take your shirt off, Billy." If necessary, pull slightly at the shirt yourself. If he starts to pull the shirt off, even if he does not succeed in getting it all the way off for the first time, say "Good boy, Billy" and give him his reward. If he does not seem to respond or understand, wait a few seconds and if he starts to shake it off, immediately say, "Take your shirt off, Billy" and reward him as it comes off [22].

During the initial stage of this kind of training, the criteria for achievement should be kept very simple and the environment should be structured to maximize the probability of reinforcement. In Billy's case, all he had to do at first to get the shirt off, and thereby receive reinforcement, was to wiggle or drop his arm.

Chaining formed the basis for the follow-up steps, too. Ball explained this as follows.

> After he has mastered the first step, the task is made more difficult by putting the shirt further on the child. Then through successive steps, you work back to the point at which he will completely remove the shirt solely in response to the verbal command. However, the task should not be considered mastered until you can say to the child no matter where he may be in the building, in or out of sight, "Billy, pull off your shirt," and he will comply with request [22].

Under Ball's program, retarded children were taught to pay attention, to come when called, and not only to undress themselves but also to dress and toilet themselves. Initially reinforcement was given for successful achievement at each step of each behavior but eventually only for completion of the entire sequence of behaviors leading to total dressing, undressing, or toileting.

Retardates often host a multiplicity of problems, and people then excuse their behavior by saying "It's no wonder the poor things don't know how to behave just look at all that's wrong with them!" The behaviorist confronted with such evidence asks, "What environmental factors are causing the patient to behave as he does?"

Wolf, Birnbrauer, Williams, and Lawler [23] worked with a patient with whom "much was wrong." She was a nine-year-old retardate with cerebral palsy, aphasia, hyperirritability, and brain damage. Approximately seven months after admission to the hospital she began to vomit during class. Within three months this behavior became an everyday occurrence and she was no longer required to attend school. Several modes of treatment were attempted without success until a behaviorally oriented instructor volunteered to work with her. He thought that vomiting was an operant response reinforced by gaining escape from the classroom situation. The girl was returned to the classroom, and her teacher was asked not to send the patient back to the dormitory when she vomited but to ignore the behavior and offer reinforcement for schoolroom behaviors in the form of candies and praise. Over the semester this procedure resulted in the extinction of vomiting.

Severely retarded patients frequently engage in acts of self-destruction. Head-banging, eating harmful articles (clothing, pins, dishes), biting and scratching one's own body, are all familiar to those who have cared for retardates. Traditional methods of treating these behaviors have usually involved construction of devices which do nothing more than prevent physical damage or make emission of the behavior impossible. Headgear is locked on a head-banger; other forms of mutilation are prevented by placing the patient in full restraint.

Psychiatric treatment has often stressed the importance of affection and understanding. Therefore, nursing personnel are instructed to provide additional amounts of tender loving care whenever a patient engages in self-destructive behaviors. The behavioral approach involves a careful examination of the patient's environment in order to determine what consequences are attendant on the patient's behavior. Sometimes the solution is simply the withdrawal of reinforcement.

Nathan Miron, a psychologist at Sonoma (Cailfornia) State Hospital, tells about working with a young boy who engaged in head-hitting as much as forty blows per minute. Miron observed that the behavior occurred only in the presence of an audience. This led him to conclude that the attention the child received from nursing personnel and his mother functioned as a strong reinforcer. Not too surprisingly, the person who had the greatest control was the mother as evidenced by the fact that in her presence the behavior was emitted at its highest frequency.

The treatment plan was to place head-banging on an extinction schedule by not giving attention when episodes occurred. This took considerable restraint on the part of everyone concerned, especially the mother. At one point she had to be forcibly inhibited from going to her son's aid. However, the extinction schedule succeeded, for within a few days the patient no longer hit himself.

Analysis of behavioral experiments of this kind not only contributes to an understanding of bizarre behavior but also shows how compassion and mother love can be destructive when made contingent on the wrong behaviors. Had the child's mother not been restrained, her son might still be mutilating himself with this deviant form he had found to control his environment. Indeed, it took much greater compassion to stand back and allow the behavior to run its inevitable course during extinction than to comfort him.

Psychotic Children

As behavioral techniques become more widely utilized, it is increasingly apparent that the type of mental illness diagnosed in no way prevents or restricts their use. Acceptance of this fact has meant that children whose behavioral difficulties result in a psychiatric diagnosis and hospitalization are now benefiting from behavioral therapy. Psychotic children characteristically have a high frequency of self-destructive and self-stimulatory behaviors which often interfere with treatment. Therefore these behaviors must be eliminated before substantial change to desirable behavior can be effected.

One method which has been explored by Ivar Lovaas at the Neuropsychiatric Institute of the University of California at Los Angeles is the integration of punishment (delivery of a negative reinforcer) into the therapeutic setting. Even though it is well known that punishment does not extinguish but only suppresses behaviors, it is used because the presence of high-frequency undesirable behaviors may leave the therapist no behaviors which he can reinforce. If the child initiates a burst of self-destruction during training, the behaviorist has no choice but to suppress these acts for the child's protection and so that more desirable behaviors can be strengthened.

The use of noxious stimuli also provides the therapist with an opportunity to establish verbal cues as control stimuli. By pairing words such as "no" and "stop" with the delivery of punishment, in time the original punisher can be faded from the therapeutic environment and words alone will serve as controls. Naturally, any course of treatment for psychotic children must emphasize the development of behaviors which are incompatible with undesirable forms of responding. If a child engages in self-stimulatory behavior he must be brought to attend to other stimuli in his environment which will interfere with this "autistic" activity. If the child is severely withdrawn, the power of external stimuli must be enhanced so that interacting with the environment becomes reinforcing.

Like retardates, severely disturbed children are characterized by an impoverished repertoire of desirable behaviors. Many fail to speak; others do not interact with their peers and fail to learn by imitating; for some, affection is not a functioning reinforcer; a few are unable to pretend. This latter problem was one of those brought to Ivar Lovaas. The patient was a boy who had advanced far enough to attend the day school at the clinic. Our observation of the child and subsequent discussion with staff members brought out the following facts.

The child did not seem to enjoy going to school and rarely talked or played with other students. At recess he would withdraw and thus avoid contact with everyone. The staff discovered that part of the problem was his inability to pretend. Obviously this made it impossible for him to participate in many of the games the other children played.

His treatment program included teaching him this ability. During his daily training sessions in verbal behavior, the therapist would periodically take time out to play baseball with the boy. Their game was unique in that no equipment or regular playing field was used. Rather, each participant would pretend that a bat had been swung, a ball thrown, or a ball caught. In addition, objects in the room were used to symbolize the bases.

At first the boy was mechanically taught the responses necessary to play baseball. If he was on defense, the therapist took him through the motions of throwing the ball to the therapist who then swung an imaginary bat. The boy was also taught the various consequences of the events in baseball. If the therapist said "Bang!" this meant the child was to act as if the ball had been hit. If the therapist was silent, the boy was expected after each pitch to act as if he had thrown a strike and to "catch" the imaginary ball that was returned to him.

Because of extensive prior language training, instructions could be integrated into the treatment program. The therapist constantly interacted with the child during the game using praise and interest as reinforcers. When the boy was the pitcher the therapist might ask, "What do you have in your hand?" Reply, "A ball." "Good. What do you do with the ball?" Reply, "Throw it." And the boy would follow his remark with a throwing motion.

"Good boy. Bang!! Look out—I've hit the ball. Run and get it before I make it around the bases!"

The child participated fully in the game and seemed to enjoy the change from his regular language lesson.

Mutism in psychotic children is another problem that has received the attention of Lovaas and the staff at the Neuropsychiatric Institute of the University of California at Los Angeles. The treatment program for this behavior is directed toward developing language patterns, not just reinstating them as is done with adult schizophrenics. (See Chapter 11.)

In the first steps of language training many psychotic children must be taught even the sounds of their language. Using primarily food as a reinforcer they are taught to imitate sounds presented by the therapist. Imitation plays a role throughout speech training because it gives the therapist a means for rapidly establishing new behaviors. For some speech sounds, prompts are used to maximize the probability of reinforcement. For example, in learning the sound $|m|$, the therapist holds the child's lips together and then makes the sound himself. As soon as the child responds correctly he is given a reinforcer. The prompt is faded as progress warrants by first leaving the hand close to the mouth and then gradually taking it farther and farther away until it is no longer needed.

Once the child has learned phonetic sounds they are combined. For example, the child may spend considerable time learning to utter $|p|$ and $|l|$ and then to combine them into $|pl|$. As soon as several combinations of sounds are learned, however, the child can usually be taught to say many words. Once some vocal behavior is established, the repertoire of social responses must be widened, which in turn will require—and thus strengthen and widen—the verbal repertoire. Just how this can be accomplished is suggested in a report by J. N. Hingtgen and F. C. Trost, Jr. [24] on the results of an experiment to determine whether or not vocal responses combined with physical contacts could be elicited from early-childhood schizophrenics. Their subjects were children who initiated no bodily contact with their peers and talked very little. During the thirty-minute morning sessions the children worked alone in a small room; in the afternoon sessions they were paired. At no time were they aware that they were under continuous observation through a one-way window. Tokens which could be used for candy and other food items served as reinforcers. The token and food vendors were in the room with the children.

The results of this study indicate that under controlled environments such children are capable of learning both physical and verbal behaviors calling for interaction. This learning was brought about by successive approximation of the desired behavior, not by instruction or admonition. No demonstrations or verbal instructions were given by the therapists during the shaping procedure.

Solely by imitation, of course, a child can also be taught to say many words whose meaning he may not know. One method for teaching meaning is called *labeling*. The therapist asks the child, "What is this?" If the child responds using the appropriate word (which he has earlier been asked to imitate), reinforcement is given. If the child gives an incorrect response, he does not get reinforced but he is asked the same question again.

Mealtime affords an excellent opportunity for this kind of training. The therapist asks the child to repeat the name of the various foods which comprise the meal. Then he might say, "What is this?" and give the child a sip of milk.

The patient's environment is made up of thousands of objects which provide stimuli which must come to control the verbal responses emitted by the child. Through painstaking hours of questions and answers these stimuli can acquire the power to control verbal behavior for the psychotic child just as they do for the normal child. In time the object elicits the name.

Obviously, labeling by itself is not sufficient to provide the child with a language. Concepts must also be taught. The child needs to learn the meaning of "I" and "you," "on top of" and "beside." Training procedures for this learning are similar to those described above. For example, the therapist might ask the child to "put a block on top of a box." When the therapist makes such a request he is first sure that the child is paying attention and then provides a model by performing the response himself. The child is reinforced for matching the therapist's behavior.

The psychotic mute child must also be trained to use his language ability at times other than during treatment sessions. Games provide an ideal method since they not only require communication but also teach the child how to play. For example, a therapist might say, "I spy something with my little eye." The child tries to guess what the therapist sees by asking, "Is it the bed? Is it the dresser?" When he guesses correctly he receives reinforcement. The situation is also reversed so that the child can ask the initial question and get the therapist to guess.

Training in language learning involves a multiplicity of questions. The patient is asked, "What do you do in the morning? What did you eat for breakfast? Who is Earl? Who is Pauline? Who sleeps in Mac's bed?" This procedure not only prompts the child to talk but also establishes questions as stimuli which control the emission of answers.

Lovaas' program is an extensive one. The children who come to the clinic at the University of California at Los Angeles' Neuropsychiatric Institute present a variety of behavioral problems. Methods must be devised which eliminate many undesirable behaviors and develop desirable ones and most of them have to be on an individual basis since every child and every problem is slightly different.

It may take thousands of reinforcements to bring a psychotic child to success in learning even a single word or any new behavior. However, once he acquires even a small repertoire of desired behaviors, learning each new one seems a bit easier. It is as if the patient not only learns to emit new behaviors but also learns to learn.

Geriatric Patients

Advanced age sometimes has behavioral accompaniments similar to those manifested by the mentally ill. Often elderly persons become less responsive to external environment and this lack of interaction is classified as withdrawal. Some old people sit and mutter to themselves; many have lapses of memory; still others act confused. These deviations from what is considered their "usual" behavior are often attributed to the aging process. Chronic psychotics who grow old in a mental institution, and persons admitted because of odd behavior ascribed to old age, are classified as *geriatric patients*.

In his paper "Geriatric Behavior Prosthetics" O. R. Lindsley [25] presents a number of thoughts regarding the role a behavioral approach can play in the treatment of the hospitalized aged. His emphasis is on structuring an environment to overcome behavioral deficits associated with old age. He points out that many devices have been developed which mitigate the debilitating effects of numerous diseases, yet little attention has been given to the design of special environments for geriatric patients. He notes that even modern supermarkets have doors which automatically open and shut as a shopper enters and leaves, yet few geriatric wards, if any, provide the same convenience. Rather, it would seem, the hospital environment is structured to increase total dependence, a factor already greatly enhanced by aging.

Lindsley draws attention to another aspect of old age—the apparent lack of "will to live" displayed by so many geriatrics. Although it may be true that aging causes breakdown in physical functioning, it may also be true that it is the typical hospital environment which contributes to destroying a desire to live. Once again, environment must be changed to overcome this characteristic of life for elderly people.

He indicates that the geriatric patient's typical inability to follow normal speech rates can be considerably alleviated. It simply requires that the speech rate of nursing personnel and all who interact with such patients be slowed down. He recommends that those providing entertainment media take cognizance of this fact and that TV programs, for example, could be presented in slow motion. Printed materials might be increased in size and the typeface made both darker and larger with plenty of contrasting white space to accommodate weakened eyes.

Our own experience suggests that geriatric patients can benefit by the establishment of contingencies between behavior and reinforcers. For example, smearing and eating feces was eliminated when reinforcement with candy was made contingent upon not emitting these behaviors. Lindsley agrees that reinforcement contingencies be established via a token system. Geriatric patients could be reinforced for the emission of self-care and social behaviors. Perhaps the results of following such procedures would counteract some of the undesirable behaviors of old people. Complementing such techniques with new prosthetic devices designed to overcome behavioral deficits could result in striking a spark which might ignite many a dwindling fire.

Jack Michael, a behavioral scientist active in clinical work, was called in by a large general hospital to advise them about a problem that existed with elderly patients. After prolonged bed rest the patients had recuperated but needed exercise to regain their strength. Like all major hospitals, this one had a department of physical therapy, and here these elderly gentleman were to do their exercises. But the problem was that patients sat around smoking cigars rather than doing knee bends and push-ups. Other psychologists called in to study the problem had concluded that the men lacked "motivation" and the "will to get better." Here again, of course, were the inner states of dualistic thinking.

The first thing that occurred to Michael, however, was that the physical therapists generally are attractive young women. He also noticed that a pretty therapist would sweetly light a patient's cigar and then try to cajole him into exercising. With another who was sitting in the sun and already smoking a lighted cigar, she would engage in banter designed to get him on his feet. As soon as a man complied with her suggestion that he exercise, the therapist abandoned him and would go to another patient who apparently needed similar urging to do what he was supposed to do.

Now, Michael, like all behaviorists, believes that behavior is governed by consequences. He saw that as a consequence of sitting and smoking a cigar, an old man would instantly attract the attention of a pretty young woman who would now fuss over him, but as a consequence of taking his exercise, the same old man would just as instantly lose the attention of this young woman. Michael paid no heed to what was actually said during all this. "Come, come, now, Mr. Smith. Time to do your push-ups. Think of how much that will do for your tummy-tum-tum!" What mattered was that sitting down had apparently desirable consequences (from the point of view, at any rate, of the patients), and that exercising had undesirable consequences. His recommendation, therefore, was simple: Instruct the physical therapists to disregard the elderly gentlemen completely while they are sitting and smoking. But let the slightest attempt on their part to get up and do some exercising be a signal for a nurse to fuss over them, exercise with them, joke with them, and in short, reward their "good" behavior. The results were spectacular. Within two days the attending physician had to advise the physical therapy department to slow down lest one of these patients succumb to a heart attack from overexertion!

There are many such examples of how behavioral techniques can be used to both treat and understand all kinds of behavior whether of persons young or old diagnosed mentally ill or mentally retarded, those suffering from old age, or simply any individuals acting in seemingly odd ways.

EXERCISES, CHAPTER 13

1. Select a simple self-care activity such as brushing teeth and describe its component behaviors.
2. You have been assigned the task of teaching a child to say the alphabet. How would you accomplish this task using the method of response chaining?
3. Prescribe a treatment plan for teaching a child to copy simple pictures.
4. Tommy is an autistic child who cannot tolerate close contact with other humans. How could you establish yourself as a conditioned reinforcer using negative reinforcement?
5. A geriatric patient on your ward is supposed to sun himself for at least fifteen minutes each day. The only way nursing personnel can be sure that he does this is to stand guard over him. He receives mail almost every day and has sufficient eyesight to read those letters himself. How can you get him to sun himself without a guard?
6. Behavior studies of Jimmy, a mongoloid child, provided the following data:

Response	Out of 45 observations
Eating	5
Sweeping porch	25
Watching TV	5
Talking	5
Playing games	1
Sleeping	4

Which of these activities is a likely reinforcer for Jimmy? How could its availability be made contingent upon low-frequency desirable behaviors?

14

The Leaving Patient

Your study of this chapter should help you answer the following questions:

1. When is a patient considered ready to leave a behavioral therapy program?
2. Why and how should the environment into which a patient is released be prepared?
3. What can be done to reduce the return rate of our mental patients?

The term listed below is introduced and defined in this chapter:

staffing

PREPARING THE PATIENT FOR DISCHARGE

It is a temptation to say that when a patient no longer emits the odd behaviors which brought him into the hospital he is ready to leave. If mental illness were like physical illness, this might be true. But if the concept of mental illness as such is a myth, the medical analogy breaks down completely. Readiness to leave a mental hospital and readiness to leave a general hospital simply cannot be compared.

In the first place, the mental patient may return to the very environment which, if it did not result in his so-called "illness," was at least present when his illness became evident. The patient whose broken leg has been set and knit together will not, of course, return to the same auto accident which caused his difficulty.

Next, the odd behavior which caused the patient to be admitted to a mental hospital may have been of such low frequency that even if society could permit an environmental stress situation into which a patient might be placed to test the extinction of this odd behavior, all possible environmental situations in which the behavior might be emitted cannot be foreseen. Bone fractures are low-frequency events, too, but it is easy to arrange for simple demonstrations that show that the damage has been remedied, and it is equally easy to prescribe the stresses that are to be avoided.

These problems stem, of course, from the dualistic way in which people are used to thinking of the mind and its workings. Yet they are problems which the patient will have to face when he leaves the hospital. They are problems for which he must be prepared, and this preparation must be part of any behavioral therapy program.

When a patient no longer emits the behaviors for which he was originally brought to the hospital, a fact which will be evident through a comparison of recent behavioral baselines with those obtained at admission, several steps can be taken. Some will test the patient's readiness to face the outside world; others will help ensure that the likelihood of the patient's return to the hospital is minimal. The procedures are essentially the same whether the patient is going on a home visit, indefinite leave, or is being prepared for final discharge.

The first step is to tell the patient formally that he is to be released. Typically the processing of patients who return to their homes takes less than a week. Release to rest homes, family care homes, and similar settings may take anywhere from six weeks to two months. This longer period occurs because of the financial arrangements which have to be made using public funds or private trust money. As soon as a patient is being considered for release, we tell him he is now in the "ready-to-leave group." This entitles him to a private room and various other privileges. They cost more, but the additional cost is kept within the range of what he can afford. The very fact that he can afford the better accommodations through his own effort is one of the criteria on the strength of which he is considered ready for discharge. We also tell the patient that barring unavoidable delays, he must leave the hospital within a prescribed period, in our case within two months. Most of our patients were chronic schizophrenics who had previously come close to discharge, but at that point they suddenly showed some or all their odd behaviors again. They were, it seemed, afraid to leave the sheltered and ordered, and indeed often comfortable, world of the hospital. In the behavioral program, a patient who reacts this way is transferred back to the orientation group.

Preparation for release always involves the social worker, and his work is of utmost importance. In sessions with the patient the social worker goes over the details of what can be expected once the patient is released. Together they review the plans made at the time the patient entered the hospital. Have circumstances arisen which require reconsidering the original plans? In the course of therapy it may have become evident that the patient's odd behavior was simply a way of escaping a situation which is unacceptable by any standards, although this **fact** may not be recognized until therapy is well under way. Sometimes neither the patient nor members of his family realize this either, and both parties eagerly look forward to the termination of hospitalization.

In one case we learned during the course of therapy that a patient had become negligent in her housework. When the husband came home evenings, he had to wait long periods for his meal. After dinner, other chores had to be done which should have been accomplished during the day. By the time she was ready to go to bed, her husband was already asleep. Soon she claimed somatic problems which forced her to stay in bed weekends. Her back hurt and she could not move. Repeated visits to doctors showed no organic trouble, but her odd behaviors began to become more pronounced. She would sit and stare for hours. She would go on walks and return without being able to state where she had been. She was unable to cook or keep the house clean. Finally she professed to hear voices. This brought her to the hospital. Her husband readily gave consent to behavioral therapy for her, and she swiftly improved. He visited her at least once a week and wrote extensive letters to nurses and psychiatrists with whom his wife was in contact. To test the theory that sexual incompatibility might have brought on her odd behaviors (since divorce for this couple was unthinkable due to their religious conviction), the patient was granted a weekend visit at the request of her husband. They went to a nearby motel from where she came running back to the hospital within eight hours.

At that time the husband was questioned in detail concerning what had happened. It became evident that without being prudish, both husband and wife were simply incredibly naïve about sexual practices. The patient was given informative literature as part of her treatment program, and the husband was told how intercourse might be arranged in a less abrupt fashion and without severe pain to his wife. Yet a second off-grounds visit four weeks later ended the same way.

In a follow-up staff meeting it was decided that the patient should be counseled not to return to her husband. When this possibility was mentioned to the patient, her odd behaviors disappeared completely. She readily agreed to being placed in a family care home. Obviously this arrangement could not have been decided upon at the time of her admission.

Perhaps the most important event during the ready-to-leave period is *staffing,* the appearance of the patient before the staff. The members of this group may be all who had contact with the patient, but most typically only the unit psychiatrist, the charge nurse, and the social worker will attend. During staffing the patient is questioned concerning the realism of his plans. Attempts are made to test the strength of his newly established behaviors. For example, patients who formerly hallucinated are questioned concerning their hallucinations. A delusional patient is asked about his delusions. If, on the basis of this meeting, the patient is deemed ready to leave, all token contingencies which are still in existence are removed. There is considerable leeway in this, however. The patient may simply be given tokens in the morning to pay for the privileges and necessities which require daily payment. Or he may not be given tokens nor asked to pay any. The purpose of this regimen is to see how well he can function when all contingencies for obtaining artificial reinforcers have been removed.

The transition is not necessarily a rapid one. Many phases of the treatment plan, however, will have been organized in such a way that there was gradual removal of artificial reinforcers (such as tokens) when the behavior in question allowed natural reinforcers to take over. For example, grooming can at first be strengthened through the use of tokens, but when once established it brings its own natural reinforcers such as public approval and social acceptance.

During preparation for release, as extensive contact as possible with outside life should be arranged. In addition to shopping in town (where the patient should be encouraged to buy judiciously and without supervision), assignments may be given which force other interaction with the public. He may be sent to the bus depot to obtain up-to-date schedules of buses which leave for a certain town. Or he may be asked to go to the post office and inquire about the cost of sending packages abroad. Sometimes it is possible to make arrangements with a store directly but discreetly to observe patients while they make purchases. From such reports, provided they are made by competent observers, it is possible to judge how well the patient performs when he believes himself unobserved.

Even though they leave the hospital, many patients remain on some form of drug therapy. Therefore, during the last few weeks in the program, special effort should be made to see that the patient continues to take whatever drugs have been prescribed. In a well-organized behavioral program the fear of drugs, which many patients have initially, has been extinguished. One technique for accomplishing this is to reinforce patients for sitting around a table without talking, hands under the table, and with the drug in their mouths. Normal salivation and swallowing assures that the pill dissolves and is swallowed. A prolonged regimen of this sort with patients who are suspected of discarding their drugs assures that the medication is given a chance to show its beneficial effects. The patient is subsequently reinforced by his improved behavior. In addition, taking the drug makes it lose its superstitious aversive attributes.

At this time the development of tranquilizing drugs promises agents which need be taken but once a month. This should greatly diminish the problems which can arise if a patient does not continue to take prescribed medication. Presently, however, the daily drug regimen still in use requires that the patient is not only willing to take his drugs, but that he remembers to do so. Most drugs for aftercare are b.i.d. (to be taken twice daily) and can easily be tied behaviorally to breakfast and the evening meal.

As soon as a patient enters the ready-to-leave-group, he is given his drug supply a week at a time with instructions to take the prescribed amount immediately after breakfast and after dinner. During the first week of this procedure he may still need to be supervised, but gradually supervision can be relaxed and following staffing only occasional checks should prove necessary. If the patient fails to take over for himself, there is reason to suspect that he is not ready for release.

During this period of preparation much of the conversation between nurse and patient should take the character of questions like, "What would you do if . . . ?" as a way of describing practical situations which may create problems for the patient. The idea is to guide the patient's thinking so that he can learn to cope with potentially troublesome situations. In fact, all discussion with the patient concerning the future should be as realistic as possible. It should be pointed out, for example, that relatives or friends who are quite amenable in the course of a once-a-week or a once-a-month visit may not, and indeed cannot, be as amenable continuously.

There is probably no better way to teach patients to interpret their own acts in behavioral terms than to have them help with the therapy programs of other patients. The involvement of patients in the ready-to-leave group with behavioral techniques is, of course, in itself a therapeutic step and therefore must be carefully weighed. Only tasks which the patient can handle without any doubt should be selected for him. Supervising patients on the drug table, for example, is a task that can be entrusted to a departing patient. Running the canteen; keeping book on various token transactions; and perhaps working with individual ward mates who are on special reinforcement schedules for speaking clearly, reading certain materials, or remaining quiet for specified periods are other tasks ready-to-leave patients can handle satisfactorily.

If the patient upon his release is expected to perform a given job, now is the time to offer him, if at all possible, additional training and thus confidence in his professional skills. Since verbal admonitions have little control over future behavior, it is not enough to simply give advice on how to avoid situations which may provoke undesirable behavior. Instead, potential trouble spots should be acted out. A forty-three-year-old female told us, for example, that her mother continually treated her as if she still were a little child. She could usually tolerate this for an hour or so but by then so much resentment would build up that she would talk back to her mother impolitely. We showed the patient how her mother's verbal output controlled her behavior in a way that was detrimental to both of them. We then acted out situations in which one of us played the part of the mother and the patient practiced quietly correcting us without getting upset. After several weeks of nearly daily practice, the mother told us (after a visit) that her daughter was finally growing up! The mother's own verbal behavior toward the daughter changed, too, now that her condescension was no longer reinforced.

Another patient had a most annoying habit of cracking his knuckles. He said that his hands did not feel comfortable unless he did this. Agreeing with him, we told him to crack his knuckles as frequently as he felt the need, but to do it in the toilet room or somewhere that nobody would see or hear him. A baseline on his behavior showed that the rate of knuckle cracking went down sharply when he followed this instruction.

This patient had shown great interest in behavioral science. After a few days he stated that he believed that this particular behavior of his must have been under audience control, because now that he refrained from doing it in public, he felt little need to indulge in the behavior at all. On his own, he then began a study to explore what kind of people would respond most to knuckle cracking. His conclusion was that people whom he intuitively didn't like responded most strongly (largely silently but visibly) against his behavior. He volunteered that instead of cracking knuckles in the presence of such people—a behavior that would reflect on *him*—it would be easier and socially more acceptable to leave situations where there were people he disliked. Or he might merely tell people to go away if doing so was appropriate. For this patient, the knowledge that it was not some mystical compulsion or deficiency of his mind which caused knuckle cracking but rather a clearly definable aspect of the environment was the sort of self-control for which every patient should be prepared.

Not all patients can, of course, be expected to show this kind of understanding. With a majority, it is the firm implanting of self-sustaining reinforcement contingencies which must be relied upon. Combined with proper arrangements for the physical environment into which patients are sent, these measures should be adequate to assure most patients' adjustment to life outside the hospital.

Preparation of chronic patients for release sometimes involves special considerations. With chronic patients the behavioral therapist should be on the lookout for behaviors acquired during many years of hospitalization which are inconspicuous in the hospital environment but which cause great alarm in a family setting. Early in our experience a patient was discharged who had a long history of hospitalization under the label "suicidal." This patient was never allowed to close the toilet door for privacy. As is not uncommon, this trivial environmental variable had become a control stimulus for normal elimination. Naturally, the patient's continuance of this habit caused consternation in the family. He was actually returned to the hospital for his "crazy" behavior. This deplorable sequence of events could have easily been avoided had we been more alert and conditioned him to defecate with doors closed, a task we accomplished quite easily upon the patient's return.

With chronic patients it is also well to be prepared for surprises during their preparation for release. The traditional hospital setting, in contrast to one that practices behavioral therapy, is such that once one has given up the idea of personal freedom, life inside the hospital can be more attractive than existence outside the hospital. The hospital provides daily subsistence, a comfortable bed, maid service, a broad range of entertainment complete with daily motion pictures, dances, lectures, and social events as well as recreational therapy such as piano, drafting, drawing, painting, and tap-dancing lessons. In the traditional setting the chronic patient faces a choice which by any reasonable standard can be made in only one way—to stay in the hospital. Such a patient has forgotten the joys of freedom, the pride of human dignity. All he sees is having to struggle for a livelihood outside the hospital or enjoying a life of comfortable retirement inside.

How can he manage to stay? Simply by acting as he did when coming to the hospital. Indeed, at least one instance is known to us where a patient knowingly used a mental hospital to provide room and board during the week while she enjoyed weekends with her husband traveling about the countryside. In a behavioral program the choice is different. It is between a normal life on the outside or the deliberate deprivations of life in an underprivileged hospital population.

PREPARING THE PATIENT'S IMMEDIATE ENVIRONMENT

If a patient is to be discharged to his family, it is mandatory that the family be informed in detail about the treatment plan which succeeded with the patient, and the rudiments of behavioral science in general. This is not always up to nursing personnel, but they can suggest reading matter such as F. S. Keller's excellent booklet *Reinforcement,* or three of B. F. Skinner's books—*Science and Human Behavior, Cumulative Record,* and the best seller *Walden Two.* A Unitarian minister and his wife claimed that reading Murray Sidman's *Tactics of Scientific Research* changed their lives and removed all difficulties they had had in dealing with their adolescent son who had been in our behavioral program. Sidman's book is not easy reading but lends itself as a basis for discussion among educated persons.

Ogden Lindsley of the University of Kansas recommends that in contacting the family it is the father with whom the therapist should work. He feels that once the father understands what is involved, information will filter down to other members of the family. Lindsley points out, however, that it is the mother who will have to do most of the work in selectively reinforcing and generally maintaining schedules, especially for retarded children who are returned to their homes.

If at all possible, the family should be referred to a behavioral therapist in private practice. Once contingency rules and contingencies have been explained, the family recognizes readily enough their own need for further advice. It is no novel idea in psychotherapy that those closest to a patient are often more in need of help than the patient himself. Still, with the mystique that surrounds traditional psychoanalysis, it is difficult to bring relatives to seek such help. With less difficult to understand behavioral techniques this problem is diminished.

Above all, in talking with the family, nursing personnel should make a strong plea for tolerance. Since in our culture everybody is for tolerance, until some specific behavior is involved, this will not be easy. Specific instances of behavior in which the patient may indulge should be cited. A mother, for example, after having agreed that she would be very tolerant, was asked what she would do if she suspected her twenty-year-old son of masturbating when in the bathroom. With great indignation she assured us that she would check on him regularly and that if she caught him "at that" she would immediately return him to the hospital. With the help of clergymen and public figures whom she respected, we succeeded in convincing her that she was neither violating religious dictates nor impairing her son's health by not monitoring his bathroom activities. We believe, too, that she finally understood it was her excessive censorship of her son's behavior which had greatly contributed to his difficulties.

In another case we persuaded parents to consent to letting their daughter use cosmetics. They were at first convinced that doing so would encourage promiscuity and that the better way was for parents to watch a (twenty-four-year-old) "girl." When the consequences of this kind of supervision were discussed, and when the parents were asked to view the situation from the daughter's viewpoint, they realized the unrealistic quality of their stand.

In cases where it is patently evident that the family is too bigoted, ignorant, selfish, and unsuited for healthy living with the patient, every attempt should be made to prevent a release to such a family. Family care facilities are available for most patients, rest homes may be suited for the elderly, and special boarding schools are indicated for children.

In California, state requirements for conducting a family care facility are sufficiently high that explanation about behavioral therapy and behavioral treatment is generally understood and well accepted by those in charge. Directors of family care homes should habitually be invited to the program from which patients come. The social worker who is in touch with these people can make the necessary arrangements and should also conduct the explanatory visits. Some family care directors with whom we talked were quite surprised to learn that we disagreed with their reassuring statement that "they understood that the patient was still an invalid and needed regular nursing like any recuperating patient." In some cases we succeeded in getting them to carry on the schedules of particular patients. In all cases the distribution of informative literature helped greatly.

When selecting a family care facility or releasing a patient to his family, the wishes and harmless idiosyncracies of the patient should be taken into account. It makes little sense to place a young man in a home that has as its only other boarders three old women. On the other hand, we have had good experiences with placing a young woman with several elderly women. The social worker must exercise his best judgment in matters of this kind. If he takes the patient on a visit to the family care facility under consideration, much can be discussed concretely that could be communicated only abstractly and with difficulty without such a visit.

Educating the Public

Aside from the immediate environment of a released patient, there is the general community and its beliefs and practices, all of which interact with him continuously. The attitude of the general public toward mental illness has come a long way from the time when lunatics were feared as mad dogs and locked in chains. But the myth of mental illness, through which this humanitarian step forward came about, is proving now to be as much an obstacle as it was once a help. It will not be possible to overcome this attitude easily since it is, like our entire culture, based on dualistic concepts which are taken as real today much as man in medieval times accepted as fact the flatness of the world. Here is an example of what can happen.

A young man in our program was returned to the hospital by the sheriff. He had stolen hubcaps. When we asked the patient about the chain of events it became evident that he knew exactly what he was doing. When apprehended he was at first interrogated by detectives. During this session he sat quietly grimacing and grinning. Finally one of the detectives asked, "What's the matter with you? You crazy or something?" The young man merely kept on grinning and grimacing as before. This caused the detective to call the hospital whose authorities readily confirmed that the young man was a patient on indefinite leave.

At that point the interrogation was instantly terminated and the culprit driven back to the hospital. It turned out he had done this several times previously. Society inadvertently was reinforcing a behavior which allowed him to avoid all the unpleasant consequences which normally accompany evidence of theft. He had only to act "crazy" and instead of being confined in a barren jail, he wound up in a fairly pleasant mental hospital. In the course of time he even learned the proper jargon about "childhood rejection," "broken home," "sibling envy," "Oedipus complex," and the like with which he could impress and convince officers that he should be treated differently from other criminals. The same society could easily have helped this young man by exploring the conditions which led to his petty thievery. As it turned out, he liked to work with animals, and when we found him a job as a helper in a nearby zoo, his thievery stopped. For the first time in his life he earned a steady if modest amount of money which made it unnecessary for him to steal.

Often the most difficult point for nursing personnel to explain about the behavioral approach to treating mental patients is that it is not the same as, and in fact in some ways is even the opposite of, "simply rewarding good behavior and punishing bad behavior." If the explanation were that simple the world would be in good shape, because that is largely what most of us do. But the evidence shows that though some behaviors have been punished for millenia, they remain utterly unaffected by punishment. On the other hand, it is equally false to say that "in a behavioral program there is no coddling of patients." There *is* coddling in a behavioral program if, and only if, coddling leads to a desired terminal behavior. In short, behavioral therapy is neither for nor against tender loving care or spartan treatment. It simply views these practices in a new light. It judges them not as absolutes which will have invariable effects on behavior, but as tools which the behaviorist can use. Like all tools, they can be used wisely or foolishly.

In their eagerness to understand behavioral therapy, many well-meaning public officials will try to draw historical parallels which are often misleading. Sometimes the criticism is heard that in a behavioral program patients are being starved into submission, much as was done in German concentration camps. When it is pointed out that patients are actually rewarded with food, another critic may make the accusation that behavioral therapy is a program of consistent bribery. Last but not least, there is the commentary that behavioral therapy may violate basic human rights since it occasionally uses food deprivation as part of its technology.

To these arguments, nursing personnel can point out that no law prescribes absolute ways of action. The situation under which something is done is always taken into account. For example, a knife can be used beneficially in the hands of a surgeon, but detrimentally in the hands of a criminal. Thus, the act of penetrating another's skin with a knife is not absolutely forbidden by law. Only the conditions under which the knife may be used are clearly specified.

In behavioral therapy it is no different. Deprivation as such should not be absolutely forbidden. The conditions under which it is used, however, should be highly circumscribed. In mental health as in physical health, it is the welfare of the patient which is and should be the decisive factor. If nursing personnel can demonstrate that a given technique can be of help, then that technique should be sanctioned for that particular case and others like it. The accent is on the word *demonstrate*. A technique can, for a very short time, be acceptable on the strength of opinion. But if it does not bring about the predicted results it should at once be questioned and, if necessary, abandoned.

To counter the argument that reinforcement therapy is equivalent to bribery, it is but necessary to point out that in bribery pay is given before the act. The reinforcer, in other words, is not contingent on the behavior, as some who have tried bribes have found to their dismay. In behavioral therapy, reinforcers are never given as a bribe, that is to say, before a desired behavior has occurred. They are only given *after* a desired behavior has occurred.

An issue that is sometimes raised in this context is that giving candy as a reinforcer is injurious to the dental hygiene of a patient. This argument points out a situation which the surgeon faces continuously. Which is for the greater benefit of the patient? To remove a gangrenous leg which will make it impossible for the patient to walk normally, or to let the leg alone and possibly cause the death of the patient? Similarly, the nurse in a behavioral program must make choices. A patient may have beautiful teeth, but if he cannot control his bowel movements or put on his own shirt, his teeth are of little practical use to him considering his total life situation. Attempts should be made, and in any field that is closely tied to research they are constantly being made, to achieve desired behaviors without introducing anything undesirable. But to counter the objection to the use of candy for retarded patients, it can readily be shown that science has by now found ways to make sugarless candy so that the jeopardy to healthy teeth no longer needs exist.

The argument that patients are being starved into submission when subjected to schedules of reinforcement involving food deprivation can be invalidated by showing that in a behavioral program a given way of proceeding is abandoned as soon as it becomes evident that it is not successful. If, for example, a patient must earn his daily meals by emitting some behavior, and if it becomes apparent that he does not emit this behavior within a day or so, one of two things is evident:

(1) The behavior required is not presently in the repertoire of that patient. Maybe the step required to emit the behavior is too large. A smaller step is tried and a behavior required that the patient can readily emit, and hence eat. Or (2) it is possible that the patient is not in any need of food at that time. In other words, food is not then a reinforcer for that patient.

No patient would be left on food deprivation in any behavioral program until he was too weak to function normally or be even near such a stage. The comparison between concentration camps and programs of behavioral therapy is simply grotesque and utterly unwarranted. Yet the public may not appreciate this difference. And since the public certainly does have a right to question novel as well as established procedures, even though used by professionals, the problem becomes one of educating the general public.

This cannot be done without an extensive sharing of the attitudes which prevail in programs of behavioral therapy by all staff members involved. Nurses can do such sharing with their fellow nurses who are not trained in behavioral technique; psychiatrists, psychologists, social workers, and administrators where behavioral therapy is practiced, can share their knowledge at professional meetings and whenever they interact with the public. Policemen, judges, lawyers, and elected officials are in daily contact with hospitals where behavioral programs are underway. In the long run, misconceptions about behavioral therapy which may arise from only limited acquaintanceship will be set right.

Dealing with the public requires tact, but on one issue the behaviorally trained nurse should be adamant; behavioral therapy may have elements in common with techniques that have been in use before, but as an approach it is quite novel. Its full understanding requires a thorough examination of one's own culturally acquired beliefs and attitudes. Compromising with statements that behavioral therapy is like this or that which has been practiced in the past may be tempting because such a technique seems to win the approval of the inquirer. But it inevitably leads to difficulties later on when the shortcomings of the method to which behavioral therapy was likened are discussed. Precisely because of these shortcomings, the other method, whatever it was, does not survive the trial of practical application.

Fortunately, results of conscientiously applied behavioral therapy have been most convincing. Patients for whom there had been no hope are now gainfully employed; male homosexuals who craved offspring from their wives but could not perform adequately are now proud fathers; once autistic children are now accepting reality. All of this should be disseminated as broadly as possible by those engaged in behavioral therapy, and the techniques by which it was accomplished should be described.

In trying to educate the public it can be pointed out that erratic behavior may be and indeed is often indicative of something wrong, except that the "something" is not a mysterious something found in the hidden realm of a person's personality structure, or nature, or mind, but is a reality in the external or internal physical environment of that person. Odd behaviors are not always obviously related to environmental variables. If they were, the mysticism which surrounds this subject would never have existed. Yet, odd behaviors are certainly not explained by reference to mystical compulsions, anxieties, or depressions, to any but the most naïve.

In the end, a person's acceptance of a behavioral point of view will be guided by his concern for his fellowman. If a given practice proves beneficial to mankind at large, it cannot help but win acceptance. Those who dedicate their lives to the helping of others, as do nurses and other professionals in the field of mental health, cannot help but use behavioral techniques to the benefit of those with whom they deal. In this fact lies the best insurance against abuse of these techniques and also the key to eventual understanding and acceptance of them by the general public.

EXERCISES, CHAPTER 14

1. List some of the criteria according to which a patient in a behavioral program is considered ready to prepare for leaving the hospital.
2. Why is it important to train patients to maintain a prescribed schedule of medication?
3. Describe a case where self-control is achieved by acting out an environmental situation.
4. Draft a letter to a family in which you announce the recovery of the patient together with suggestions for the family's responsibilities toward the patient after discharge. Stress points of tolerance and understanding of the patient's problems.
5. Why are visits to a family care home desirable *before* making definite arrangements to send a patient there?
6. Give examples of trivial behaviors, which might not be considered unusual in a hospital setting, but that might get the discharged or visiting patient into difficulty at his home or with friends.
7. What is the most difficult point in discussions of behavioral therapy with interested laymen who know nothing about behavioral therapy? How can this point be dealt with?
8. Give an example of how the public in a well-meaning way thoughtlessly reinforces undesirable behaviors.
9. What does the behaviorist regard odd behaviors indicative of?

Part V

Behavioral Techniques in a State Hospital Setting

15

The Patton Experiment

Your study of this chapter should help you answer the following questions:

1. What is the Patton experiment?
2. How was the Patton experiment set up and how does it operate?
3. What is being learned from the Patton experiment?

The terms listed below are introduced and defined in this chapter:

tender loving care
tokens
orientation group
therapy group
ready-to-leave group

As techniques for behavioral therapy become more widely known, many ask precisely how one might start a program that uses these techniques. There is, of course, no answer to this question that would suit every situation. From the foregoing chapters it should be clear that many factors—nurses, patients, climate, location, size, available buildings, in short, all of the environment—contribute to the format of such a program. Two factors are generally essential: (1) No behavioral program must be undertaken without thoroughly training the already professionally competent staff in behavioral techniques, and (2) there must be an administration willing to face the novel challenge of such an approach, and farsighted enough to believe strongly in man's potential for learning, spiritual growth, recovery, and rehabilitation.

By 1967, there were more than fifty major behavioral programs active across the United States alone. Many of these programs had been in effect for many years and had gathered much valuable experience in that time. The potential initiator of a behavioral program would be well advised to visit several of these programs to profit from their experience. In the spirit of such helpful sharing we are giving here a description of the development of the behavioral program with which we are most familiar.

HOW THE PATTON EXPERIMENT BEGAN

Patton State Hospital in Southern California sprawls across 600 acres of sloping foothills at the base of the San Bernardino Mountains. On its grounds approximately 4,500 patients can be housed in some sixty buildings. From the exterior, many of the older buildings are duplicates of the modest two-story frame houses and Spanish-style stucco dwellings frequently seen in the surrounding communities of Highland, San Bernardino, Colton, and Redlands. The newer, larger, glass-and-red-brick structures closely resemble modern schools and offices found everywhere in the United States.

All of Patton's inmates are there because at one time or another they consistently behaved in ways unacceptable to themselves or to the members of the communities in which they lived. Some pace unendingly back and forth or around a room; some stand rigid; some dress in highly bizarre clothing or not at all; some hear voices or are deluded into thinking themselves a Hitler or a Christ; many keep up incessant nonsense talk in a loud voice, while others fail to speak even when spoken to.

Although those petitioning for the commitment or admission of such a relative, friend, or ward often state that the prospective patient suffers from "mental illness," "retardation," "a neurosis," or simply "old age," only after medical and psychiatric examination by professional staff members is the "sick" individual's behavior labeled and his or her assignment made to a hospital unit. Little if anything factual is known regarding the causes for the oddities of behavior for which many of these patients are committed. At one time all that could be done was to feed, clothe, and confine them.

A nationwide breakthrough for the treatment of patients in all mental hospitals came during the late 1950s with the widespread use of therapeutic drugs. Patton Hospital, like so many institutions of its kind, gradually changed its primary efforts from custodial care to treatment which promised recovery and the subsequent discharge of its patients.

Short-term hospitalization for psychiatric patients became the rule rather than the exception. Still, one group—and a large group—did not fit this new pattern. Like the majority of patients, its members came to the hospital for care and were frequently discharged after a relatively short stay. But over and over their names reappeared on the list of admissions and their histories had to be taken from the record file. These patients had a diagnosis of chronic schizophrenia.

Typically such a patient entered the hospital, was put under medication, participated in the work and activities associated with rehabilitation, and eventually reached a point where he or she was considered ready for discharge. The patient then returned to his home or went to a halfway house and job that had been located for him by a social worker. However, unable to fend long for himself, or subject to the same environment which originally influenced his behavior adversely, such a patient habitually returned to the sheltered existence of the hospital voluntarily or involuntarily. Here, with all decisions made for him, he once again left the real world and gave himself up to the hallucinations and delusions, the apathy and withdrawal which marked the behavior that originally brought him to commitment.

During the last three years this circularity has been changed for some 200 patients at Patton State Hospital who were diagnosed chronic schizophrenics and assumed to be incurable. The difference has come about because of the application of techniques developed in the field of behavioral science. Planners of the Patton program took into account the work done by B. F. Skinner and O. R. Lindsley with psychotics at the Metropolitan State Hospital, Waltham, Massachusetts; by C. B. Ferster and Marian DeMeyer with autistic children at the University of Indiana Medical Center in Indianapolis, Indiana; by Nathan Azrin and his coworkers with selected patients at Anna State Hospital, Anna, Illinois; and by many others. By carefully controlling environment and by working out individual schedules of reinforcement, the Patton program was set up to break the repeated cycle of admission, care, discharge, and readmission of chronic schizophrenics.

GENERAL CHARACTERISTICS OF THE PATTON EXPERIMENT

The Patton program was initiated in 1964 by O. L. Gericke, M.D., the superintendent of the hospital. The details of its design and its continued operation and subsequent expansion are guided by a special committee headed by the senior author, the hospital's chief of research.

Two buildings, each capable of housing from seventy to seventy-five patients were selected for the experiment: one for men, the other for women. Though relatively old they were chosen in preference to newer facilities because of their cottage-type appearance and a floor plan which permitted small lounges, intimate dining areas, and sleeping quarters suited to semiprivate and private as well as ward arrangements.

The original nursing personnel was recruited from among the experienced nurses and psychiatric technicians already employed at the hospital. Because of the simplicity of the behavioral techniques being tried out, no additional funds were sought and the established ratio of approximately one staff member to each ten patients was maintained. In practice, of course, this ratio does not mean that one nurse takes care of ten patients only, since never more than five staff members are on duty at any one time and sometimes even fewer. Ideally, during waking hours, a ratio of one nurse or psychiatric technician to at most ten patients should be sought.

The first step in the program was the training of all personnel involved, including nurses, social workers, psychiatric technicians, the ancillary support staff, and also hospital administrators, food service administrators, and other personnel with whom the patient would in one way or another interact. During the initial stages, several charge nurses, the chief of social services, and selected social workers formed the nucleus of the training group which met twice weekly for an entire afternoon. Members of the hospital administrative staff appeared irregularly but contributed immeasurably.

It is quite probable that the subsequent success of the program is in no small part due to the practicality which aspects of an envisaged program took on in the face of objections which came from the staff. As far as the objections were real and referred to such factors as available manpower, available space, etc., they served to modify the plan for the program so as to make it feasible and realistic. As far as the objections were imagined or unreasonable, they usually focused interest on points that needed discussion. It was soon realized that under a program based on the application of behavioral techniques the nurse's traditional role of merely following a doctor's specific instructions would need revision. To be sure, the doctor (psychiatrist) would still give instructions. But his instructions would be of a much more general nature. Instead of ordering that a patient be walked down the hall and back at 3 P.M., the doctor now might simply ask that a patient be made to exercise. The kind and amount of exercise, the time the behavior was to take place, and how it was to be elicited and reinforced was left to the discretion and ingenuity of the nurse or technician responsible for the patient involved. In operant conditioning, a quick decision as to what to do with a patient is often needed in order to immediately reinforce a desired behavior. At such times nursing personnel must *be* free to make decisions and *feel* free to do so! Accordingly, such differences from traditional procedure were discussed at length during the training period.

Nursing personnel at every level learned to take part in deciding exactly which behaviors would be sought and which would be extinguished. Their ideas and experience were called on regarding the establishment and maintenance of schedules of reinforcement. The notion of *tender loving care* so much stressed in nursing education took on new dimensions. Instead of being instructed in how to perform all the usual personal services routinely given patients in hospitals, nursing personnel were now urged to consider how much more loving, if not more tender, it would be to see that patients assumed responsibility for their own care, since this is what would be expected of them once they were discharged from the hospital.

Barring immobilization due to extreme emotional disturbance or an outright physical disability, psychiatric patients are perfectly capable of bathing, dressing, toileting, and grooming themselves. They can make beds, shine shoes, keep their quarters neat and clean, use eating utensils, and operate simple machines. There is no need for them to be waited on hand and foot. During the course of their new training the nursing staff soon saw that only by shifting responsibility for personal care, being on time, taking medication, etc., to the patient, would they really be helping patients prepare themselves for life outside an institution.

Early in their course, the staff as students considered the reinforcers available for their work with patients. They decided to use food, beds to sleep on, going outdoors, visitors, cigarettes, TV, and various luxuries and minor privileges. A system of tokens (as generalized reinforcers) was introduced as a means of paying for specific reinforcers. In other words, the patients from whom the staff wished to elicit a smile would be paid in tokens when they smiled, rather than by being given something to eat or a cigarette or whatever reinforcer had been decided upon. In turn, the patients could use their tokens to pay for the necessities or the luxuries they considered most important.

Each student in the training course was required to draw up a list of desirable behaviors that he expected to influence through the reinforcers that had been decided upon. At first students listed such goals as "good personal hygiene" and "adequate social interaction." Gradually these broad concepts were translated into behavioral terms. "Good personal hygiene" and "adequate social interaction" became lists such as those shown in Table 15-1.

Table 15-1

Behavioral Descriptions of Epithets

Good Personal Hygiene	Adequate Social Interaction
No dirt on feet	Asking questions
No dirt on legs or knees	Responding "Good morning"
No dirt on hands or arms	Saying "Thank you"
No dirt on neck or face	Saying "Please"
No evidence of body odor	Asking the time
No residue in the navel	Speaking during group therapy
Clean fingernails	Playing card games
Nicely combed hair	Watching TV with others
Daily change of underwear	Talking about something besides oneself
Clean socks or stockings	Visiting on the grounds
Neat and recent shave (men)	
Suitable cosmetics (women)	

The course of instruction in behavioral techniques that was given all nursing personnel lasted eighteen weeks. It included not only the fundamentals of operant conditioning but also lectures and discussion covering simple behavioral experiments and a description of the research work and teachings of Ivan Pavlov and B. F. Skinner. While undergoing this training the students worked right along on their regular assignments in the experiment. The course has since been offered each year for training new personnel and as a review for old.

At this date all patients selected for the experiment have come as transfers from other wards. They are only alike in that they meet the following criteria.

1. **A diagnosis of chronic schizophrenia**

   This datum is either taken from the patient's medical record or given by the psychiatrist who treated the patient in the hospital.

2. **Hospital habituated**

   A judgment based partly on the fact that the patient had been in the hospital for at least six months and had not responded to therapeutic attempts, and partly on personal statements of the patient which revealed that he had accepted the hospital as his home.

3. **No organic brain damage**

   A fact drawn from the patient's medical record.

4. **A prognosis of low hope for therapeutic success**

   A judgment recorded in the patient's medical file, typically by the original examining psychiatrist who treated the patient and social workers who interviewed the patient on occasion.

5. **Able to function on an open ward**

   A value judgment based in part on the psychiatric evaluation but due also to the long hospital record of these patients some of whom had been at Patton for as much as twenty-two years. More typically on nurses' impressions as recorded in nurses' reports.

In physical appearance, intellectual ability, personal skills, interests, and cultural backgrounds the patients were as diverse as any 200 or 300 persons in any general community.

Once the patients had been selected, practical considerations determined many of the procedures adopted by the nursing personnel as they began to work out the details of the experiment. It soon became clear that close attention is required for effective use of reinforcers. Yet no psychiatric nurse or technician can be expected to pay close attention to more than ten or twelve patients. With at least seventy patients twenty-four hours a day, and at most five staff members on duty at any one time, some kind of grouping had to be arranged which at some stage would make close attention possible for all patients.

To accomplish this purpose it was decided to use three groups in each ward. These were thought of as an orientation group containing approximately 60 percent of all patients, a therapy group of about 20 percent, and a so-called "ready-to-leave" group of the final 20 percent. All patients upon coming into the program are assigned to the orientation group. Naturally it took several weeks before the first two therapy and ready-to-leave groups were activated, but since that time there has been a steady feed-in at all levels.

Careful control of the physical environment of each of the three groups makes possible the effective use of reinforcers. It also provides high motivation for patients to take more and more responsibility for themselves so they may "work up" to the next group until they are ready for release.

In general, a patient in the orientation group is provided with only the minimal requirements that human dignity and common sense require. He sleeps in an unadorned dormitory on a simple bed that has no spread, only sheets and blankets. There is no storage space provided for his personal belongings. He is admitted to the dining room only after members of the other two groups have entered and eats from a sectioned plastic dish at a crowded, long, bare table with his single utensil a large spoon. His food, however, is exactly the same in quality and quantity as that available to all patients. Only hospital-provided clothing is permitted him. Likewise he is restricted in the number of visitors he may have. He does not attend movies or any of the hospital parties or off-the-ward activities available to patients in the other groups.

Patients in the therapy group have more comfortable beds, a bedspread, draperies at the windows, a small dresser for personal belongings, and a rug on the floor. They may wear their own clothing. In the dining room they sit at tables set for four, use flatware and dishes such as are found in many middle-class American homes, and are served family style. They may attend social functions, entertain visitors, and move freely about the hospital grounds.

Every member of the ready-to-leave group is provided with a private room which he may decorate as he pleases. He may leave the hospital grounds during the day and frequently does so because he commutes to a job in a nearby community. His group enters the dining area first and eats at tables spread with a tablecloth and decorated with flowers. He is expected to seek entertainment off the grounds, to use busses, attend movies, go on shopping trips, and generally plan and carry out a variety of outside activities.

In every group the patients "pay" for necessities, luxuries, and privileges. Payment varies, however, from group to group, patient to patient, and even time to time. Patients are never permitted to get in ruts that are too predictable or comfortable. Behavioral techniques clearly call for variable ratios of reinforcement if the desired behavior is to become permanent.

While in an orientation group, patients learn that they must pay not only for bed and board, as is expected everywhere in human society, but also for such "privileges" as lying down during the day (if this has been judged an undesirable behavior for an especially apathetic patient) or for *not* getting up, or *not* being on time for medicine, or even for the privilege of smoking the cigarettes and eating the sweets that are rightfully theirs!

At all levels, payment is made in tokens which have been earned for "good" behaviors. Initially white, red, and blue poker chips were used as tokens until it was possible to install automatic equipment, such as turnstiles in the dining room, timers on the TV, food and toiletry dispensing automats, and automatic door openers. These accept brass tokens which are about the size of a nickel but manufactured to specification so as not to fit in any of the other vending machines on the hospital grounds. They are blank on both sides but can be imprinted. At Patton blanks were preferred since for some studies tokens were marked with patients' names to make it possible to trace what had been purchased and by whom.

The "good" behaviors which elicit reinforcement in the form of tokens differ. For a catatonic, "good" behavior may be simply opening his eyes, or smiling, or saying "Fine" when someone asks, "How are you?" For a ready-to-leave patient, "good" behavior would more likely be an entire week of proper dress and reporting for work on time.

From the moment he enters the program, a patient is never summoned, coerced, or continually reminded to do something. He is not called in the morning; he is not told to dress or wash; he is not taken to the toilet or rounded up for meals. If he fails to do what is expected of "normal" people in such matters, he simply does not earn the tokens customarily given for such acts—tokens needed to pay for a pleasantly served meal, the next night's sleep in a luxurious bed (rather than on one that meets minimum requirements), the privilege of going outdoors. He is initially told of such routine matters and thereafter expected to keep track of them for himself even as he will be once he is released from the hospital.

Since the goal of the program is to make patients independent, they are gradually weaned from the artificial support of always being paid in tokens for every "good" behavior. Friendly praise, extra privileges, and the approval of staff and patients for acceptable behavior replace tokens at every opportunity. Gradually, habitually passive patients are reached because they realize something is expected of them and that their efforts will be taken seriously.

Patients normally find life in an orientation group so aversive that within only a month or two their behavior is sufficiently changed to warrant their inclusion in a therapy group. It is in this second group that they receive the most attention, that they are subject to the most intensive operant conditioning possible within the limitations of daily life in a large, public institution. Decisions for reassignment are up to the charge nurse of a ward in consultation with nursing personnel and, if necessary, the advice of the professional staff of the hospital.

Leave planning is begun just as soon as a patient moves into a therapy group. The social workers are called upon to be in contact with the patient's relatives, to locate a halfway house and employment if that is deemed advisable, and generally to help prepare the patient for his life outside the hospital.

Once in a middle, or therapy group, a patient has a maximum of five months to reach the discharge stage. Two of these five months are generally spent in a ready-to-leave group. If at the end of three months in a therapy group a patient has not shown that he is willing or able to face living outside the hospital, he is returned to an orientation group.

Not all patients in the Patton experiment like the demands placed upon them under a program based on behavioral techniques. But each readily admits that his or her life is now directed toward release, not regression.

ASSESSMENT OF THE PATTON EXPERIMENT

Without question, the heart of the program was the daily staff session in which patients' cases and treatment problems were discussed. In addition, weekly two-hour sessions brought together staffs and other interested personnel throughout the hospital.

The importance of empirical proceeding rather than reliance on authority was another important aspect of the program. If a question arose, a brief experiment became the best authority for an answer. For example, are nurses' uniforms desirable? In the course of a two-week ancillary study it became evident that at least in the conduct of this work and under the situations prevailing, it would be desirable for nurses *not* to wear uniforms.

Many of the initial fears which professional personnel had had concerning the effects of various forms of deprivation on the patient evaporated as it became evident that these effects, if anything, were highly beneficial. The value of quantification became abundantly evident. The question, "What do we really mean by schizophrenia (or apathy, anxiety, etc.)?" became so commonplace that its mere appearance usually instantly suggested various behavioral definitions and, consequently, valuable insights.

The social workers who would eventually be responsible for the placement of the patient outside the hospital were involved throughout a patient's therapeutic progress and worked directly with patients in the ready-to-leave group. The social workers appreciated the factual behavioral data which, unlike impressionistic general statements, gave them solid information which could be used in placing a patient.

At this writing the Patton experiment is still progressing, and there are no plans for its discontinuance. Patients are being transferred into the program from other wards and discharged from the ready-to-leave groups at the rate of approximately 9 percent per month.

Because the experiment has been accepted as a regular part of the total hospital program, no final assessment can be made as to its success or failure. However, certain data are available and certain results known.

Experiments involving mental patients are frequently considered a success or failure based on how many of its patients are permanently returned to society outside the institution versus the number of readmissions. No definitive data are available which make possible a totally valid comparison of this kind. However, for the first thirty-one months of the behavioral program, the readmission rate for the 248 discharged patients is approximately 16 percent. During the same period, the average for readmission of mentally ill patients in all public mental hospitals in the United States is estimated at 35 to 40 percent. Regardless of the percentages, the Patton figure is significant in that all the patients in the experiment were at one time considered "incurable."

These figures are, of course, highly gratifying. Combined with the opinions expressed by the nursing personnel, as well as statements made by patients and their families, they suggest that the application of behavioral techniques should have a permanent place in the treatment of patients now confined in our mental institutions. Perhaps the words of O. L. Gericke, superintendent of Patton Hospital since 1954, most clearly reflect the prevailing opinion as to the value of the experiment.

> One of the most gratifying aspects of the project was the personal interest the nursing staff took in working with individual patients. . . . Early in the program the charge nurse of the women's unit wrote the following. "I have known some of the patients for five years, and for the first time I am seeing real progress made with them. I feel quite encouraged with our program and we are learning as we go along. . . . All the staff are extremely enthusiastic and feel that their own thinking is tremendously stimulated by what they are learning in this project."
>
> Although the problems on the men's units are different, the results are the same. Perhaps the most striking difference on the men's unit is that the men are undoubtedly now the cleanest group of men on an open unit anywhere in the hospital. There is none of the stale odor frequently encountered when large numbers of men live in one unit. Everyone wears neatly pressed clothes and is shaved and well scrubbed.

Cases we have dealt with give us great confidence in the unorthodox techniques we are now using, and we point to them whenever we are called upon to explain and justify a therapy that requires the patient to pay for what he used to regard as his due.

Not the least benefit of a program involving behavioral science techniques is that everyone involved is often forced to ask, "Why am I doing what I do, and how does it affect the patient's behavior?" Ever since mental hospitals came into being, the great leaders in psychiatry have asked this question. But in the course of time, as routine and habit make it easy to move along the path of least resistance, perhaps many of us do not really question as seriously as we should our roles in the recovery of patients. Some even defend the view that technicians and nurses should never ask questions. To be sure, there are situations in life, such as with the military, where the success of an operation depends on a person's ability, not to reason *why* but to *do*, if necessary without understanding. But such situations hardly apply to the problems we face in the mental institution. Operant procedures rest primarily on the analysis of behavior and, thus, on questioning our own responses.

With the complexity of human behavior it is, however, no task for one single person to explore all the reinforcers, all the control stimuli, and all the response contingencies even for a single patient. A team is needed to provide baselines of the behavioral repertory of the patient, to structure the physical environment, and to arrange schedules of reinforcement that lead to acceptable behavior and to recovery. Nurses and psychiatric technicians are a vital part of this team.

In initiating this project we questioned whether behavioral techniques are practical and useful in a mental hospital. We are now satisfied that this question has been affirmatively answered. As our knowledge increases, we are beginning to ask to what degree these techniques can be applied to deal with individual problems and, in particular, how *permanently* we can change a pattern of behavior. The discharged patient usually returns to an environment that is not very different from that which prevailed when his difficulties began. This environment is not under our control. Our job must be to prepare the patient to cope with this environment. Will behavioral techniques enable us to do this? We shall try to provide empirical answers to this question by continuing and expanding the project [26].

EXERCISES, CHAPTER 15

1. Discuss the reasons and background for the Patton experiment. Why was it begun? What did it hope to accomplish?

2. Prepare an oral or written report on any of the following:

   a. The experiment conducted by B. F. Skinner, O. R. Lindsley, and M. T. Mednick with psychotics at the Metropolitan State Hospital in Waltham, Massachusetts

   b. The experiment conducted by C. B. Ferster and M. K. De Myer with autistic children at the Indiana Medical Center in Indianapolis, Indiana

   c. The experiment by N. H. Azrin with closed-ward patients at Anna State Hospital in Anna, Illinois

3. Describe the step-by-step procedures followed in setting up the Patton experiment. Compare the considerations encountered here with those to be met in your hospital.

4. Discuss what needs to be considered in terms of buildings, staff selection and training, selection of patients in order to institute in any mental hospital a treatment program based on behavioral techniques.

5. Consider whether you feel the results obtained to date warrant the continuation of a program such as the Patton experiment. Are patients fairly treated? What changes, if any, should be made if further application is made of behavioral techniques to the treatment of mental illness. Be prepared to defend your viewpoint with logical reasoning, specific examples, and reasonable hypothesis.

6. What relationship does the behavioral program at Patton Hospital have to the rest of the hospital?

7. In what principal ways does the Patton experiment differ from traditional treatment of patients diagnosed as schizophrenics?

8. What is the role of nursing personnel in the Patton experiment? How does this compare with the traditional role of nurses?

9. What is the rationale on which the behavioral program at Patton Hospital rests? What arguments are there that support this rationale? That deny it?

10. What preparations were made before treatment was started with patients?

REFERENCES AND NOTES

1. Szasz, T. S.: "Mental Illness Is a Myth," *The New York Times Magazine,* June 12, 1966, p. 30.
2. Wolpe, J.: *Psychotherapy by Reciprocal Inhibition,* Stanford University Press, Stanford, Calif., 1958, p. 34.
3. Watson, J. B., and R. Rayner: "Conditioned Emotional Reaction," *J. exp. Psychol.,* 3:1–14, 1920.
4. Jones, M. C.: "A Laboratory Study of Fear. The Case of Peter." *Ped. Sem.,* 31:308, 1924.
5. Salter, A.: "The Theory and Practice of Conditioned Reflex Therapy," in J. Wolpe, A. Salter, and L. J. Reyna (eds.), *The Conditioning Therapies,* Holt, Rinehart and Winston, Inc., New York, 1965.
6. Wolpe, J.: *Psychotherapy by Reciprocal Inhibition,* Stanford University Press, Stanford, Calif., 1958.
7. Lang, P. J.: "Experimental Studies of Desensitization Psychotherapy," in J. Wolpe, A. Salter, and L. J. Reyna (eds.), *The Conditioning Therapies,* Holt, Rinehart and Winston, Inc., New York, 1965.
8. Wolpe, J.: *Psychotherapy by Reciprocal Inhibition,* Stanford University Press, Stanford Calif., 1958, p. 71.
9. Kraft, T., and I. Al-Issa: "Behavior Therapy and the Treatment of Frigidity," *Amer. J. Psychother.,* 21:116–120, 1967.
10. Wolpe, J.: "The Systematic Treatment of Neurosis," *J. nerv. ment. Disorders,* 132:189–203, 1961.
11. Cowden, R. C., and L. I. Ford: "Systematic Desensitization with Phobic Schizophrenics," *Amer. J. Psychiat.,* 119:241–245, 1962.
12. Coleman, J. C.: *Abnormal Psychology and Modern Life,* Scott, Foresman and Company, Chicago, 1956, p. 643.
13. Coleman, J. C.: *Abnormal Psychology and Modern Life,* Scott, Foresman and Company, 1956, p. 646.
14. This situation is too tempting for not at least someone to suggest cynically that the patient was freed of her psychosis only to give her cancer of the lungs. The fact, of course, is that this patient would have smoked as much if not more outside a behavioral program anyway. If smoking is regarded as a health problem, as well it should be, it is also a behavior and thus can be weakened or strengthened by behavioral techniques.
15. Bachrach, A. J., W. J. Erwin, and J. P. Mohr: "The Control of Eating Behavior in an Anorexic by Operant Conditioning Techniques," in L. P. Ullman and L. Krasner (eds.), *Case Studies in Behavior Modification,* Holt, Rinehart and Winston, Inc., New York, 1966.
16. Ayllon, T., and J. Michael: "The Psychiatric Nurse as a Behavioral Engineer," *J. exp. anal. Behav.,* 2:323–334, 1959.
17. Tredgold, A. F.: *Mental Deficiency,* The Williams & Wilkins Company, Baltimore, 1956.
18. Bijou, S.: "Experimental Studies of Child Behavior, Normal and Deviant," in L. Krasner, and L. Ullmann (eds.), *Research in Behavior Modification,* Holt, Rinehart and Winston, Inc., New York, 1965.

19. Birnbrauer, J., S. Bijou, M. Wolf, and J. Kidder: "Programmed Instruction in the Classroom," in L. P. Ullmann and L. Krasner (eds.), *Case Studies in Behavior Modification,* Holt, Rinehart and Winston, Inc., New York, 1966.

20. Progress Report: "A Demonstration Program for Intensive Training of Institutionalized Mentally Retarded Girls," Parsons Project No. 4443, Bureau of Child Research, University of Kansas, Parsons State Hospital, Parsons, Kansas. U.S. Department of Health, Education, and Welfare, Public Health Service, Grant No. MR 1 801 B67.

21. Fuller, P. R.: "Operant Conditioning of a Vegetative Human Organism," *Amer. J. Psychol.,* 62:587–590, 1949.

22. Ball, T. S.: "Behavior Shaping of Self-help Skills in the Severely Retarded Child," in J. Fisher and R. Harris (eds.), *Reinforcement Theory in Psychological Treatment: A Symposium,* State of California Mental Health Research Monograph, No. 8:21, 1966.

23. Wolf, M., J. Birnbrauer, T. Williams, and J. Lawler: "A Note on Apparent Extinction of the Vomiting Behavior of a Retarded Child," in L. P. Ullmann and L. Krasner (eds.), *Case Studies in Behavior Modification,* Holt, Rinehart and Winston, Inc., New York, 1966.

24. Hingtgen, J. N. and F. C. Trost: "Shaping Cooperative Responses in Early Childhood Schizophrenics: II. Reinforcement of Mutual Physical Contact and Vocal Responses," in R. Ulrich, T. Stachnik, and J. Mabry (eds.), *Control of Human Behavior,* Scott, Foresman and Company, Chicago, 1966, pp. 110–114.

25. Lindsley, O. R.: "Geriatric Behavioral Prosthetics," in R. Kastenbaum (ed.), *New Thoughts on Old Age,* Springer Publishing Co., Inc., New York, 1964, pp. 41–60.

26. Gericke, O. L.: "Practical Use of Operant Conditioning Procedures in a Mental Hospital," *Psychol. Studies & Proj.,* 3:1–10, 1965.

RECOMMENDED READINGS—CHAPTER ONE

Grünbaum, A.: "Causality and the Science of Human Behavior," in R. Ulrich, T. Stachnik, and J. Mabry (eds.), *Control of Human Behavior*, Scott, Foresman and Company, Chicago, 1966.

Krasner, L.: "Behavior Control and Social Responsibility," *Amer. Psychol.*, 17:199–204, 1962.

Rogers, C. R., and B. F. Skinner: "Some Issues Concerning the Control of Human Behavior: A Symposium," *Science*, 124:1057–1066, 1956.

Skinner, B. F.: *Cumulative Record*, "Freedom and the Control of Men," pp. 3–18; "The Control of Human Behavior," pp. 18–23; "Some Issues Concerning the Control of Human Behavior," pp. 23–36; "Psychology in the Understanding of Mental Disease," pp. 194–202; "What is Psychotic Behavior?" pp. 202–219; Appleton-Century-Crofts, Inc., New York, 1961.

Ullmann, L. P., and L. Krasner, (eds.): *Case Studies in Behavior Modification*, "Traditional Therapy and Behavior Therapy," pp. 35–39; "Characteristics of the Behavior Therapist and Social Values," pp. 39–44; Holt, Rinehart and Winston, Inc., New York, 1966.

CHAPTER TWO

Holland, J. G., and B. F. Skinner: *The Analysis of Behavior*, pp. 1–62, McGraw-Hill Book Company, New York, 1961.

Keller, F. S., and W. N. Schoenfeld: *Principles of Psychology*, pp. 15–66, Appleton-Century-Crofts, Inc., New York, 1950.

Skinner, B. F.: *Cumulative Record*, pp. 37–142, Appleton-Century-Crofts, Inc., New York, 1961.

CHAPTER THREE

Holland, J. G., and B. F. Skinner: *The Analysis of Behavior*, pp. 97–110, 181–202, 245–271, McGraw-Hill Book Company, New York, 1961.

Keller, F. S., and W. N. Schoenfeld: *Principles of Psychology*, pp. 67–114, Appleton-Century-Crofts, Inc., New York, 1950.

Mechner, F.: "A Notation System for the Description of Behavioral Procedures," *J. exp. anal. Behav.*, 2:133, 1959.

CHAPTER FOUR

Holland, J. G., and B. F. Skinner: *The Analysis of Behavior*, pp. 72–77, 137–180, McGraw-Hill Book Company, New York, 1961.

Keller, F. S., and W. N. Schoenfeld: *Principles of Psychology*, chap. 5, "Generalization and Discrimination," Appleton-Century-Crofts, Inc., New York, 1950.

Skinner, B. F.: *The Behavior of Organisms*, pp. 167–307, Appleton-Century-Crofts, Inc., New York, 1938.

Skinner, B. F.: *Cumulative Record,* p. 178 (description of cumulative record), p. 404 (regarding control stimuli), Appleton-Century-Crofts, Inc., New York, 1959.

Ulrich, R., T. Stachnik, and J. Mabry (eds.): *Control of Human Behavior,* chaps. 2, 4, 6, 7 (for practical examples on stimulus control), Scott, Foresman and Company, Chicago, 1961.

CHAPTER FIVE

Bond, I. K., and H. C. Hutchison: "Application of Reciprocal Inhibition Therapy to Exhibitionism," *Canadian Med. Ass. J.,* 83:23–25, 1960.

Cautela, J. R.: "Covert Sensitization," *Psychol. Rep.,* 20:459–468, 1967.

Cowden, R. C., and L. I. Ford: "Systematic Desensitization with Phobic Schizophrenics," *Amer. J. Psychiat.,* 119:241–245, 1962.

Cowden, R. C., D. J. Reynolds, and L. I. Ford: "The Verbal-Behavior Discrepancy in Schizophrenia," *J. clin. Psychol.,* 17:406–408, 1961.

Franks, C. M. (ed.): *Conditioning Techniques in Clinical Practice and Research,* Springer Publishing Co., Inc., New York, 1964.

Lang, P. J.: "Experimental Studies of Desensitization Psychotherapy," in J. Wolpe, A. Salter, and L. J. Reyna (eds.), *The Conditioning Therapies,* Holt, Rinehart and Winston, Inc., New York, 1965.

Wolpin, M., and L. Pearsall: "Rapid Deconditioning of a Fear of Snakes," *Behav. Res. Ther.,* 3:107–111, 1965.

Wolpin, M., and J. Raines: "Visual Imagery, Expected Roles and Extinction as Possible Factors in Reducing Fear and Avoidance Behavior," *Behav. Res. Ther.,* 4:25–37, 1966.

Yates, A. J.: "The Application of Modern Learning Theory to the Treatment of Tics," *J. abnorm. soc. Psychol.,* 56:175–182, 1958. Also reprinted in Eysenck, H. J. (ed.): *Behavior Therapy and the Neuroses,* Pergamon Press, New York, 1960.

CHAPTER SIX

Ellsworth, R. B.: "Manual for the MACC Behavioral Adjustment Scale," Western Psychological Services, Los Angeles, 1957.

Honigfeld, G., R. Gillis, and J. Klett: "NOSIE 30: A Treatment Sensitive Ward Behavior Scale," *Psychol. Rep.,* 19:180–182, 1966.

Schaefer, H. H., and P. L. Martin: "Behavioral Therapy for 'Apathy' of Hospitalized Schizophrenics," *Psychol. Rep.,* 19:1147–1158, 1966.

CHAPTER SEVEN

Ayllon, T., and N. H. Azrin: "The Measurement and Reinforcement of Behavior of Psychotics," *J. exp. anal. Behav.,* 8:357–383, 1965.

Holland, J. G., and B. F. Skinner: *The Analysis of Behavior,* pp. 72–77, 117–136, McGraw-Hill Book Company, New York, 1961.

Premack, D.: "Toward Empirical Behavior Laws: I. Positive Reinforcement," *Psychol. Rev.,* 66:219–233, 1959.

Skinner, B. F.: *Cumulative Record,* pp. 76–99, 100–130, 272–285, 393–403, Appleton-Century-Crofts, Inc., New York, 1961.

CHAPTER EIGHT

Anonymous: "Operant Conditioning Roundup; Its Diverse Applicability," *Roche Report: Frontiers of Hospital Psychiatry,* 4: No. 9, 1967.

Atthowe, J. M., Jr.: "The Token Economy: Its Utility and Limitation," paper read at Western Psychological Association, Long Beach, Calif., April, 1966.

Ayllon, T., and N. H. Azrin: "The Measurement and Reinforcement of Behavior in Psychotics," *J. exp. anal. Behav.,* 8:357–383, 1965.

Gericke, J. R.: "Problems for Behavioral Therapy in Mental Hospitals," *Psychol. Rep.,* 20:534, 1967.

Martin, P. L., and D. Farish: "Behavioral Control of Early Morning Rising on Hospital Wards for the Mentally Ill," *Calif. ment. health Res. Digest,* 5:109–110, 1967.

Miron, N.: "Behavior Shaping and Group Nursing with Severely Retarded Patients," *Calif. ment. health Res. Monogr.* 8, 1966.

Skinner, B. F.: *Science and Human Behavior,* chap. 16, "Thinking," The Macmillan Company, New York, 1953.

Sommer, R., and H. Osmond: "Symptoms of Institutional Care," *Social Problems,* 8:254–262, 1961.

CHAPTER NINE

Ayllon, T., and J. Michael: "The Psychiatric Nurse as a Behavioral Engineer," *J. exp. anal. Behav.,* 2:323–334, 1959.

Baer, D. M.: "Laboratory Control of Thumbsucking by Withdrawal and Re-presentation of Reinforcement," *J. exp. anal. Behav.,* 5:525–528, 1962.

Berne, E.: *Games People Play.* Grove Press, Inc., New York, 1965.

Harris, F. R., M. M. Wolf, and D. M. Baer: "Effects of Adult Social Reinforcement on Child Behavior," *Young Children,* 20:8–17, 1964.

Hart, B. M., K. E. Allen, J. S. Buell, F. R. Harris, and M. M. Wolf: "Effects of Social Reinforcement on Operant Crying," *J. exp. Child Psychol.,* 1:145–153, 1964.

Wickes, I.: "Treatment of Persistent Enuresis with the Electric Buzzer," *Arch. Dis. Child.,* 33:160–164, 1958.

Williams, C. D.: "The Elimination of Tantrum Behavior by Extinction Procedures," *J. abnorm. soc. Psychol.,* 59:269, 1959.

Wolf, M. M., T. Risley, and H. Mees: "Application of Operant Conditioning Procedures to the Behavior Problems of an Autistic Child," *Behav. Res. Ther.,* 1:305–312, 1964.

CHAPTER TEN

Barrett, B. H.: "Reduction in Rate of Multiple Tics by Free Operant Conditioning Methods," *J. ment. ner. Dis.,* 135:187, 1962.

Brady, J., and D. L. Lind: "Experimental Analysis of Hysterical Blindness," *Arch. gen. Psychiat.,* 4:331–339, 1961.

Kushner, M.: "The Reduction of a Long-standing Fetish by Means of Aversive Conditioning," in L. P. Ullmann and L. Krasner (eds.), *Case Studies in Behavior Modification,* Holt, Rinehart and Winston, Inc., New York, 1966.

Lovaas, I.: "A Behavioral Therapy Approach to the Treatment of Childhood Schizo-phrenia," in *Minnesota Symposia on Child Psychology*, J. T. Hill (ed.), vol. 1, University of Minnesota Press, Minneapolis, 1967.

Quarti, C., and J. Renaud: "A New Treatment of Constipation by Conditioning: A Preliminary Report," in C. M. Franks (ed.), *Conditioning Techniques in Clinical Practice and Research*, Springer Publishing Co., Inc., New York, 1964.

Rafi, A. A.: "Learning Theory and the Treatment of Tics," *J. psychosom. Res.*, 6:71, 1962.

Richard, H. C., and M. B. Mundy: "Direct Manipulation of Stuttering Behavior: An Experimental-Clinical Approach," in L. P. Ullmann and L. Krasner (eds.), *Case Studies in Behavior Modification*, Holt, Rinehart and Winston, Inc., New York, 1966.

Also recommended in this context:

Lovaas, I.: "Reinforcement Therapy," an educational motion picture (16 mm, B&W, sound) produced by Smith, Kline and French Drug Co., Philadelphia, 1966. Available from SK&F Public Relations Department on a loan basis.

CHAPTER ELEVEN

Ayllon, T.: "Intensive Treatment of Psychotic Behavior by Stimulus Satiation and Food Reinforcement," *Behav. Res. Ther.*, 1:53–61, 1963.

Ayllon, T., and J. Michael: "The Psychiatric Nurse as a Behavioral Engineer," *J. exp. anal. Behav.*, 2:323–334, 1959.

Flanagan, B., I. Goldiamond, and N. H. Azrin: "Operant Stuttering: The Control of Stuttering Behavior Through Response Contingent Consequences," *J. exp. anal. Behav.*, 1:173–178, 1958.

Isaacs, W., J. Thomas, and I. Goldiamond: "Application of Operant Conditioning to Reinstate Verbal Behavior in Psychotics," *J. Speech & Hearing Disorders*, 25:8–12, 1960.

CHAPTER TWELVE

Ayllon, T.: "Intensive Treatment of Psychotic Behavior by Stimulus Satiation and Food Reinforcement," *Behav. Res. Ther.*, 1:53–61, 1963.

Brady, J. V.: "Ulcers in Executive Monkeys," *Sci. Amer.*, 199:95–100, 1958.

Ferster, C. B., J. I. Nurnberger, and E. B. Levitt: "The Control of Eating," *J. of Mathetics*, 1:87–109, 1962.

Lang, P. J.: "Behavior Therapy with a Case of Nervous Anorexia," in L. P. Ullmann and L. Krasner (eds.), *Case Studies in Behavior Modification*, Holt, Rinehart and Winston, Inc., New York, 1966.

Loeb, L.: "Anorexia Nervosa," *J. nerv. ment. Dis.*, 131:447, 1960.

Nemiah, J. C.: "Anorexia Nervosa: Fact and Theory," *Amer. J. dig. Dis.*, 3:249, 1958.

CHAPTER THIRTEEN

Bandura, A.: "Behavioral Modification Through Modeling Procedures," in L. Krasner and L. P. Ullmann (eds.), *Research in Behavior Modification*, Holt, Rinehart and Winston, Inc., New York, 1965.

Barrett, B. H., and O. R. Lindsley: "Deficits in Acquisition of Operant Discrimination and Differentiation Shown by Institutionalized Retarded Children," *Amer. J. ment. Deficiency*, 67:424–436, 1962.

Kerr, N., and L. Meyerson: *Learning Theory and Rehabilitation*, Random House, Inc., New York, 1964.

Kerr, N., L. Meyerson, and J. Michael: "A Procedure for Shaping Vocalizations in a Mute Child," in L. P. Ullmann and L. Krasner (eds.), *Case Studies in Behavior Modification*, Holt, Rinehart and Winston, Inc., New York, 1966.

Metz, R. J.: "Conditioning Social and Intellectual Skills in Autistic Children," *Calif. ment. health Res. Monogr.* 8, 1966.

Patterson, G.: "An Application of Conditioning Techniques to the Control of a Hyperactive Child," in L. P. Ullmann and L. Krasner (eds.), *Case Studies in Behavior Modification*, Holt, Rinehart and Winston, Inc., New York, 1966.

Patterson, G.: "A Learning Theory Approach to the Treatment of the School Phobic Child," in L. P. Ullmann and L. Krasner (eds.), *Case Studies in Behavior Modification*, Holt, Rinehart and Winston, Inc., New York, 1966.

Risley, T., and M. M. Wolf: "Experimental Manipulation of Autistic Behaviors and Generalizations into the Home," in R. Ulrich, T. Stachnik, and J. Mabry (eds.), *Control of Human Behavior*, Scott, Foresman and Company, Chicago, 1966.

Zimmerman, E. H., and J. Zimmerman: "The Alteration of Behavior in a Special Classroom Situation," *J. exp. anal. Behav.*, 5:59–60, 1962.

CHAPTER FOURTEEN

Keller, F. S.: *The Definition of Psychology*, Appleton-Century-Crofts, Inc., New York, 1937.

Sidman, M.: *Tactics of Scientific Research*, Basic Books, Inc., Publishers, New York, 1960.

Skinner, B. F.: *Science and Human Behavior*, The Macmillan Company, New York, 1953.

Skinner, B. F.: *Walden Two*, The Macmillan Company, New York, 1966 (11th printing).

Skinner, B. F.: *Cumulative Record* (enlarged ed.), pp. 3–36, 185–220, 391–426, Appleton-Century-Crofts, Inc., New York, 1961.

CHAPTER FIFTEEN

Bruce, M.: "Tokens for Recovery," *J. Nursing*, 66:1799–1802, 1966.

Farish, D.: "Remotivation Through Behavioral Technology," *Calif. ment. health Res. Digest*, 5:110–111, 1967.

Martin, P. L., and D. Farish: "Behavioral Control of Early Morning Rising on Hospital Wards for the Mentally Ill," *Calif. ment. health Res. Digest*, 5:109–110, 1967.

Schaefer, H. H.: "Investigations in Operant Conditioning Procedures in a Mental Hospital," *Calif. ment. health Res. Monogra.*, 8:25–39, 1966.

Schaefer, H. H., and P. L. Martin: "Behavioral Therapy for 'Apathy' of Hospitalized Schizophrenics," *Psychol. Rep.*, 19:1147–1158, 1966.

Index

Absence without permission (AWOL), 134–135

Acrophobia, 54

Aged patients, 189–191

Alarms, enuresis and, 130–131
tics and, 140

Al-Issa, I., 56, 58

Animals, behavior of man and, 6–9

Anna State Hospital, Anna, Illinois, 209

Anorexia, 172–175

Antagonistic response, fear and, 53, 54

Anxiety, definition of, 51
desensitization and, 52–57
[See also Fear(s)]

Apathy score, definition of, 73

Autistic children, behavioral therapy for, 141, 209
use of seclusion with, 130

Aversive control (see Control)

Aversive stimulus, definition of, 32
punishment and, 32–36

Awareness and thinking, reinstating, 109–112

AWOL (absence without permission), 134–135

Ayllon, T., 85, 112, 113, 126, 127, 151, 158, 164, 174

Azrin, N. H., 85, 112, 113, 209

Bachrach, Arthur J., 173–175

Ball, T. S., 183–184

Barrett, Beatrice, 139

Baseline, definition of, 67, 69
on smoking behavior, 79–80

Baseline data, obtaining, 69–76
sources of information for, 67–69

Bathing, treatment plans and, 85
(See also Showering)

Behavior(s), antagonistic, and fear, 53
causal order in, 9–10
changing, by reinforcement, punishment, or extinction, 35
concomitant, 71, 73, 74
control of, 10–13

Behavior(s), definition of, 3–4
deprivation and, 29–32
developing new (shaping), 104
ignoring, technique of, 122–123, 125–127
initial and terminal, in handshaping, 38–39
treatment plans and, 82–85
of men and animals, 6–9
mutually exclusive, 70–71, 73, 74
odd, treating, 120–176
(See also specific behavior)
reinstating, 104
responsibility for, 10
(See also Self-care)
science of, possibility of, 9, 10
(See also Behavioral science)
scientific causality in, 10
self-destructive, treatment of, 184–185
superstitious, 46
terminal, in handshaping, 38–39
treatment plans and, 82–85
in work assignments, 116
values of, 74–75

Behavioral analysis, important merit of, 26–27

Behavioral data (see Data)

Behavioral science, objections to behavioral approach and, 6–10
value of, 4

Behavioral Study Form, 72, 73

Behavioral techniques and ward routine, 103–119

Behavioral therapy, aim of, 306
desensitization in, 55–61
objections to, 6–10

Behaviorist, role of, in control of human behavior, 11–13

Birnbrauer, J., 184

Breaking and throwing as manipulative device, 132–133

California, family care facilities in, 199–200